Eat Away at Anything
for Redemption

By
David James Watt

Soul Asylum
Poetry and Publishing Inc.

Note for Librarians: a cataloguing record for this book that includes
Dewey Decimal Classification and US Library of Congress numbers is
available from the Library and Archives of Canada. The complete cataloguing record can be obtained from their online database at:
www.collectionscanada.ca/amicus/index-e.html

ISBN# 978-1-926876-04-7

Published in Canada by
Soul Asylum Poetry and Publishing Inc.
79 De La Salle Blvd, Jackson's Point, ON L0E 1L0
www.soulasylumpoetry.com

10 9 8 7 6 5 4 3 2 1

Project Editor: Kenneth Wm. Cowle
Cover Design: Kreso Cavlovic

Foreword

Charlie was mentally lost and emotionally struggling in his average middle class life. So suddenly he set out on an amazing yet unintentional journey to re-discover his life's path. Along the way he encountered many people; some old, some new and some long ago forgotten. He analyzed every detail along the way, every relationship and every occurrence. He pushed himself to his emotional limits, until he was almost completely broken. In the end he discovered the wisdom to learn about some of life's most valuable lessons and he became all the better for it. This is his story...

My special thanks go to Alma, Ava, Corrinna, Elizabeth, Fernando, Georgie, Glenda, Katharine, Kreso, Lee, Mark, Meredith, Randy, Ronnie, Teresa, my mother and my children. I love you all very much and none of this would have been possible without each one of you in my life.

Chapter 1

<u>Sweet Clarice</u>

Into my world came a beautiful child,
floating in and around,
so lost so wild.
Embracing dancing two worlds collide.
the strike of lightening,
I can not hide.
Protect the innocence in the pit of crushing tool,
shelter the flower,
from the evil gun of a fool.
Each time paths in a different direction,
always forever,
this undying affection.
Beauty beyond what any eyes can see,
words that inspire,
elevate me.
Pain inside always prompts an end,
but I will never turn away,
from this truest friend.
Begin again my soul once so cold,
every little moment lingers,
my heart is sold.

Clarice is this gorgeous beautiful creature that I met through my sister when I was about 18 or so. She was then my sister Janine's friend from school; I never paid her much thought when I first met her as Janine was a good looking girl and good looking girls run in packs. Janine had so many cute little friends around back then and Clarice was just another one to me. A couple of years passed and Clarice floated in and out of our lives from time to time always being very nice and pleasant whenever she was around.

But my true memory of Clarice starts when she came around at age 16 and this time she was in trouble, big trouble. She had this older boyfriend she was living with and he was abusing her physically; abusing her bad, very bad! Looking back I seem to remember a story with her receiving such a beating that it put her into the hospital. Clarice would stay with us from time to time as mom had the tendency to help any of my sister's friends who were in trouble in some way; the same would go for my friends, but there always seemed to be one of Janine's friends who needed help. She became a friend to me and we would chat a lot. Somehow, I don't remember how she found the strength to separate herself from that guy, but he left her with a gift, she was pregnant. She was 16 years old and she was pregnant. It was very unfortunate and my family continued to help her whenever we could, although we were never really in any position to help anybody.

On June 25 1993, when I was 20 years old; my best friend Larry and his girlfriend Brenda had decided they were going to get married and I was to be an usher at their wedding. I was single at the time and I was pursuing this girl Kim, who wasn't into me at all. I didn't even have the nerve to ask Kim to the wedding. So one day while discussing going stag to the wedding with Janine; she suggested why don't you ask Clarice? She's pretty and not really showing yet; she'll look great on your arm, why not? I thought about it and said yeah, why not? Clarice was gorgeous! 5 foot 7 maybe,

140 lbs, beautiful face, long blond hair, very shapely, a chest like you wouldn't believe and very feminine. So I asked her to be my date for the wedding and she accepted instantly.

So it became that Clarice was my date for one of the biggest parties I can remember; ever! I was so trashed for 2 days straight during the course of that wedding! The bachelor party was the groomsmen drinking shooters all night long, at least 20 apiece; we had a recipe book for shooters and we followed it. We had the party at Larry's sister Patricia's place and she had a fully stocked bar, and the bar was open for business! Plus while all this drinking was going on, I had this 5 gram vile of marijuana oil that I was smoking non stop for those 2 days. I remember at the bachelor party that one of the other groomsman Matt disappeared and all the other guys were saying; where's Matt, where's Matt? Hey Matt, Matt, where are you? Then from behind the bar, up flops over this one arm and then another, and then slowly up pops Matt all staggered and hammered and he says hey guys what's up. Oh man did we ever laugh for like 10 or more minutes; the look on his face and the surprise of where he came from was just hilarious.

The next day at the wedding, things did not slow down in the least when it came to the partying sense. We drank so much and we smoked so much, more than I can even describe. I can remember Larry's dad Ken yelling at us groomsmen to get out of the parking lot, because every few minutes we were out in that parking lot smoking a joint. Or we would disappear to the bathroom to role those joints that we were smoking. Ah memories; this went on all night long and by the end of the night I could barely stand or see, I was that trashed, beyond that even. And the whole time this was going on Clarice was off socializing having a good time on her own. She didn't complain about my behaviour, she just let me be to have my fun. She really treated me with respect that night as she knew how important that day was to me and how important it also was in the grand scheme of things. Clarice was and is, still is to this day a real sweetheart when it comes to how she treats me.

Then it happened, the moment that would change my life forever. Everything was calming down for the night and Clarice and I finally got up to dance, well maybe we did before that but I don't remember it, all I remember is this: Never Tear Us Apart by INXS came on and it was a song that I knew all the lyrics to; I could and still can sing that song from memory, and I did sing it, while Clarice and I danced. Then Clarice rested her head on my shoulder and we continued to dance and I continued to sing the song and it was now her I was singing it to and then something started to come over me. It was that feeling that is just so hard to describe, that feeling that hopefully drives us all. And boom that was it, as bombed as I was, my mind just clicked on, and my heart just clicked on and my soul just clicked on and from that moment forward I was forever in love with Clarice. It was right then and there just like that, in a split second of time.

I remember after the drive home hugging her goodnight, and maybe I even kissed her on the cheek but I was too drunk to remember exactly. What I clearly remember is the feeling of watching her walk to her basement apartment and afterwards and missing her as soon as she was out of my sight. So after that day I began to pursue Clarice; but there was a problem. Clarice had a new boyfriend, this guy Sean and Clarice liked Sean. Sean was this tiny little rodent of a guy that I had known for years and if I really wanted to I could have annihilated him in a second to scare him away; but I didn't, that wasn't me, it was not too often or ever that I would use violence for personal gain. So I didn't care about Sean and I pursued Clarice anyways; my pursuing Clarice would become a theme for hers and I relationship for many years to come.

I did it subtly at first; but then slowly the gestures began to grow and I did all the pursuing under the guise of friendship. I'd make her dinner, I'd buy her small things if she needed them, and most importantly or what I thought to be most important was that I gave her someone to talk with that wasn't a stoner idiot. While she was going through her pregnancy crisis, as she had decided to keep the baby, I always gave her and treated her with all my respect. We

4

shared so much, everything, the connection between us became very deep very quickly; but I was sure to never try to kiss her or do anything out of order.

I remember Clarice, a large group of our friends and I going to this amazing Tool concert together and I stuck with her the whole night. I vividly remember putting my arms around her and guiding her through the mosh pit so we could get up close to the stage. What a mind blowing concert it was to see Tool, who is now this huge band and one of my all time favourites, in this little venue before they became really famous. The concert was even before their second album Undertow came out and it was an awesome concert that is one of my all personal time favourites. After the show I remember the feeling of an intense negative energy release and feeling so exhausted while having my arm around Clarice for the journey home on public transit.

There was also this one time that Larry, Brenda, Clarice and I took a trip to Shelburne to stay at the trailer that Brenda's parents owned on this piece of land. It was a couple's weekend and even though Clarice was quite pregnant and showing by now, I continued my pursuit of her. In the past the party crowd had done a couple of big party camping weekends there, but this was to be a more relaxed atmosphere. Larry and I spent the day drinking beers and smoking joints just like we always did back then and the women bonded over pregnancy as Brenda was also pregnant at this time. The trip was cut short though as Clarice began to feel ill and we returned home without even spending the night; it was even quite possible she was confused at my behaviour and or just tired of my advances.

I was truly in love with Clarice the entire time and slowly but surely I told her so, but I never told her clearly how I felt. She still somehow got the message of how I felt and she was shocked, but I still think to this day that she was somewhat interested. She explained to me of her situation with Sean, but I continued my pursuit of her and pushed her. I always treated her with respect, but I wanted her so badly. The depths of my love for Clarice were endless and so it got to the point where I put her under the gun, so to say, and she felt the need to take off and think about things. I believe I remember that she went to Scarborough to hang with a family member or a friend and to stay with them for a while as she thought about things.

I was going mental inside while she was gone and I don't remember the exact moment when she came back and told me or if she even did tell me; but somehow I got the message, Clarice was staying with Sean. It was so crushing and devastating to me but now that I look back that whole time it's a blur. I think that's probably because I drank and smoked myself silly to kill the pain of Clarice's rejection. And from that moment on I stayed away from Clarice, it's generally what I do when I fall in love with someone and am rejected. Soon thereafter I quit doing drugs for good and at first no one believed me, but I had strong will power and was determined to be clean and was successful. Everyone was shocked, maybe even including me. To this day I know of friends who have never pulled themselves out of that lifestyle and I feel sad for them at times.

And so I stayed away from Clarice, even though I heard she was in all kinds of trouble at times; horrible horrible troubles. Christina, her daughter, was born and some serious issues took place in her home where Christina was taken away from her by Children's Aid and I could have easily supported her through that, she could have used my help for sure, but I stayed away; I think even Janine asked me at one point to help her but I said no. Even when some idiot burst into her apartment at one point brandishing a gun; I still stayed away. Soon after that Clarice moved to a new apartment and then slowly over time any news of her became few and far between.

It stayed that way for a long time, 4 years actually; then one day right when I was in the middle of my relationship with Laura my first fiancée, there was Clarice again. She had run into my room-mate Jessica, and Jessica told her that I was living with her and then Clarice decided she wanted to visit me, if that was ok with me. I was surprised, very surprised to hear all this but I started to talk to Clarice again nonetheless; she came to my apartment, I met her daughter Christina and we started to become friends again.

Once again a huge party was to take place; a real monster and this time it was at my apartment. It was a party like you wouldn't believe. This apartment had this huge living room dining room combination and were able to fit a complete band in there and then still have room for 50 or more people at any given time during the night. What a party it was, everyone in the whole building came, so many of my friends came and Clarice came.

On this night there was a new development that shocked and surprised me; Clarice now had eyes for me now. She was being affectionate, and not like I had ever seen before. Laura was off socializing, as she could be quite the butterfly when it came to socializing and stuff and that left me all to Clarice. I remember her sitting in my lap and putting her arm around me and stroking my hair which I had at the time. I honestly couldn't understand why Laura was not getting upset because Clarice was being very very attentive towards me, almost to the point that she was like my girl-friend.

Then it happened, another big moment between Clarice and I; we were in my bedroom at one point just standing there and talking and Clarice spoke to me. She explained that she felt that she had made the wrong choice all those years prior, in choosing Sean over me and she said that she really regretted it all at this time. She said that she now felt like she wanted to kiss me and uh oh as inside I went into panic mode. I truly was head over heals in love with Laura at that point and now here was Clarice about to complicate things huge. Complicate things huge because I knew those past feelings for Clarice were still very much present; so I told her that I couldn't kiss her or whatever gibberish came out of my mouth because I loved Laura. And with that Clarice left; well, as far as I know she did because after that the party is mostly all a blur. I remember singing with the band that night; Wish You Were Here by Pink Floyd was the song, my second favourite song of all time.

There were so many friends around and it was a real happening. If you know me personally from the partying days and you weren't at this party well you should have been; it was one of the best parties ever.

So fast forwarding to 2009 it had been 3 years or so since Clarice and I had again made contact through the website facebook, but it had always been just small talk or the odd message here and there up until the chatroom feature was added to the site. Once the chatroom feature was added we started having conversations online from time to time and our friendship began to develop again as the conversations became more frequent and longer as time passed. Less than two weeks before I moved out of the house Clarice and I finally agreed to meet for the coffee that we kept saying we were going to get together for. Well it was actually going to be tea for me as I gave up drinking coffee after my father passed away from a heart attack, and that was a low hanging fruit item when my doctor told me to give up certain unhealthy things as a preventative measure for my own protection.

By this time in my marriage I was at the point where there was only the faintest glimmer of hope that my wife Carrie and I would be able to reconcile things; maybe I was even at the point of acceptance that the marriage was over because I prepped myself fully for the meeting in the sense of if Clarice and I were to have sex I would be ready. Clarice had dropped many comments that she was unhappy in her relationship and that she was frustrated sexually and even believed that Steve her husband might be cheating. So I was not totally sure of what her intentions were; but I was ready for sex if that was what she was after. I even shaved my testicles in preparation for the big event just in case, as my attraction to Clarice was still very strong after all these years.

I didn't tell Carrie where I was going that day; just that I had an appointment as we were now at the point in our marriage where the honesty was gone between us. I headed out that morning to meet Clarice and I was only 5 minutes away from my home when Clarice called to let me know that she was almost at the agreed upon meeting place which was Wal-Mart. She said that she wanted to pick up some Valentine's day cards for her youngest daughter once I got there; I said ok and continued on my way. It was the first time I had heard Clarice's voice in 10 years and she sounded exactly the same and I only grew more excited at seeing her after all this time. She had looked gorgeous in the pictures that she had posted on her facebook page, a little bit older of course, but she had not lost her looks at all in my opinion.

I arrived at the store and Clarice was waiting for me outside and did she ever look great, just totally gorgeous. She looked almost exactly like I remembered her so I parked my car and headed directly to her and she hugged me. We went into the store and started chatting away about small talk but we couldn't find any Valentine's Day cards so we decided we would look at another store during the course of the day. We agreed to go to a coffee shop close by and I followed her there in my car.

We got our drinks and sat down at a table and just started gabbing away about everything; about my marriage, about her marriage, about our kids, about the past and which friends we were still talking to or had added on facebook, just everything. It was another one of these strange moments that I have been experiencing a lot lately where I hadn't seen a person for so long but it felt like almost no time had passed between us at all. I explained about what had happened in my marriage and put the focus on an online sexual experience I had and I was totally honest as I felt I didn't have anything to hide. I told Clarice that I knew it was over with Carrie and now my only concern was the well being of my children and she listened intently offering her opinions and advice.

She then went on to tell me about her suspicions of Steve being unfaithful to her and I was pretty sure they were not unfounded. There was this woman Janice, that Steve and Clarice knew through a mutual friend and Janice had been around them a bit over the last little while; up at their cottage in Owen Sound and just hanging out with them in general. Clarice had picked up on a vibe that Janice was interested in Steve through a conversation that she and Janice had had about a swinging lifestyle and Clarice had been very repulsed by this conversation as Clarice was monogamous. She didn't like Janice very much after that conversation and was always on her guard with Janice from that point forward.

Then just recently Steve had told Clarice that he was going to go away for a skiing trip with Janice alone; he felt that since he was being honest and telling Clarice about it, that it was Janice he was going with as a friend, that Clarice should not have a problem with it. Well Clarice did have a problem with it, a big problem with it and she forbid him to go; but he said he was going to go anyways and they had a huge fight over it. The way Clarice described the situation seemed awfully strange to me and since I had basically cut off almost all my female friends during the course of my marriage out of respect for Carrie; I found it so odd that Steve was intentionally putting Clarice into a position like this since it upset her so much so I told her that I agreed with her completely.

The only real female friend I had during my marriage to Carrie was Connie and even that friendship caused some distress between Carrie and me at times. I first met Connie when she worked at the same place as my best friend Don and I do; she worked in sales and she joined the work softball team at its inception. We quickly became friends through there and then more so through emailing each other over the last 5 years and during that time she has grown to become one of my best friends. Connie is a highly intelligent person and probably one of the most cheery people you could ever meet anywhere and for that matter she's totally cool to boot. Connie also became involved with and married Don and I'm proud to say that I had a major hand in the initial connection between them. Connie has listened to me and offered me advice through all the tough times with Carrie and never once did she judge me. Honestly I could probably use every positive adjective I could think of to describe Connie's personality and it still wouldn't do her justice in my opinion; she's top drawer all the way and her and Don make a wonderful couple together. It's awesome to have two of my best friends married and I so enjoy all our time together always.

During one "discussion" Carrie actually detailed to me why she thought I had a crush on Connie and I was really taken aback by it. Carrie grew to believe that I was an absolute male chauvinist pig during our marriage and that I had no respect for women whatsoever; as she thought and she was right about, that I didn't think much of any of her friends. And yet I always spoke so very highly of Connie, which was cause for thought on her part. Carrie also knew that I had a fetish for Latina women and since Connie is Latina; well Carrie just connected the dots and boom I had a thing for Connie as she saw it. Well I won't lie; I do find Connie to be an attractive woman, she is; and possibly under different circumstances maybe I would have been interested in her from a romantic point of view had I been single when I met her. But there is one thing that I could never ever ignore even if that thought ever crossed my mind; she is with my best friend Don and I have a code about that stuff. Connie is forever off limits no matter what the circumstances are and I would never ever attempt anything with her no matter what, ever!

So I've honestly never looked at Connie in any other way during our friendship other than just being friends but she really did mess me up during a meeting at work this one time using her considerable assets to her advantage. In the not too distant past before that meeting; Don, Connie and I attended a Velvet Revolver concert in Hamilton. We were just standing around having a few beers before the show and I was staring at women like I always did whenever I go to concerts. Connie picked up on what I was doing and that started up a conversation about Don, Carlos and I and our girl watching habit when we go to concerts. I started discussing with Connie which women I found attractive and such and of course being the type of man I am; most of the women I was pointing out had large breasts.

So soon the conversation turned to me telling this old story that I would tell every once in a while about my friends Larry, Brenda, Charlene (my first girlfriend) and I being at a fireworks display at Square One shopping center in Mississauga and then with me getting in trouble for getting caught at one of my favourite pass times to do while I'm out in public. Well some things never change and I was staring at women that day too; especially ones with large breasts. I was probably stoned or drunk or something and while sitting there with everyone, I spotted this one woman walking by and I started moving my head up and down along to the hypnotic movement of her breasts. Then for some reason I just said out loud; bouncy, bouncy, bouncy as she jiggled on by. Well did I ever get smacked by Charlene and then I was given what for by Brenda and I really dug myself into a huge hole that day. Well Connie laughed her ass of at that one for a while and I guess the story or my interest in watching women with large breasts really stuck with her.

It was at the work meeting she really got me; it was the type of meeting where I had to stand up and address everyone in the room. I think I was reading some report or something from a focus group I was in and I was trying to be a good public speaker. I was looking around the room and making eye contact with everyone and Connie was sitting across the table from me. So when I got to her; we made eye contact and then she gave me a smile and a little wink and then she stuck out her chest ever so slightly and then did a little shake. Oh bitch! I was right in the middle of a sentence and I honestly went blah, blah, blah as I started mumbling what I was saying because I was so distracted. Oh man did she ever have a laugh after that meeting and many times since at my expense.

So Clarice and I continued on with our day and we went and purchased the Valentine's Day cards for her daughter and then she joined me in my car and we went to a fish and chips place for lunch and continued to chat away for hours. This was even though Clarice still wasn't feeling too well as she had just gotten over bronchitis and the bronchitis had actually motivated her to finally quit smoking after many years; although she said that she still smoked the odd joint nightly to help her sleep. We reminisced about old times and old friends and gave updates to each other on what we knew about the ones who were closer to us. It was a very nice day and after lunch I drove her back to her van and we hugged and said we would see each other soon and headed on our different ways.

Clarice and I continued to chat every once in a while and she started to become a good friend again. She was very supportive when the actual split between Carrie and I took place and listened and offered advice after I left. The next time I saw her was when Janine came down for a visit while Kimberly, my niece, was off for March Break from school. Janine, Clarice and I, plus another old friend Gene all went out for lunch one day. It was another nice time, Gene and I joked around acting feminine because the women were talking about who had gotten fat from the old gang, and all the other gossip that women talk about. It was a very nice lunch and it was like once again that no time had passed for all of us; I guess when you make those kinds of bonds of friendship, where you invest a lot of time with people that bond never really goes away.

Clarice and I had already started instant messaging each other periodically before that lunch as that was how Clarice said she predominantly stayed in touch with most of her friends. On the way home, after we had parted ways Clarice sent me a message that really caught my attention and motivated me to explain a little bit deeper the unknown history between Clarice and I to Janine. The IM said that the lunch meeting had really reminded Clarice just how much she missed having Janine and I in her life and she hoped that we would continue to see more of each other in the future. I told her that we would be tight from now on and sent her hugs and kisses and she did the same and that truly began rekindling my feelings for Clarice. Our next series of connections only would cement what was to come.

I knew that things were now starting to develop between Clarice and me and at one point I made and cancelled another meeting with her for coffee after waking up that day a little sore and tired after a night of basketball. We were only going to get together for an hour or so and at that point a couple of factors made me cancel the meeting. Mom and Connie were both advising me that it would probably be not be the best idea to get mixed up with Clarice again as she was married to Steve and had a daughter with him. They said since I was only just newly removed from my marriage I should steer clear of a complicated past love like her since I told them I was becoming interested in Clarice again. Plus things were going pretty well with this other woman Roberta at that time and honestly my attention was more focused on Roberta than Clarice. So I messaged her and cancelled the meeting with her and she said it was ok; but it probably wasn't and I'm still not sure to this day how she felt about that as it never has come up.

Every once in a while I throw out random music quotes out as my update on facebook and it was just a random song lyric that would change my life. One of my favourite all time female singers is Shirley Manson from the band Garbage, oh man I've seen Garbage in concert many times and every time I see them I just become hypnotized by that woman's beauty and does it ever help that the music of Garbage just totally rocks my world. My favourite Garbage song is Vow off their first album and that was the song that I had chosen to quote that day. The lyric went, "I can't use what I can't abuse and I can't stop when it comes to…"; and I stopped and left the rest blank even though the lyric finishes with the word, "you". Well up pops Clarice commenting on my status and she says, "SEX? laugh out loud". So I answer back oh my god Clarice I'm shocked at your dirty mind; I was referring to sunshine and lollipops and then she answered back, laugh out loud, oh please, you can't be shocked, I think sunshine and lollipops are much better though, next time finish your sentence. I then dedicated the song to her through facebook and replied to her, listen to the song I sent YOU Clarice and then YOU will understand.

Further to that, I then sent her the entire lyric as an instant message and she replied that she was flattered and blushing. So I replied that I live to please and told her to see if she could discover the meaning behind that statement, to which she replied, live to please Clarice? And I said no but you're close and honestly the truth might shock you. That is when she said the two little words that started nearly four weeks of off and on X-rated instant messages going back and forth between the two of us as she said, nothing you can say will shock me, EAT AWAY. Oh my goodness I thought, here we go, and honestly I truly enjoy performing oral sex on women, I mean I love it! Poor Clarice just didn't know what she had signed herself up for with those two little words.

I started subtly at first just telling her that it was one of my favourite things to do and asked if she would like to hear a description about it to which she said yes and I proceeded to give her the soft core version of my technique at that time. I was very careful to never go too far too quick and would apologize if I thought I had crossed the line at any point, but she always told me not to worry that she was enjoying it and there never seemed to be any line to be crossed at all. So I continued getting more and more graphic with my descriptions until I basically got to the point where I was just flat out describing scenarios to her. She was not as good with the words as I was and I was basically the one driving the bus so to say the whole time, but I heard things from her like you've gotten me wet or I've creamed myself or after the last set of texts where I had described her squatting on top of me, grinding her vagina into my face; she called me the king. And right after that she continued with I'm still coming over tomorrow right, as prior to that day we had arranged a lunch date at my new place for her first visit there.

Right around the same time as the X-rated instant messaging started going on between Clarice and me; Clarice did some good detective work and she found her long lost father on facebook. I remember the day I saw her update saying oh my god oh my god I found my real father and then messaging her to see what had happened and then telling her how happy I was for her. I also cautioned her to be careful that this family did not hurt her again to which she replied she was already preparing herself for the same.

Clarice's father had left her in life when she was still not more than a baby due to the complications of life, his drug abuse and some extreme relationship issues with her mom. He had never been able to find Clarice because she had her mother's maiden name as her last name, and her mother had since remarried and changed her last name. Clarice's name was not listed in the phone book anywhere and that only complicated things for her father further.

Clarice had gotten some basic information from her mother about her father and had always longed to find him. Then one day out of the blue she searched everyone with his name on facebook and then pieced together who he was by checking to see who his friends were and then looking for similar names to which her mother had told her whom she thought his relatives were. She was right and she had found him! Soon thereafter Clarice drove to Lindsay to meet her father's family at a huge happy family reunion; in particular it was her grandfather that Clarice said she wanted to meet. Her father lived in Alberta and little did Clarice know that he had flown in for the reunion and then snuck up right behind Clarice when she wasn't expecting it and surprised and shocked her. Clarice posted all the pictures of the reunion on facebook and she looked so very overjoyed and was glowing at being around her new family.

I awoke very early on the day that Clarice was coming over for lunch and only told Connie what was going on with her. I went out early that day to pick up some condoms as I didn't have any and hadn't had any possible use for those things in ages, but I wanted to be prepared in case the scenario of sex came up because after all the X-rated messaging that was going on I wasn't sure what to expect that day. Clarice arrived around 10 am while I was preparing some kabobs for lunch; I was chopping up the chicken and veggies and putting the stuff on the skewers. After I was done we went outside and sat on the patio furniture and started chatting. Clarice had told me in a text the previous day that she had almost cancelled on me because she had slightly fallen down the stairs and hurt her right foot a couple of days prior to our lunch so I told her that when she came over I would rub her foot for her. When we sat down I asked her which foot it was and reached down and pulled it to my crotch to give her an hour long foot massage while we talked; also pulling up her other foot after a while. She thought nothing of it I guess but having her feet up against my crotch made my genitals twitch and leak for the entire length of the massage and I didn't want to stop rubbing her feet for a single moment as I was in heaven.

We started out discussing my marriage to Carrie again and what the new developments were and then I asked her about her marriage with Steve and what her feelings were on that subject now. She told me that she loved him but was in no way in love with him and that she had grown to call him dumb ass and had lost all respect for him because of his drug use and that he was taking her for granted. She further said that they had not had sex for 6 weeks. She continued that sometimes she wished that she could find the courage to leave him and that she was going to use her visit to her Dad's in Alberta as the one last chance to see how she truly felt about Steve and to see if she missed him while she was gone. She felt that was how she was going to know if she should stay with him or not. I gave her my opinion; that I felt that if I was saddled with the choices that I made when I was 20 years old, I would be absolutely miserable.

We chatted and she told me about her dad and the reunion and expanded on who everyone was and in particular the stories of meeting her dad and her grandfather. She spoke of her mother's reaction to the whole thing and how her mother had not been very pleasant with Clarice about Clarice meeting her dad. From all the stories she has told me over the years my opinion of Clarice's mom is not very high; and I wasn't at all surprised by what she told me her mom's reaction was. I further explained why I was especially happy for Clarice in this particular instance referring to my history with my father and the story about his death. Clarice said she didn't really know the whole story about my father as she wasn't even sure that Janine and I had the same father; so as we sat there I told her the whole story of my life as it pertains to my father.

My father up and decided to leave our family in 1978 when I was just a very young boy; I can still remember the day he told my mom he was leaving as I was sitting at the top of the stairs leading to the lower level of the house watching as he told mom while she had Janine sitting on her lap and that mom was crying so very much. Mom said my father just said he was leaving and he handed her $20 and left a pack of pork chops in the fridge, took some of his clothes and left. Mom was devastated and to make matters worse my grandfather, her father, passed away around two months later and to this day I can't really fathom what she went through that year or how she got through it.

At first my father would come and take my sister and me for visits on a semi regular basis; to his apartment or out with his new girlfriend Margaret and I always felt very uncomfortable when I was out with him. Over time the visits with my father became less and less frequent and then even very erratic as sometimes he would show up for every consecutive visit for a while and then I wouldn't see him for months on end. I would be sitting there waiting for him on the porch on scheduled visiting days only for him not to show up and be heartbroken. For three years this was the pattern and I gradually lost the connection I felt towards him and he honestly became a stranger to me. While I have memories of my father; they are really just of images of his apartments or of places we went or the people that were around. I don't remember his voice, or his mannerisms or his personality at all; just what he looked like and what we did together, which really was not all that much.

As the divorce proceedings finished up mom addressed the issue of visitation through the lawyers and how it was having a very negative effect on my sister and especially on me. I was an overly emotional child and was teased to no end when I was young and I was very quick to cry when I was a boy. I felt very alone and was quite embarrassed of my home life as a child as I only knew of one other child whose parents were divorced and it was not at all that common back in those days to have divorced parents, not even anywhere as close to as it is nowadays.

Mom then made a request through her lawyer to have scheduled visits that were frequent and concrete or if not that my father needed to stop coming around because of the effects things were having on Janine and I. It was just a ploy on my mom's part to try and resolve the issue but to her surprise my father decided to discontinue the visits with Janine and me. Mom once explained that during the previous years Christmas holidays that my father had become incensed with mom because she had taken Janine and me to Nova

Scotia with her boyfriend at the time and his boys to visit her boyfriend's family. Mom said that she had tried to contact my father about scheduling a visit but he was not returning her phone calls and so she went without him knowing. I don't know if it was to get back at mom or if he didn't care about us or what but I never ever saw my father again after that; I was not even 10 years old at the time.

My grandparents moved back from England in the not too distant future from that point and they began taking my sister and me for visits to their new home in Cobourg. Never did my father ever show his face during those years while my grandparents had us at their home. I clearly remember my grandmother questioning me about my feelings towards my father one time and I flat out told her that I hated him. She said that that was my mother talking and there was no way that I could feel like that about him, but by this time I was at least 13 years old and I was not stupid and I said to her then where is he grandma, where is he? It's not like we've moved far away and he doesn't know where we are, we're in the same house and all he has to do is knock at the door to see us, just like you did. I guess I caught her off guard and she tried to make up excuses for him and further explained to me that he had told me about leaving before he did and I honestly faintly remembered the scene that she painted; but I could not at all remember a single word that he had said to me during that discussion. I was truly furious with him; years are like dog years to children at that time in their lives and it had felt like a lifetime to me since I had seen my father and I wasn't going to give into grandma no matter how much I loved her.

When I was 16 years old my grandparents passed away within 5 months of each other. After suffering her second stroke my grandma passed and mom asked me if I wanted to go to the funeral, but I was so scared and confused about everything and I didn't know what to do so I said no and we didn't go. Five months later when my grandpa passed it was a different story this time around and I was ready to face my father if that was to be the case because I wanted to say goodbye to my grandparents as I loved them both so dearly. So mom called my father in Ottawa, as that was where he had moved to, and told him that we wanted to attend the funeral; and he refused her, he flat out refused. He told mom that he didn't want to see us children under these circumstances and for us to not come. Had I been older I would have gone to the funeral anyway whether he liked it or not, but at 16 what was I to do? So we went to a viewing and was received by my father's brother Craig and I was able to say my goodbyes to my grandpa thankfully. But it was during that same conversation with my father that mom asked him if you aren't going to see them now are you ever going to Charlie? (That is his name; Charles William actually and further more his father and grandfather were both also Charles Foster) She said that we were getting older and she thought that he should see us at some point but he said that he just couldn't think about that right now and that was to pretty well be the last contact that was ever directly made with him.

The child support money was always there but he was sure to cut us off quickly after Janine and I finished school. The whole scenario around my grandparents' passing really devastated me and I remember writing a short story in English class that year about a fantasy sequence where I murdered my father. Yeah and some teacher I had; I was screaming out for help and he completely ignored me; well for that matter pretty well everyone did. So not too long afterwards; surprise surprise go and cue all the drug and alcohol abuse and then you can throw in an abusive stepfather and a slightly mentally damaged mother into the mix and there you have it, what a total mess I was in the 16th year of my life.

The years passed and the thoughts of my father always stayed with me but I never once gave it much of a second thought to try and go see him right up until about one month before he died. I was at Larry's dad's 50th birthday party at Patricia's house and the brother-in-law of the neighbours who had lived directly attached to my family home for years; began asking me questions about my father as he had personally known him years prior. I was pretty open about the situation with him as he was a nice man and I knew all his kids; especially his gorgeous blond daughter who I stared at every chance I got; but he got me thinking aloud that I should go see my father and he agreed with me. But I was hesitant and I wasn't sure if I was mentally ready to see my father yet as I was only less than two years clean by that point. It just so happened too that this was the day before my father's actual birthday but little did I know on that day that my father was to be dead within less than a month's time.

One day after work I returned home to hear a strange message on the answering machine; it was a police officer from Ottawa looking for a Miss Foster regarding a case and he had left a phone number to contact him. Mom had just been in Ottawa with her current boyfriend Fred a month or so prior and so I wondered if something had happened while mom was in Ottawa. Since mom had changed her last name when she was re-married though I was pretty sure that it had something to do with my father. So I called mom at work and told her about the message and she said no, nothing had happened while she was in Ottawa and she also became convinced that it had something to do with my father. She said wait until she got home to inquire as she would leave work immediately and then we would call together to find out what was going on; but the curiosity was killing me and I didn't wait for her to get home. I called the police officer.

I was right and it was about my father; the police officer had found my grandma's phone book in his apartment and she had listed my sister's name first in the book and that's why they had asked for Miss Foster. The police officer was hesitant to tell me what had happened but after I explained the situation to him he finally relented and told me that my father was dead. He had died in his apartment and was discovered when the newspapers and mail began to accumulate at his door, no one knew where he was or saw him for a while and a bad smell was coming from the apartment. That was when the police were called and he had been dead for five days when he was finally discovered and his body had begun to decompose. I took down the information and the officer asked if I was going to come to Ottawa to take care of matters and I told him that he needed to contact my father's brother Craig to take care of things as I wouldn't have any idea of what to do and hung up.

I then immediately called Janine who I believe just happened to be living at Clarice's place at that time and asked her to come home right away; things were strained with Janine at that time for some reason and I honestly don't remember why. Mom returned home from work and I met her at the door and told her at once that my father was dead and she started to cry and so did I and we hugged and cried. It was at this time that Janine entered the house with a puzzled look on her face as to why mom and I were crying. I then told her our father was dead and she just turned around and went right back out the door, I guess she couldn't handle it. The next little while is obviously a blur; I called into both my jobs to say I wasn't coming to work for the next little while; well actually I couldn't even remember the phone number for my part time job and ended up calling my friend Gene because we worked together, to get that number. Mom figured I was right that it had to be Craig who was the one that had to take care of things in this matter; but we had no way of contacting him and he wasn't listed in the phone book. So mom pulled out her detective cap and started sifting through old phone books looking for the phone numbers of my grandma's closest friends Irene and Jan; she thought if anyone might know where Craig was that it might be one of them.

So in a round about way we finally got in touch with Irene through her daughter and then through Jan's daughter were able to locate Craig and he finally called us. He had already known about things for a day; and thinking back what a bastard he was for not contacting us! Irene warned us when we were on the phone with her that Craig and his wife Maureen, were a bunch of money grubbers and that we should be very cautious of them. Craig was already leaving in the morning and I asked if I could tag along but he said he didn't have the room. So he gave me his number and said things would be alright and that he would look after everything and to let him know of my plans. It didn't take long for me to snap out of the daze I was in, and mom and I got it together real fast and decided to head to Ottawa in the morning. Fred drove us there and our first stop when we arrived in Ottawa was the morgue; we asked at the counter and they told us that Craig had already been there and had identified the body but we asked to see it anyways as I had to know without a shadow of a doubt that my father was dead.

We were lead down to the basement and the attendant went and got the body and then put it in the viewing area. Now what you see on TV or in the movies is not the way it happened at all, the attendant warned us that the body was already decomposing when it was discovered and that it might be a good idea not to see it; but I persisted and mom agreed and so they pulled back the curtain to show his face. He was in this little side room behind glass and I'm pretty sure I know why because after we left and went to the apartment the smell of death that filled the morgue was just as ever so strong in his apartment. Mom took one look at him and said she couldn't recognize him at all and turned and cried in my arms but I looked closely because I had to be sure. His skin was a dark dark shade of green, like that of an evergreen tree and he was all bloated and there were sores all over his face. I knew it was him though as I had grown to look like him as I grew older and he still had the moustache and the same color hair. Mom took a second look but it was very hard on her and she leaned on me heavily and after I was done we exited the building.

We next headed to his apartment and met up with Craig, Maureen, their son Shane and my father's old friend Bob who had come along with them. Craig looked the same as I remembered him, just older but Maureen looked completely different. She had gained at least 100 pounds from the last time I saw her 13 years ago. Bob explained who he was and I remembered him from going on a fishing trip with him once when I was a kid and he remembered the same trip. I took a special interest in my cousin Shane, as I had never met him before but had always seen pictures of him and his brother Craig; who had unfortunately passed away in a tragic accident many years prior, at my grandparent's house. Shane was

13 or 14 years old and I spoke to him as much as I could during my time at my father's apartment as I was thinking of my grandparents and that they would probably want that.

The usual pleasantries were exchanged and things were actually very pleasant amongst us all. I remember mom getting quite the shock while we were there as these two blatantly gay men who were friends of my father came to the door and asked some questions. Mom never truly knew my father at all and she wondered if he had turned gay and if that was the reason why he had deserted us. So this only added fuel to the fire with regards to her theory. The evening progressed and we all sat down to dinner and reminisced about stories and as always my memory was solid and I was able to go along with almost all the stories that were in the timeframe that I was alive and that really astounded Craig and Maureen. Mom and Fred went and stayed with some friends of Fred and I stayed at the apartment with everyone and did so for the entire weekend even after mom and Fred returned home; I would be taking the train home with Bob on the Monday as it was Canada day weekend. I also unfortunately ended up in the hospital that weekend with a serious asthma attack as my father had a short haired black cat who had become seriously ill during the time he spent alone in the apartment with my father's body and the cat was shedding everywhere. The excess hair had seriously bothered my allergies to the point that my asthma kicked in and by the time I got to the hospital I could barely even breath.

It was a weird time for me but I needed it to finally come to terms with who my father was and I found out who exactly he was. He was a professional man which was made evident by the Armani suits that graced his closet and basically by the upscale condominium that he owned. Bob filled me in on his lifestyle as he had still been friends with my father for all this time and he had no reason to hide anything from me; my father was a womanizer and he had always had been so.

He had always been heavily involved in marching bands and I
remember taking a trip to Denver when I was very young for a
competition that he was involved in; and as well that was one of the
few places that he would take me during the small number of visits
that he actually took my sister and I on. Well the family didn't
always go on the marching band competition trips and Bob said that
when they used to go that my father was always was picking up
women and cheating on my mom with them. Bob told me of one
story where he and my father were smoking some dope one time
and he questioned my father about his womanizing and wasn't my
father worried that he was going to get caught sooner of later.

So that also filled me in about my father's drug use and low and
behold I soon found his stash of marijuana in a little box on the
shelf under the coffee table. I knew it was good stuff too by
smelling it and so I flushed it down the toilet right there and then.
When I told Craig about it later on; when of course he, Bob and I
went out for a walk to the beer store and they started puffing a joint,
Craig actually got upset and said why would I have done that, as he
would have smoked the stash. Yeah real good smoke the stuff that
probably gave your brother the heart attack that killed him. There
was also a stack of beer cases in the closet in the kitchen, it seemed
the old man liked Coors light and he still smoked the same brand
cigarettes to the day he died as there were a lot of packs lying
around.

Even after it al,l though; after everything he did to me I still lit a
candle for him and said an our father for him at one of the old
churches in the downtown core. I spoke to Janine on the phone as
she had not joined us for the trip and she asked me to describe the
place to her. She was particularly interested in the many books he
had on the shelves while I was more interested in the record albums
he had, as I had a lot of the same albums myself. Janine also wanted
me to take the cat for her but it was very sick and I told her I wasn't
going to take it.

I slowly came to dislike all that I saw around me and only found solace looking down the street at a church that was in the distance and hearing the bells ring out periodically. I gradually grew to just wanting to focus on taking care of the business end of things, but Craig stopped me every time I opened a drawer or started snooping around. Irene was right about him and he totally confirmed it when he produced a copy of my father's will towards the end of my time there saying that my father had made no provisions for either my sister or I. Perfect, just perfect; it was the final insult from him and it was just fitting. Soon after that I left and returned home.

The day of his funeral in Whitby, the rage welled inside of me and I sat near the back of the almost empty chapel; as there had also been a memorial in Ottawa where I guess all of his work associates and friends had attended. He must have had some friends, as he worked for Bell Canada for 35 years and had just retired early and was preparing to move back to England to retire. For the entire funeral I was screaming at him from inside me, the minister said how nice it was that my sister and I were there and my absolute disgust at that just filled me with every negative emotion possible. I left the service and waited outside until that farce was done and then we all headed to the cemetery where his ashes, that were in a marble cube were to be placed.

I honestly don't know and don't care where that place is that he is laid to rest; all I remember is standing there looking out over the countryside at this beautiful sight and then Maureen gave me a flower to put in the hole. When I was left alone for my moment with him to reflect, I did not shed one tear for him and with all my anger and rage I damned my father to hell for all time and I spat on his grave and then forever walked away from the man who had cursed two beautiful little children and the little boy that bore his own name no less, to a life of sorrow.

I came to know later in life that my father did not get off Scot free for the misery he had caused. Janine had experienced a different type of emotional trauma than me because of my father's total abandonment of her; as she has almost no memories of him whatsoever. However her resentment of him is still of the greatest substance and she let him know that she was still out there on her 17th birthday. She got his number from my mom and called his home and he answered and she simply said happy father's day and hung up on him.

Jan, the other friend of my grandmother's also informed us of a visit my father had made to her house while on a trip to England and a conversation that had taken place. You have to understand that Irene, Jan, my great aunt Cheryl and my grandma were a tight knit group of ladies and they knew everything about each others families and Irene and Jan were like my father's aunts. So Jan said when my father sat down with her at her table that she started to question him about my sister and I out of respect for my grandma, because she knew my grandparents were very upset with him about abandoning us. And when Jan questioned him she said his hands started to shake and he got very upset and told her that he had written a letter to Janine recently saying god knows what, but that he didn't have the courage mail it.

So I pieced it together that the timing of the phone message from Janine, the trip to England and visit to Jan's and then his death all took place in a six month period. Then add in the smokes and all the empty beer cases and the stash of marijuana and you have a coward who hid behind his addictions and led his life of pleasure with no remorse for his actions or even a second thought for his children until it was far too late and I forever stand by my actions at his resting place.

So after telling that story to Clarice; well it was probably abbreviated; I proceeded to chef up some excellent kabobs that we chowed down in no time flat. Clarice really impressed me with her eating as she kept right up with the fastest stomach in the west and I really enjoyed watching someone other than my mom truly appreciate my cooking for once. I love to cook and especially for someone that enjoys and appreciates it as much as Clarice sure did.

We spent the afternoon chatting some more, snuggling up close on the couch looking through all my old photo albums that I dug out to show her. She listened intently as I went through the historic family album I had put together to see who everyone was and said aw at my baby and childhood pictures and loved looking at the ones from the old days 15 to 20 years ago. Unbeknownst to me I had saved a picture of Christina's that Clarice had given me back in the days in Burlington; and I became so happy with myself that maybe saving that picture showed Clarice that it had meant a lot to me that she had given me that picture.

We also discussed Sean for a period of time as wouldn't you know it; on the exact same day that I moved into my house, the very first moment that we began to unload the truck; here comes Sean riding up to me on a bicycle saying Charlie, Charlie Foster how are ya buddy? Oh boy, I didn't tell Clarice about it for a while because I hate hearing about the old days with Sean as it still hurt me that she didn't choose me outright; but I told her on this day because I could never lie to Clarice or hide something from her. She got me very excited though about telling me how she would role play for Sean from time to time to get him excited and that just totally drove me wild.

I threw on a couple of AC/DC DVD's that I had; as the conversation turned to music and AC/DC is Clarice's favourite band. Since it was one of mine too I could talk about them to every length and produced cd's and ticket stubs and all kinds of information. I said that there was something about AC/DC's music that just made women want to take their clothes off and Clarice agreed with that. The first three vinyl records that I ever owned were Dirty Deeds Done Dirt Cheap, Highway to Hell and Back in Black and I consider AC/DC to be my 3rd favourite band of all time. So Clarice and I continued gabbing away about music and she went through my entire ticket stub collection which I keep in an old photo album. It's at 137 tickets and still going strong, and it should be up over

140 stubs, baring any unforeseen circumstances, by the end of this summer. We discussed going to concerts at length as that is a huge passion in my life.

We were sitting right next to each other on the couch now and I had placed my arm around her but time was winding down on our visit and she kept a close eye on the clock as she had to leave in time to pick up her daughter from school. I knew there wasn't going to be any fooling around going on but I was feeling extremely close to Clarice at this moment and something inside me just told me to reach over and grab her hand to hold it and I did. And when I did she squeezed my hand very hard and with that I felt my genitals squirt and I ejaculated every so slightly. My god I thought what was that and I cherished each second that we sat there until she said I have to go.

She started talking about my kids and I coming over to her house for a barbeque sometime soon but I told her that I thought that was inappropriate as I didn't want to be looking at her the way I do in front of Steve. She said who the hell cares what he thinks; but I still said that I did not think that was a good idea. So I walked her out to her car; hugged her goodbye and headed back to my home.

As I walked away from her I could literally feel my heart breaking inside and that was it; here I was again full blown in love with Clarice; just like that night while dancing at Larry and Brenda's wedding. I returned to the house and proceeded to message her telling her about this horrible feeling I was having now that she was gone and I also said that this should all be kept very quiet with regards to Steve. She quickly messaged me back and said that I had a great heart and she would never want to hurt me and that she couldn't make any promises to me but if she was ever single that I was the guy who would probably have the chance at her heart. She continued that if what she thought what was going to happen happens, then we should focus on becoming best friends as that is the basis of a great relationship and then in the future we could complicate things; she furthermore said that she trusted me more than almost anyone. I replied to her with some stuff but I told her that the foundation is already in place baby and she said that's good to know. I floated upstairs to the computer and wrote the poem Sweet Clarice for her and sent it to her in under four hours as it was and is so easy to write about her. She was ecstatic when she read it and further told me that she had been, up until recently, carrying around a poem that I had written for her years prior but I could not recall that poem at all.

For the longest time Clarice has had this gorgeous picture of herself as her profile picture on facebook and I could just stare at it endlessly and that picture inspired me to write four more poems about her over the next 4 days. I decided that night to go to basketball just to get her out of my head for a little while and no matter what basketball always does that for me, it clears my mind. I get on that court and all I see for those 60 minutes is the game and nothing else; playing basketball has to be one of the truest passions of my life and I would probably play it every single day if I could and if my body would let me; but I'm getting older and the body does not always cooperate at times. I can't believe I only started up playing again just this year, what was I ever thinking! And it worked for the entire night, she was the last thing I thought of when I hit the court but she was also the first thing I thought of once I got off the court after playing for 60 minutes solid and she dominated my mind for the entire drive home.

That night I decided to write another poem for her but this time I decided I was going to try my hand at doing something erotic in the same fashion as the instant messages. So I sat down at the computer and started to write my topic paragraph to get my basis for the poem but something happened and instead of just writing a paragraph it became two paragraphs and then a page and then I found I was right in the middle of this short story; so I decided to just run with it and by the end of it I had three pages of almost pure pornography describing what it might be like if Clarice and I had sex for the first time and I really liked it. It was like something right out of one of the dirty magazines I used to buy, so I decided to send it to Clarice and pasted it onto a message on facebook. The only problem was though that the message was too big and the site wouldn't accept it so I had to break it up into 6 parts to get it to go through. With that it was like 3 am and I was very tired and went to sleep for the night.

The next morning there was a message from Clarice saying somebody was a busy boy last night, what you couldn't sleep? I said no and asked her if she liked it and she said honestly no, sorry but she wanted to be honest. She couldn't visualize it, although she expected me to act out that fantasy line for line in the future. She continued on that she liked the poems better and would appreciate more of those; and that was ok with me as I was the same way when it came to reading and told her I would have more poems for her in the near future. Yes you heard right, I am a writer but I hate to read, I honestly would prefer to listen to music or watch a movie rather than reading a book, how ironic is that?

I then further told her that I wanted to see her again as soon as possible and asked when a good time might be? She said that Steve was supposed to be heading up north to the cottage with her daughter for the weekend and that she might be able to come by the next day in the afternoon before she headed to St. Catherine's to meet up with her best friend. She wasn't at all sure what her plans were and wouldn't know until later that day and she would text me later that night while I was at work to let me know of her plans. I then headed to the computer to continue writing the poems and out came the piece Patience that afternoon; that was the third poem now and I was really starting to get excited about the results I was getting and I continued to write that night at work whenever I was on break and out came the piece All With You just after midnight. At the same time I was still waiting to hear from Clarice and kept checking my phone all night long and a text from her never came. I started to get anxious and upset and that started the next poem whose title is actually a play on words and it should actually be Con Text, but I thought context was more appropriate and it was ok that I changed it as I knew what it really meant. The upset feeling lasted with me for a while right up until my 3 am break and that's when my epiphany occurred.

I was standing by my car listening to My Heart Can't Tell You No by Rod Stewart for the umpteenth time of the night, staring up at the moon and then it just hit me:

What are you doing? Are you going to let this happen to you again? And again and again? When is it going to stop? Have some self respect man; just look at that writing you're doing, really look at it! It's amazing, just amazing! Those four poems are absolutely the best work that you've ever done, ever! Give it up, who cares if she messages you or not? Go after Roberta again or go after someone else or be alone who cares! Just keep on writing and see what happens. You are going to be happy no matter what happens! No matter if Clarice loves you or not, no matter if Roberta loves you or not, or whomever! It doesn't matter anymore, you don't need someone to tell you that you are worthy because you are no matter what anyone says especially Carrie! YOU ARE WORTHY!

And with that; out came the piece Return in a matter of hours and I was happy. I would continue to bang away at that keyboard for the next 4 days until I encountered a different kind of problem. Clarice did finally text me the next day and said she might see me later in the week if she had time as she was tied up. But I didn't care by that time as I now had a new love in my life and it was writing; and writing was a demanding mistress calling for 9 more poems over the next 4 days and I was up to the task even though that new problem was lurking in the shadows, ready to rear it's fearsome ugly head.

Chapter 2

<u>Found</u>

Irrelevant a phrase it might have been,
but transport that commentary through all you have seen.
It resonates to your soul,
recall those words when evaluating the gapping hole.
Find the kindred!
Discover the formula!
Forget the torment!
Once so afraid of expression,
dominated by the fear of rejection.
Wishing for a time of the free,
dreaming of a place in the scheme.
Hide no longer in the shadow!
Rise above the ashes below!
Return oh lost child!
Cast out the chains restraining a conscious wild!
Forever more only present what is true,
strength my friend I now give to you.

Ever since I can remember I've known Larry Walsh; there has been very little time in my life when he has not been involved in some way. I actually have pictures from my 2nd birthday party and he is in those pictures. Growing up we lived 4 doors apart on this street Kennedy and were part of the group of kids on our street playing baseball, hide and go, bike tag and all the other stuff kids did while growing up. Larry is 4 years older than me but back in

those early days I was still included in a friendship with him and
this other guy Peter who was the same age as Larry. For many
years the three of us hung out pretty exclusively just playing as
kids, swimming in Larry's pool, or playing dinky cars in the sand
pit in Peter's backyard or hanging out in the forts that we built in
my crawl space. The crawl space forts were a favourite of ours for
years as we had discovered a huge stack of my father's old Playboy
magazines and we plastered the centerfolds all over the crawl space.
I was always the tag along being the youngest kid and sometimes
Larry and Peter could be pretty cruel to me and would take advantage of me; but in the end they never were too cruel to the point
where they beat me up, just a lot of teasing which I guess is normal
for kids.

My first clear memories of Larry are from when I was 12 years
old chasing girls at the Streetsville arena. God did we ever look
funny back then with our sense of style; we were what you would
call Preppies and did we ever look the part, like something out of a
John Hughes film, (specifically think Duckie, but not as charming).
I remember Larry with his pink polo shirt, green hospital pants,
brown penny loafers and his box hair cut; oh god how ridiculous he
must have looked. And I wasn't any better with my skater dead eye
hair cut, my blue fedora type hat with the white stripe, plaid col-
lared pink shirts, walking shorts and my deck shoes. We really
looked the part and lived the part too by listening to Depeche Mode,
U2, the Smiths, the Pet Shop Boys and everything else that was
trendy at the time; but it worked for us and there were always girls
around. Larry was very successful with the girls back then and he
was able to land the most beautiful girl of my age group at the
Junior high school. I guess looking back he was cradle robbing as
he was already in high school dating a girl in grade 7 or 8; but man
was Chrissie ever gorgeous. There were other girls too after
Chrissie dumped Larry for getting to close to having sex with her as
he was a smooth operator.

As the summer approached that year Larry and I parted ways for
about 4 years because like I said he is 4 years older than me and he
had many friends from high school. One friend in particular was

this guy Matt, someone Larry had played baseball with growing up and Matt honestly was a cool guy. His family was better off financially than Larry's or mine and so he was afforded a more privileged lifestyle and of course Larry was drawn to that and he spent a lot of time with Matt. I was still around but slowly Matt became Larry's best friend, which was ok because I had friends from school it wasn't like he just ditched me and left me all alone, we were in different worlds and Larry was older. The last thing I remember around that time was one day I came over to Larry's house during the afternoon to find Larry and Matt smoking joints and watching porno movies from Larry's dad's collection and it really spooked me as I was very naive at the time; so I kind of just accepted fading away.

Four years passed and Larry and I would always stop and say hi to each other when we saw each other but we didn't hang out anymore. Larry changed his style and became a long hair rocker during these years and started hanging out in the rough crowd that dominated the area we grew up in. It wasn't always to his advantage to do so and it got him into a lot of fights and troubles with the kind of guys you didn't want to mess with. They were the kids of bikers and they were drug dealers and guys who basically just enjoyed beating up younger kids and stealing whatever they could from them. This period of time for Larry ended with him being declared a rat and having to look over his shoulder for years wherever he went. Having personally witnessed how a person in the area could be declared a rat; I think, well actually I should say I know, that Larry had just basically stood up for himself against a bunch of idiots who were taking advantage of him and it ended very poorly for him.

As my high school years progressed I also started to adapt to the rocker lifestyle as well and I still remember pretty well the exact moment when it happened for me; it was the first time I listened to the album Sonic Temple by the Cult. That was it for me, the album just rocked my world and after that Carlos just let me copy tape after tape of his and I turned into a total rocker listening to Led Zeppelin, Metallica, Motley Crue, Van Halen and the list went on.

My hair was already almost half way down to my shoulders and I just let it grow, never cutting it for years. I used to walk around high school with my walkman on all the time blaring my music as loud as I could, partly trying to be cool but mostly because the loud music always gave me relief from the stress of day to day life as it still does to this very day.

The first time I ever got really drunk was when I was 15 years old and of course as always it was over a woman. My third ever job was working at Zellers at South Common mall and I worked there for almost 3 years as a stock boy and then later on in the Toy department. During this time I had 2 main interests, music and girls and I would say that's pretty normal for any teenager. So at one point during my time at Zellers there was this cashier named Stella and I fell for Stella in a big way. She was one of the most beautiful girls I had ever seen. She had the most beautiful eyes, like Elizabeth Taylor's; and she had long curly black hair. She was 5 feet 4 and weighed about 120 pounds and had a body to die for; a perfect hourglass figure. I mean when you are 15 and you see a 17 year old girl stacked like she was; well… I had a crush on her almost instantly. Stella was only 17 but she looked like and acted like a mature woman and for some reason, she found me to be cool and we started hanging out at work and taking our breaks together all the time. It was the summer time so we would work nights and weekends and have our days free and hang out from time to time. I remember one night she was babysitting at some house and we talked on the phone until like 6 am and I seriously fell into puppy love that night with Stella.

Then one day she comes over to my house dressed up in this black pant suit with a negligee showing at her cleavage and I went gangbusters inside and slowly but surely we start making out. During the course of making out she let me get her topless and I fondled and kissed her breasts for what seemed like hours. Stella explained that she was on her period and asked that I didn't touch her vagina so hence we did not have intercourse or I think I would

have most definitely had that afternoon. Well maybe or it might
have been that she was lying and that I was too inexperienced and
was fumbling around too much killing the mood for Stella.

So less than a week later we're back at work one night talking
while on our break like we always did and all of the sudden out of
the blue during the conversation she just starts talking about how
she had just had sex the previous night with one of her brother's
friends who was in the army and was being shipped out in a day or
so. WHAT? I couldn't believe it as here I am in love with her;
thinking we're dating or even boyfriend and girlfriend and she starts
telling me about fucking some guy. I was just a kid but I did man-
age to tell her how I felt and she just laughed me off saying that I
was just some sort of play thing to her or something to that extent.
Oh man was I devastated and it's a wonder sometimes why I
haven't sworn off women for good after all the hell they've put me
through.

Well, word spread around the friends I had working in the store
real fast and little did I know that there was this other girl Sophia
who had a crush on me at that time. Sophia was already a friend
and she sought me out to give me her sympathy about what Stella
had done. It just so happened that Sophia was having a party at her
house that night and invited me to come over and drink and hang
out. So after my shift was over my buddy Carl and I headed straight
to Sophia's house and I proceeded to drink myself silly almost
immediately. A whole bunch of my work friends were there and it
was mostly just them as it wasn't a huge bender or anything. They
all shared what they had with me and I was a lightweight at this
time and the combination of beer, liquor and wine coolers just
ruined me and I was stumbling and falling all over the place.

It was at this point of course that Sophia took me for a tour of
her house which was this pretty huge place in one of the better parts
of Mississauga. Oh stupid me I was oblivious to what Sophia's
intentions were and of course we ended up in her bedroom; but I
was so drunk that I just flopped on her bed almost passing out.
That didn't stop Sophia as she was really into me and she lied down

beside me and started kissing me; but I was honestly was too drunk to do a damn thing. Which in hindsight was a good thing for me because a couple of days later her boyfriend came looking for me at Zellers and thankfully I was able to tell the truth and got out of that one because he was like 20 or something and was ready to give me a beating.

It was just after Sophia had gotten frustrated with me that I was-n't able to perform and left the room in disgust that Carl came and retrieved me; he dragged me to his car and we headed home. Carl was all perturbed at me as he had wanted to leave much earlier but I had kept pushing him off and drinking more and more. I arrived home and stumbled into the house and proceeded to head down to my bedroom in the basement as it was around midnight or so. As I headed down the stairs, there was my stepfather Bill in the den watching the TV and he said where have you been, your mom is frantic out driving around looking for you? Now I didn't like Bill at all; he had become quite the jerk over the first couple of years of marriage to my mom and he was always intimidating me and in my face. My tongue was quite loose at this point so I said to him what the fuck business is it of yours and I probably called him another name or two in the progress.

Well up jumps this 5 foot 10, 200 pound bear and I mean he was a very strong man, I saw him do things while working with him over the years that was really quite impressive; lifting a 200 pound solid glass table being one example. So Bill became really incensed and grabbed a hold of me and threw me down the next flight of 6 stairs to the basement and I landed with a thud. I was really hurt and really upset and I said something else to him at this point, prob-ably calling him an asshole or something and he came down after me dragging me into my room while I was still swearing at him and then that's when he really went after me. He got me down on my back, got on top of me with both his knees on my shoulders and proceeded to punch me straight in the face over and over and over again. I don't know how many times it was; it seemed like it was 10, but luckily because I was so drunk I barely felt it. He continued to drive me in the face until I was knocked out.

When I awoke a couple of minutes later I began to vomit, and he had left the room by this point and did I ever vomit, everywhere, all over my room. I tried to get up; but I was in such a mess that I just fell back down into a puddle of my own vomit and after a while I passed out. The next thing I remember was mom coming into my room and she was yelling as she entered but then her yelling soon turned into oh my god Charles what happened to you? All I could get out was mom he beat the shit out of me, he punched me in the face over and over again; sobbing while I told her and with that I passed out. This is what I am left with as the memory of the first time I got really drunk, oh happy times.

Life continued on with the usual events a teenager goes through and about a week before my 17th birthday I was walking home one day and passed by Larry's place and he was sitting on his porch; I said hey to him and he waved me over and we chatted for a bit. It was really nice to talk to him and I invited him over for my birthday party at my house which was going to happen that weekend and he said he would come. Later that week I still remember the phone conversation between Larry and I that I had in the kitchen in front of my mom; he told me he was going to bring over some joints and we could get stoned at the party and I said yeah of course as I had already smoked a few times prior to that and had enjoyed it. As soon as I got off the phone, mom had caught wind of the conversation and said what is Larry bringing the drugs to the party and I totally denied it, but mom was smart and she was right.

The first time I had gotten really stoned had already happened about 6 months prior to that when I was at school during the winter time. My best friend Raymond and I had bought a gram of hydroponic marijuana from this guy at school and went up to the coffee shop to smoke it. I rolled it up into 4 joints and we headed out in this blistering blizzard to get high. We smoked the joints out in the forest behind the school and didn't really feel anything at first, well maybe it was because we were standing out in the middle of this blizzard and the freezing cold temperature had numbed us; but once we returned to the coffee shop oh boy did it ever hit us. I remember sitting there at a table and Raymond was just freaking out scared at some hallucinations he was having and he had good reason to be scared, that stuff was killer. It felt like every muscle in my body was being stretched and pulled and I could barely think straight at all. Raymond and I later returned to school and finished out the day fried out of our trees. After that day I started buying and smoking dope on a sporadic basis; but alcohol was still the main drug of choice for Raymond, Carlos, another friend Rick and I at that point in time.

My 17th birthday party was quite the event, my mom and step-father left the house and many of my friends showed up and we all got very very drunk as I had gotten this older friend of mine from Zellers to buy all the alcohol for the party. Larry came to the party and he brought some dope and we got very stoned and so started our path to becoming brothers. The next day I went over to his house and continued on from where we had left off the night before. We drank tequila slammers and smoked joints all night long just having a good old time until I puked all down the side of Larry's bed in the basement after consuming just a little bit too much. It was also during that summer that Larry began to date Brenda his long time girlfriend and future wife.

That summer was one big long party and of note especially had to be the regular pool parties we had in Larry's backyard during the afternoons. One classic had to be this time that this guy Brian bought four 24 cases of canned beer and dumped them all into the pool and we all spent the entire day jumping in and out of the pool fishing out beers and just getting smashed. Then as the night pro-gressed on there was the infamous story about this girl going out behind the bushes at the end of Larry's backyard to perform oral sex on many of the guys that happened. It was pretty well anyone who would present themselves and many of my buddies gotten taken care of that night although I honestly did not get involved.

There was very heavy drinking and smoking in the storm sewers which we called the crack pipe and every weekend the crowd of friends grew bigger and bigger; but at the center of it all was an integral crowd of friends that included Larry, Brenda and I; Janine, Freddie, Eagle, Robbie "Mr. Smirnoff", Frank the Birdman, Brian and Eric "what's the count at?". We came to call ourselves the party patrol and the name totally suited us. It was a summer to remember for all times and I remember it fondly. The summer faded away and Larry and Brenda focused on building their relationship as a couple as there had been girls during the summer who had become very interested in and then pursued Larry and that had caused issues between Brenda and him.

That fall I began dating and fell in love with my first real girl-friend Charlene whom I had met through Carlos as he had dated her very briefly. Charlene was an absolute knockout at 5 foot 6, 130 lbs with long beautiful blond hair and a gorgeous face and an amazing body. She was a rocker chick and looked the part by wearing leather and black all the time. After meeting her and hanging out like twice I asked her to become my girlfriend and she accepted and I can remember the first kiss between us after I asked her out. I had just walked her home with a couple of my buddies and we kissed in her room after I asked her out and as I left I floated up the stairs and jumped around on my way home as I was so excited.

Charlene and I became very close very fast as mutual interests, especially music, and a similar life made things very easy on us. I lost my virginity to Charlene within almost a month of us going out and the event itself honestly was nothing too special from a roman-tic point of view. It was just us in my room and we had sex and after that we started having sex on a very regular basis as it got bet-ter after the first couple of times. Charlene and I spent almost every moment we could together, having sex, smoking cigarettes, playing video games and just being teenage lovers. Charlene's family really accepted me and I spent an inordinate amount of time at their house. They fed me; they gave me beers, or smokes or whatever because as time went on Charlene made it clear that she wanted to marry me. Geez I was 17 and I wasn't thinking about marriage but I went along for the ride as I loved having regular sex with Charlene and what 17 year old boy wouldn't?

As the months got warmer I started seeing Larry and Brenda more and Charlene and I would hang out with them from time to time then becoming a foursome. We all went to a Whitesnake and Kiss concert together at the CNE with Larry's older sister Patricia and her boyfriend Travis and we had a blast. Charlene was two years younger than me and sometimes it caused issues because she didn't know how to act around older people and she would just blurt things out from time to time that would seem foolish. She also started to give me grief about my drug use when I was around Larry; but I would just brush her off and do what I wanted to as I had her pretty well wrapped around my finger for those first six months of our relationship. I remember her even coming into my room one time, going to where she knew I hid my stash and pulling it out and yelling at me just like she was my wife. Another issue that she continually gave me grief over was I didn't have the money to purchase tickets to see Motley Crue during the Dr. Feelgood tour as Motley Crue was her favourite band and she would never forgive me for missing that show.

Charlene also became integrated into my family as well as we clearly became a couple and mom came to know her and treated her well right up until the moment she found out Charlene and I were having sex. Mom had a queen size waterbed in her bedroom and one time while she was out I talked Charlene into having sex on mom's bed as I wanted to try sex on a waterbed. So we did and after we finished I went to the bathroom to dispose of the used condom. Normally and believe me ever since, I would have flushed the condom down the toilet; but for some odd reason I didn't that day, I don't know why or what my thinking was but I didn't. I opened up the trash receptacle and went to drop the condom in, but as I did I saw a discarded jar of Vaseline and grabbed it and put the condom in there and returned it to the garbage.

Later that day or the next day I'm not sure; my mom asks to talk to me and she starts to tell me how she had been getting ready to take off her makeup. Mom used Vaseline to help remove her make-up and she explained to me that she had forgotten her new bottle of Vaseline in the car or something and remembered that she had thrown an old one out in the garbage can in the bathroom that had a little left in it and... With that my heart dropped to the pit of my stomach, and then raced back up to my throat and then dropped back down just as soon again and mom could see by the look on my face that I knew what she was about to say.

And so the rant began; how dare you on my bed and how dare you in my house and so on and so on, oh the yelling and could mom ever yell. The end result was that mom said Charlene and I now had to tell Charlene's parents that we were having sex; because if we didn't she was going to. So when I told Charlene about what had happened with mom she lost her mind too, oh my god what were we going to do? So we told Charlene's parents after a lot of deliberations and her dad was pretty cool about the whole thing right up until the point where he threatened to kill me if he ever caught me doing it in his house. Sometimes I have the worst luck I swear; who else could say something like that happened to them? Well, who am I kidding about sometimes having the worst luck?

This didn't stop Charlene and me from having sex though; I still remember this one time that we were in her basement on the couch going at it after a barbeque and her parents had gone for a walk. The curtains were closed to the basement but the window was open and when her parents returned from their walk, her dad yelled in the window hey what are you guys doing down there? For those few minutes when I didn't know if he had seen us or not, as he hadn't, I sure was freaked out, or shitting my pants as the expression goes. Charlene began to wear a lot of skirts and track pants around that time so she could get dressed real fast after sex and we developed a good system, although we sure did take risks. She used to grab the belt loops on my jeans during intercourse to help pull my penis up into her as far as it could possibly go, as it got to the point that I just undid my fly most of the time so I could also help her get dressed again fast if needed.

A similar situation occurred when once again her parents went for a walk and we were in her bedroom having sex. The window in her bedroom faced to the back yard and was about 5 feet from the floor and her bed was right up against that window on the floor. The curtains at this point in time were wide open and so after we finished having sex I stood up on the bed to head to the bathroom. I was facing out to the backyard as I stood up and weren't her parents and another couple sitting right there on the patio furniture having some drinks. Oh crap! I hit the bed as fast as I could and told Charlene that everyone was right there so we quickly got dressed and it was a good thing too because it was only just a moment later that her dad was at her bedroom door looking for us. I can even remember one night performing oral sex on her and then having intercourse with her right at her front doorway while I was leaving to head home after her parents had gone to bed; oh man the risks I would take, but I honestly didn't care.

It wasn't all happy times for Charlene and I though; one incident really signaled the end for us and I don't think we ever recovered from it as a couple and it also triggered the heavier drug use on my part while hanging out with Larry. Mom had really gotten into the bible thumping at this time and you could say she had even been somewhat brainwashed by Bill and the Baptist church they were going to. The Baptist religion dominated almost every facet of mom and Bill's life and of course they were on Janine's and my case all the time to go to church and read the bible. I despised that religion; it was exactly that same garbage you could see on TV watching the televangelists like Jimmy Swaggert or Jim and Tammy Faye Baker. Honestly over time it would make me laugh as the choreographed crying for money almost happened on cue every single week; it got so bad that I could predict when the crying would start on cue while sitting there with Janine bored out of our minds. Then there were these people speaking in tongues and I don't know what the hell they were saying but everyone would just stretch out their arms to them and be quiet as these people were supposedly filled with the spirit of god and speaking in Aramaic or some other ancient language. It was like we were all supposed to understand what they were saying or something. What a joke it all was and mom bought into it hook line and sinker. Man what torture these two plus hour sermons were, absolute torture and not one ounce of fun did I ever have and any interest in it that I ever displayed would just be to appease mom. Mom met some nice people who became long standing friends there though as mom made friends and was loved by all wherever she went for that matter. Growing up Catholic though and then losing my faith at a very young age, this whole scene was just ridiculous to me and I despised it.

One day when I wasn't around, mom got her hooks into Charlene and started spewing off all this stuff about religion to her. Charlene's family was not a religious one and she was interested in religion and she wanted to make friends with mom; so after some preaching mom got Charlene to agree to go to church with the family that coming Sunday. When I was told this by mom and Charlene I was like yeah ok and Charlene and I retired to my room where I immediately blasted Charlene, saying what the hell are you doing? Charlene knew me as a Catholic as I went to a Catholic high school and wore a cross for an ear ring but she didn't realize just what she had agreed to. Charlene thought we were going go to a Catholic mass and when I explained to her what she was in for, she changed her tune about going to church real fast.

I then angrily told mom that we were not going to church and that's when mom lost it and became absolutely furious. I left the room and returned to my bedroom and mom followed me down to the basement yelling at me all the way with Bill right behind her. Charlene was already in the room along with Janine and I sat down in an easy chair as mom and Bill entered the room to continue the verbal assault. Mom yelled and screamed about how we were going to hell and then proceeded to start to rip down all of the posters of my favourite bands that donned my walls; all the while yelling about the devil's music and how it had a hold on me. And of course with me being as disgusted with the whole religion as I was and what mom was doing to my possessions; I fired back and tried to stop her from tearing down my posters as did Charlene and that's when Bill stepped in.

He stood in front of me with his eyes bulging out and his face turning red, as it always did whenever he got in my face, and he started yelling and spitting at me just as he had done so many times before. I don't know what triggered it, I probably mouthed off, but the next thing I knew he had me by the throat in the chair, crouched over me and choking the life out of me. That really sent the scene into a madhouse, Janine started crying and Charlene started freaking out yelling at Bill to let me go and mom actually held Charlene back, all the while still yelling a bunch of religious garbage at me. Then it happened, Charlene called mom a fucking bitch and cocked back to punch mom in the face and mom shrieked as the fist came at her, but Charlene didn't hit her as much as she wanted to and should have; but in that split second that mom shrieked it distracted Bill just enough that he loosened his grip around my throat. So quickly I raised up both my legs and pulled my knees into my chest and when Bill turned back to face me again I kicked him full force with both my feet right into his stomach. Now I was not yet a man but I had some pretty good strength to me, and the force of the blow winded Bill and put him down to his knees giving me the opportunity to escape. With that Charlene, Janine and I got the hell out of the house as fast as we could run.

Oh god were we ever freaked out, and looking back rightfully so; what a scene that was and I couldn't calm down after all that and neither could the girls. I had forgotten my stash at the house and I really wanted to smoke a joint to help me relax, but there was no way I was going back to the house; so I convinced Janine to go back to the house and get the stash while I waited for her. Charlene headed home to be with her parents while the retrieval was going on and we told Charlene we would catch up with her in a bit. Janine got the stash and we smoked a joint and calmed down a bit and then headed to Charlene's. By that time Charlene had told her parents the entire story and they were both extremely concerned; but due to the sex stuff between Charlene and me they told me that I could hang out there for a while but not stay for an extended period of time.

It was ok I told them and I got on the phone with Larry and told him about what had just happened and he freaked. He was going to kill Bill; but I told him no, just to please come and get Janine I. He did and then we spent who knows how many days just baked out of our minds afterwards. I didn't return home for a week or so after that incident, until mom called me up one day crying and begging for forgiveness for what had happened. Reluctantly I returned home; but believe me I never went to that church again after that incident and Bill never laid another hand on me again after that incident. However Bill would still tell me every once in a while that I was going to hell because I didn't believe in his religion; and it got to the point, that once I started getting braver, that I started telling him to fuck off and started standing up for mom and Janine as well whenever he would focus his anger on them. I even chased him around the house swinging a tennis racket at him this one time when he got physical with mom and shoved her into a closet.

The writing was on the wall though for Charlene and me after this; she would still get on my case about my drug use and I honestly didn't care about her anymore as getting wasted had become my whole life after that incident. I despised living with Bill and mom and Larry allowed me to crash at his place whenever I wanted. I became a permanent fixture on his couch and slowly I just stopped calling or seeing Charlene altogether. Charlene and I went away for a week together with her family, late that summer, to a cottage that her parents had rented in Port Perry; but I spent the whole week drunk and stoned. It was also around this time that Charlene decided that she didn't want us to have sex anymore because we had a pregnancy scare not too long before that and so she just cut me off.

Well, between nagging me about drugs, having no sex and how I was feeling inside about everything that was going on; that was it for me and I was done with Charlene. A couple weeks after we got back from the trip to Port Perry I just picked up the phone one night, called her up and told her that was it, I was breaking up with her. I didn't even blink an eye or give it a second thought and it destroyed her. I found out later on that she spent almost an entire month in her room just crying all the time; but it didn't matter to me as I was stone cold and just went on with my life smoking my brains out. I really hated myself and my life and at this point I could have easily became a teenage suicide statistic; but it was Larry my brother who was the one that kept me going through all those tough times even if he didn't know exactly how I felt inside.

I would hear stories of what Charlene was going through since our break up periodically and she had unfortunately gotten mixed up with the wrong guy while on the rebound from me and had gotten pregnant only a couple of months after our break up. And this guy was a real loser too; he beat her up and treated her like total shit. It took a while for these stories to filter to me, I think it might have even been Charlene that told them to me directly; but once I heard about them I became incensed and put the word out to Cathy, (Brenda's girlfriend) to notify me when he was around at Streetsville high school as I heard he was hanging out around there a lot. Then one day Cathy called me saying he was there and I high tailed it down to the school while taking my lunch break from work. Cathy pointed him out to me in the cafeteria and I grabbed a hold of him by the hair and dragged him out to the front of the school to give him the beating of his life. He played innocent at first not even knowing who I was but then I told him exactly who I was and his tune changed awfully quickly. He told me that Charlene was lying and that he hadn't done anything to her and he started to cry and beg me not to kill him. I slapped him a few times and punched him in the stomach but I was so disgusted that he was down on his knees crying that I couldn't kick his ass and left.

I met up with Charlene again after Christopher her son was born and we went for a walk and talked and I told her I wanted her back but she said she wasn't interested in me anymore and that she was thinking of dating my good friend Rick. With that Charlene and I parted ways for good and the hurt of her rejection lasted with me for many years. She would come around the restaurant I worked at with her soon to be husband and I would see her somewhat frequently with that being constant reminder of the remorse I felt for the way things ended and how I missed her so. Up until just recently we never really spoke again after that and it's nice that we're becoming friends again now through facebook.

Janine was not so lucky in life though as she also hated her life and made an attempt at suicide by overdosing on pills a couple of years prior to all this. Janine was taken to the hospital and spent three months under psychiatric evaluation and I was quite horrible to Janine during that time as I had always felt that Janine was a selfish little brat ever since she was a little kid. I believed that her suicide attempt was a farce; and I told my mom so when she asked for my help the night Janine made her suicide attempt. I shunned Janine during this time and didn't visit her in the hospital or give her any sympathy to what she was going through. She moved in and out of the house all the time during her teenage years as she was not at all equipped to deal with the emotional trauma that had enveloped our family. I was so blinded by my own trauma and consumed by my own world that I never saw clear to what everything had done to Janine as well. Things were and have never been good between Janine and me as we have just coexisted over the years; which has been very easy at times since we are almost exactly alike. If anything she's the more intelligent person of the two of us.

Day after day during my senior year of high school; well, those days that I actually went to school, Larry would meet me at the bus stop after school with a case of beer or a bottle of booze or some dope and we would get smashed. I had quit my job at Zellers after three years due to building frustrations with management and for the longest time until I got a part time job, Larry carried me financially and shared with me whatever he had, no questions asked. Larry and Brenda boarded at my house for a while when I was 18 and then moved in with his sister Patricia for a while and then they finally got their own place a couple of years later. Once they left my place, I was a permanent fixture on their couch or a third wheel to them, Larry's sidekick as I saw it. They'd feed me, take me wherever they went and I'm pretty sure that Brenda would get annoyed at times that I was around so much; but I was never told to get lost and I tried my best not to cause much trouble.

I lost my part time job after a while and deservedly so as I was skimming money, with the guys I was working with, and spending it all on drugs which we were all doing basically all the time even at the store while we were working. One time I even did LSD while I was working. My time working at that job, if you can call it that; was flat out drug fuelled madness and one long free party and it didn't bother me that I had lost my job one bit.

I graduated from high school that summer and spent the next four months bumming money from my mom and just getting by. Larry carried me again at this time while I was out of work as mom didn't have much money and reluctantly gave me whatever she could, as I was basically the one doing most of the chores around the house. That September I started a job at a local restaurant and I stuck with that job for nearly 5 years. It was mind-numbing boring work and I was terrible in the kitchen. I just basically put in time there to get paychecks to feed my drug habit and to attend the occasional rock concert.

It was at this time that I first developed my friendship with Don who was Raymond's brother and a busboy in the restaurant. It is a friendship that still endures to this very day. Don and I became friends while taking turns scratching lottery tickets while working Thursday nights. I was still good friends with Raymond at the time but Raymond and I were drifting apart as Raymond was dishonest and terrible with money which bothered me to no end. Don's and my friendship only grew with our similar interests in music and we began going to rock concerts together without Raymond and soon just started hanging out in general. Once Don returned from his college years in Guelph with a new party hearty attitude that only brought us closer together. Then a couple of white water rafting trips to the Ottawa river over the next 2 summers just cemented our friendship, as on one of those trips I actually helped save Don from drowning with the help from another guy. I began to consider Don as my closest friend, after Larry, and I began to integrate Don into all aspects of my life. Looking back Don has really helped me through a lot of tough times in my adult years and I can honestly say that he is the only person in my life that has never ever wronged me intentionally and for that I really respect him as a human being.

Life continued the same for me for a while; I was getting stoned to block out all the misery inside of me but no matter how hard I tried to block it out, the reality of my home life would not go away. Mom and Bill's relationship was always strained and that relationship has forever damaged the individual relationships between my mom, my sister and I. We were always lashing out at each other, mostly verbally but sometimes even physically. I was in no way able to communicate the feelings I had inside; as I couldn't even understand them myself as they were so muffled because of all the drugs I was doing. The one thing I knew though was that I despised Bill with every ounce of my being, as he was a disgusting man and not just because of his unbearable foot odour; he abused our dog and he had now just started to abuse Janine physically as well as mom.

One night while I was down in my room and it was late; I was trying to get some sleep for work the next day and mom and Bill started arguing once again. Mom wanted some money from Bill to pay the bills and Bill made a sarcastic comment to her asking if she had been a good little girl to deserve the money. Mom just lost it on him and started screaming and yelling. I lied there with a pillow over my head trying to block out the yelling but it was no use and the worst kind of rage began to build inside of me. Rage, that just burned through my heart and into my soul and as the argument stopped and mom returned to her bedroom something just snapped inside me. I couldn't take one more single moment of my life and I headed upstairs for what has now become the defining confrontation of my life.

I headed straight for Bill as he sat there so smugly watching TV; I was so full of rage and disgust for everything he had done to my family over the last 5 years. I stood in front of him and while looking down I calmly said to him you know what Bill you're a fucking asshole and with that he clicked on and jumped up to confront me and just as quickly as he was up I shoved him back down with all my might. The force of the blow actually made his feet flip up and I said yeah you heard me you are a fucking asshole and by this time I was now yelling at him and mom heard the commotion and came running from her room. By the time she got there I had my finger in his face and continued to yell at him; I want you to get your fucking shit and get the fuck out of my house right now or I'm going to fucking kill you. And he jumped up again and got right in my face as he had done so many times over the years trying to intimidate me; but this time it wasn't going to work and I shoved him back down again. I then repeated it again and said get your fucking shit and get the fuck out of my house now; and that's when mom piped up behind me and said yeah get out now.

This was it for me; either he was going to leave or I was going to die trying to kill him; I could not take one more moment of my home life, all the abuse, the mental cruelty, the fear, it was over NOW! He started yapping and I just kept repeating it over and over again; shut your fucking mouth, get your fucking shit and get the fuck out of my house now. Well I guess he finally got the message and I don't know why, maybe he was scared but I don't think so, he probably could have easily kicked my ass, but maybe he knew that I was at the point where I just might have slit his throat in his sleep, and so he did it. He continued yapping off periodically and I just kept telling him to shut his fucking mouth and to get the fuck out as I sat on the couch with mom watching his every move very careful-ly; but he did it. He packed it all up right then and there; every last piece of crap he had in the house and he put it all into his cube van; and he left. It was finally over; hallelujah it was finally fucking over! And so, soon a new chapter would begin for my family but the damage that that man had done lingered for years; long after he was gone and I don't think it will ever truly be gone.

Bill had quite the hold over mom and she asked in the not too distant future for forgiveness for him and asked if he could return to the home but Janine and I stood united; we told mom that if Bill returned to the home that we would both leave the home and she would never see us again. Bill never came back again. I didn't see Bill again until 4 years ago when I ran into him at a grocery store and we spoke and at that time in my heart, even though I didn't say so; I forgave him. With all that was bad during those 5 excruciating years there were some good times too, but they were very few and far in between, but they were there. I have made attempts at understanding how Bill became who he was, the son of an abusive immigrant mother, abandoned by his father, but he is responsible for his actions and he is not my responsibility. I never plan on seeing him again. I took one positive thing from my time with Bill though; I learned how to work hard. I'll always remember that about him, he was as strong as a bull and a very hard worker.

After I had thrown Bill out of the house mom couldn't cover the household bills on her own as Bill had been pretty terrible with money and they had accumulated considerable debt over the course of their marriage. So I had to assume the responsibility of paying the mortgage or risk losing the family home and for the next 3 years I worked 2 jobs to help make ends meet. It was a tough time for me handing over considerable sums of money to my mother every payday and I felt I was given very little respect during those years by either mom or especially Janine. They aura of entitlement that those women displayed to the family home really hurt and disgusted me. I was now the man of the house, but inside I was still just a scared child, I was very lonely and sad. I continued with the same drug fuelled lifestyle for 2 years and would repeatedly lash out at my mom and my sister. Over time and it soon came to the point that I felt little to nothing in regards to love for either of them anymore. Our family was broken by the years of misery with Bill and we were incapable to understand or repair the damage.

As time passed I quit doing drugs and over time it became a reality that I was going to stay clean. So Brenda began to ask me if I could possibly help or influence Larry to quit his addictions as well. Larry was spending most of their free money on dope and beer and there wasn't much left over for anything else. Plus there was another side to it too, Larry had always been quite the Wildman

in our younger days doing stuff like running up and over cars, getting into fights and losing his cool in many circumstances; but now
all that behaviour was translating into moodiness and quite the short
fused temper. The only thing that was moderating this behaviour
was his substance abuse. I started making comments from time to
time about how good I felt to have quit smoking dope and questioned him as to why he continued on with it, but it never really
went any farther than that as he always justified his using. The
years continued to pass much the same with regards to Larry's
addictions.

Larry and Brenda's second child was born and I then connected
with and eventually married Carrie and then Charles was born and
we all continued to grow up. But once I was married to Carrie;
Larry and I started to grow apart and I started to see our relationship
in a different light. I started to resent all the little jokes that Larry,
Brenda and Patricia were making at my expense; the fat jokes and
especially the nickname that I had been given; Squid Loaf. Larry
had started call me squid years earlier as a joke, saying that I was a
shit or something because that's what squid's would do. The name
then got combined with loaf one night after one of the dances at the
Streetsville arena where Larry and I would bartend. Patricia was
absolutely trashed and started trying to call me an oaf, but she was
slurring her words and instead of saying oaf she started to call me a
loaf. Not soon there after Squid Loaf was born and at first I didn't
mind it; I thought it was funny but as the years progressed and I
would get presented as Charlie the squid loaf or sometimes just as
squid loaf or squid alone it started to bother me.

Over time I started to really get upset about the name and once I
started bringing Carrie around Larry and Brenda's home, Carrie
started joining in on the jokes about me. It just seemed to me like I
was at the center of all the ridicule; and I actually had to tell Carrie
to stop joining in on the joking and teasing because I really didn't
like it anymore and I was getting very infuriated about it inside. I
felt like I was changing, like I was garnering some respect in life;
but whenever I went around Larry, Brenda or Patricia it was like I

was this pathetic 18 year old kid again, and that 18 year old kid was not too far off from killing himself back then. I didn't want to be that person again.

So slowly over time I saw less and less of Larry and we drifted apart. I didn't call much anymore and I barely ever went over to his place and mainly just concentrated on my family life with Carrie and Charles. I still involved Larry in everything in my life as he was my brother; how could I not involve him after everything we had been through together over the years? He was the best man at my wedding, he was the first person I called when Charles was born and he was the first person I turned to whenever I was in crisis with Carrie; but I had lost all respect for him and he was now in the same classification as mom and Janine, and that's grrr family. Larry's and my relationship became exactly like Janine's and my relationship; we were so much alike that it was easy to coexist and when things were good, everything was fine but when there was conflict the rage I felt inside towards them was intense.

Things really started to go bad for Larry and I when we all went on the third big white water rafting trip with a whole slew of friends of Don's and mine from work. Carrie and I drove to Ottawa with Larry and the rage I felt towards him manifested itself during the trip, right out in the middle of the river while we were paddling through the rapids. I was steering the boat as I was experienced at it from the previous two trips that Don and I had been on and I was trying my best. It isn't such an easy thing to do to steer the boat no matter how good at it you are; and of course we would go out of control from time to time. So Larry, being the genius he is at times decided that it was easy to steer and he started criticizing me to no end about steering and that just set me off and I started yelling at him and telling him I wanted to fight him and stuff. Everyone on the boat did not enjoy themselves much and Carrie tried her best to calm me. I turned over the steering job to Larry and he soon found out that it was not so easy after all. After that scene I was just pissed at him and then further to that confrontation it didn't help matters that there was this other guy who was a drunken moron and was just pissing everyone else off to no end as well. That guy got so obnoxious that Carrie actually came close to kicking his ass. Seriously the woman that was so friendly and that everyone liked so much; she wanted to kick the crap out of him. So tensions were very high that day and that weekend could not have ended any sooner for many of us; but the damage was done between Larry and I and I didn't forgive him for that scene out on the river and that set the scene for the confrontation that was to become the end of our friendship for many years.

I had and have been running a complex baseball pool for many years and most of my guy friends were and are involved in the pool. Larry, Don and Carlos had all been members of the pool since its inception; although Larry didn't ever really have the passion for following baseball that I did. I think he joined the pool to be close to me and to also feel somewhat like a normal guy who fit into the crowd. I always helped him with his decisions on player moves within the confines of the league such as trades and acquiring free agents and he became an integral member of the league and became friends with most of the guys in the league.

That Christmas following the summer of the rafting trip, Don had one of his now historic holiday DX parties and Larry went to the party. Unfortunately for me, Don and I have been working on opposite shifts at work for the last 8 years and he scheduled the party on a Saturday night that I was working so I was unable to attend. I heard that it was another classic bender, as Don's DX parties have always been spectacular and the next time I saw one of the guys from the baseball pool at work I listened intently as the stories that were told. I then heard something come out of this guy Mike's mouth that just made me snap; he was telling one of the stories and then all of the sudden he referred to me as squid loaf. When he said that my eye brows rose up and I started feeling angry and I said where the hell did you hear that? He then told me that Larry had been telling stories about me to the baseball pool guys at the party and that he had heard my nickname was squid loaf. Mike continued on with the stories but all I was seeing now was red; I became enveloped in rage and I was so furious with Larry that the moniker squid loaf was now following me into my workplace. I told Mike to never call me that again and went home to write a very nasty email to Larry.

I was no longer Charlie the squid loaf, I had long ago cut my hair and was a family man and a shift lead at my work who had an excellent income and I wasn't going to be the butt of their jokes any longer. I fired off a very nasty email blasting Larry for his drug abuse and how his jokes were only an avenue for putting me down to make him feel better about his situation. I continued on with how pathetic I felt he was for his treatment of me and for how he was so proud of the results garnered by his fantasy baseball team even though I was the one who was pulling his team's strings from behind the scenes. It was quite the brutal email and maybe I did go too far but I was furious with him and the feelings of resentment I had developed towards him over the last 5 years had just boiled over. In hindsight had I been a better communicator maybe things would have been different; but I was still clouded to all my thoughts and was not yet mature enough to express the true hurt and fear of my past that I was running away from and how Larry was continually pulling me back there with the way he saw me and how I was treated by him and his family.

His response to that email was one of the most hurtful things that had ever been said to me in my life and both devastated and enraged me. He said that I was a porn freak and that I disrespected Carrie and Charles continually and that there was no way my marriage would ever last; he further called me a mental degenerate and said that I would continually be in crisis for my entire life and that I would always require therapy as I was so pathetic. Then just for good measure he really went to the worst possible place he could go as he referenced to when we were children and how I was such a cry baby when we were younger and that was probably what I was going to do now and for that matter he didn't care what my reply was going to be as this was the end of our friendship. Well there's no doubt it was and other than speaking briefly at a mutual childhood friend Billy's wedding and then seeing each other from time to time at some baseball diamonds, but never speaking to each other, we walked for 6 years on separate paths.

That is until one day while surfing through facebook I saw Brenda's name on the people you might know list and so I said what the hell and added her as a friend as I had never had any real problem with Brenda at all. Just after doing that I found Larry on that list too and I thought about it for a moment and then added him too. Over time I had gotten a few updates from mutual friends such as Mary as to what was going on with Larry in his life while we had been apart. I knew a few years prior he had developed mental illnesses, but no one could really tell me what was going on and honestly I was curious but in the end I didn't care all that much. So I listened to hear what was going on from people but I never made contact with him except for the time that I found out that Brenda's mom had passed one month after the fact and sent an email of condolence to her through Larry. Brenda's mom and dad were/are upstanding people and I would further go to say that they are the best kind of people.

After Larry accepted my friend request, the message that he posted on my wall on facebook really made me question my thinking about him; he said hey dude, I missed your positive existence involved in mine, nice mug. So not too long after that first contact and a lot of thought and conversations about it with Connie, Don, mom and Janine; one morning after I returned home after a night shift there was Larry in the chatroom and we started talking. The conversation quickly became very intense, as we both were very tired and the topic of his mental illness was discussed freely. He said he didn't see the same person looking back at him in the mirror anymore and outlined all 5 of his diagnosis and their symptoms. I told him that the only thing new that I was hearing in my opinion was the extreme depression that he was experiencing and that I had observed all those qualities of behaviour in him long ago. The conversation while being pleasant soon became upsetting to both of us and he said he was crying a little and I was slightly doing the same. He said he had to go because he couldn't handle things right now and we said our goodbyes and exchanged phone numbers and I told him that I would see him soon. But I was worried because I didn't know what his state of mind was like and I wondered if he had lost it and become a shell of a person? I wasn't sure, so I decided to send Brenda the following message before I made anymore contact:

On the qt or not please. I am aware of Larry's situation mental health wise although not to what degree. Stacey, Mary and Cliff & Erin have told me snippets over time. Will it be ok to rekindle our friendship and will he be able to handle it? He did say he was crying a bit when we chatted Saturday morning and that it was a little much too handle and I even teared up myself a little bit to be honest. He did say though that he needed my contact. I guess what I'm saying is I don't want to hurt him or send him into any type of a bad mental state if we poke and prod into him any further or into I for that matter. Please advise of your thoughts on the matter as I wish to be respectful of your family and home.

Brenda responded with the following message in the next couple of days:

Hey, all is good. He needs the support if you can give it, especially you. There will always be ups and downs but you can't really hurt him or do any more damage. He would actually be more worried about hurting you.

So I decided that in the future, when everything had settled down as I was right in the middle of the move to the new home with mom and was just calming things down after a big confrontation with her; that when I felt ready I would approach Larry again and see what I could do to help him. Little did I know what was to lie ahead when I finally saw my brother after all these years.

Chapter 3

<u>Answer</u>

Awoke anew,
in the first beautiful sunrise;
angel passed over,
to complete surprise.
Here lies the pitiful heap,
of degredation;
clear of the clouds,
of hallucinations.
Abused by the confusion,
of hypocrisy;
brutal is the war,
of a traumatized family.
Voyage is leading,
to the promise of a cage;
intellect can not comprehend,
this uncontrollable rage.
Loving arms embrace,
can grant the tortured mercy;
but profound trails,
scream for the epiphany.
Sobered and cleansed
in the face fear;
blown smoke of the spirit,
now disappear.
Change the engraved,
to become whole;
save yourself,
and free your soul.

I guess it is somewhat odd looking back at the old partying days that it was at Clarice's place of all places that I came to the realization, not too long before Larry and Brenda's wedding, that I was going to quit using recreational drugs. Oh man did I ever party back then; it was every weekend, it was all week long, and it was every night. Around the time of my realization there were 2 major spots to hang out and party, my basement and Clarice's apartment. This period carried on for a while; when looking back it seemed like it was forever. I had been going 4 years pretty hardcore mainly just smoking hash or weed, sometimes I would drink myself silly and there was the odd time that I did LSD. The final and last time I did LSD was when I came to the realization that I needed to quit doing recreational drugs for good.

My drug abuse at this time was pretty well out of control, I spent almost every unaccounted for dollar on purchasing hash. I had 3 different circles of friends that I could call up and within hours we would be hanging out smoking dope. I had eight friends that you could almost call my best friend in a way, (Gene, Chad, Sandy, Pete, Zack, Buddy, George and obviously Larry), and they would hang out with me for days on end and we would just smoke our brains out. These guys were all interchangeable too and they all knew each other so we were in a way like a big commune as every one shared with everyone. It was a pretty cool lifestyle in some ways, but in others it was not. Over time I began to not enjoy the feeling that I would get when I would initially get high, or over dosing as I saw it, so I just stayed a degree of being high all the time rather than going through that initial feeling and it was easy having so many close friends who were doing the same.

It was at this biggest monster party weekend that I can ever remember when I really started to downward spiral into extreme abuse. One of the circles of friends that I ran in decided as a group that we were going to rent some cottages up north in this party town and then after all the planning was done we headed there for the first long weekend of the summer getting ready to rip it up for a whole weekend. And did we ever; I personally had 2 cases of beer and a quarter ounce of hash and consumed the whole sha bang in 2 days. Wrecked, oh man let me tell you my friend, whoa. The drunken madness was forever unequalled; I did mescaline, I walked around town for hours going to party after party, I cooked up the biggest batch of French toast you ever saw for all my buddies, it was just a great weekend; well kind of. The reason it was kind of, was because once we returned from the weekend; that hardcore party mentality didn't stop for weeks afterwards. The crowd just went overboard, and then the other 2 crowds I ran in got pulled in as well and it just became one giant party for weeks on end.

Then one Friday this buddy of mine comes by my place and he's got some purple blotter LSD; so a large group of us dropped it. Whoa, that had to be the strongest LSD ever, I saw trails like you wouldn't believe and honestly a few hours of my memory is lost to that experience. Usually I can remember every single detail about everything whether I was drunk, stoned or whatever, maybe it gets blurry with age but if it was a major happening I can remember it.

So the next thing I remember is watching Cheech and Chong movies in Clarice's apartment and hallucinating while watching them. Those guys sure do know how to manipulate people on drugs, seeing the movie under the influence really blew me away. I had lots of hallucinations that night; the major one being what I believed to be the ability to see people's souls, as I kept seeing red glows around my friends that night. Slowly but surely I started to come down off the LSD and wanted to start smoking again as did the 15 or so guys that had congregated at Clarice's place as while we were on LSD, smoking dope was having no effect on us. So one of the biggest joints I had ever seen in my life was rolled up. For some reason all the guys just started throwing in hash from their personal stashes probably because they were lazy and didn't want to roll their own joints.

What a monster joint it was and it seemed like it lasted for ever but after it was done I remember sitting on the floor in the kitchen with this dude Jay, and I didn't feel so good so I went outside to get some fresh air. Well I didn't make it outside as I blacked out at the door and I mean right out. The next thing I remember was that the crowd had become much smaller as many of the guys had left. There were now about 6 people left or so and it was like 4 in the morning maybe, I don't know exactly. If you've ever done LSD when you come down you feel like talking, and me I love to talk and chat; and I did so to no end. I was now thinking about how much I hated what I was doing to myself with all the drugs; and smoking cigarettes too for that matter. It was also around this time that I noticed something in the eyes of all my friends, it was really strange but it looked like each one of their left eyes was drooping a little on their face. Somehow I put together that the damage that each one of them was doing to themselves with their drug abuse was being reflected in their eyes, since I believe that the eyes are the window to the soul. It was like we were all having little strokes from the use of drugs and our faces were becoming slightly para-lyzed on the left side. Janine's eyes; who was around for all this, especially freaked me out as she looked the worst of all of us to me and I said to her Janine what the hell have you been on?

Then out of the blue, from the back of my mind somewhere out rang this phrase, "cigarettes isn't that cocaine", and it just kept ring-ing through my mind, over and over again. I then started saying the phrase over and over again and my buddies, who were trying to sleep, were like what the fuck Charlie, go to sleep. I later found out from mom that it was Bill's voice inside my head as that was what he had said to me when he initially found out that I was smoking. But there was no sleeping for me in the cards as my mind was going a mile a minute and I started thinking about the hierarchy of people in the area and just who and where all the drugs were com-ing from. Then it hit me, "anyway you do it; it's all just the same". Anyway you do it; it's all just the same. Any way you get high, the end result is the same, you're getting high; whether you drink, smoke, snort, ingest, inject, it doesn't matter because you're getting high. I was always so proud in a way that the crowd had basically only smoked and drank; but this realization really freaked me out, and it became Whoa, Whoa, Whoa; and my friends looked at me like I was loosing it and then I jumped up and said I gotta go. I headed out the door, to the elevator and outside. Just after I was

outside my chest felt heavy and I thought I felt something go pop
and then I blacked out again. I honestly thought at that moment, as
I was falling to the ground, that I was about to die.

Later on I awoke to the sun beating down on my face as I was
lying there in the parking lot. I was scared out of my mind and I
got up and high tailed it home. I was now almost completely sober
except for the lingering effects of the LSD and I burst into my
house and ran upstairs to my mom's room and woke her up. I told
her something about my drug use although I'm not sure what I said
exactly. Mom knew what I was up to somewhat, just not the extent.
I was totally freaked out and ended up crying in her arms until I fell
asleep. When I awoke later that day I just kept on smoking, it was
just too engrained in me to just give it up on the drop of a dime, but
it was that acid trip that changed everything in my life. A few
months later after all the summer parties were over and I had prepared myself mentally I just gave it all up one day, well August 23,
1993 to be precise.

I always remember the exact day I quit doing drugs because it
was 5 days after one of the best concerts I have ever been too; Neil
Young, Pearl Jam, Soundgarden and Blues Traveler at the CNE sta-
dium in Toronto. What an awesome day that was, and what a mosh
pit there was in the general admission floor area, that being where I
had tickets to. Neil Young and Pearl Jam were on the stage at the
same time, the pit was so intense when Soundgarden played the
song Gun and I made it right to the front when Pearl Jam played the
song Alive. It was just a mind blowing day and that was the last
time I ever got completely stoned out of my mind.

There was however one slip up the next January after a woman,
oh isn't it always a woman with me, crushed me. It was the second
woman I ever had sex with and I fell head over heals in love with
her. Stacey was this gorgeous woman whom I met through Patricia
as Patricia and Stacey worked together. Stacey was 25 at the time
and was a total knockout; the first time I saw her, my eyes almost
popped out of my head. I came over to Larry's parent's house for a
swim and a barbecue and there she was in the backyard lying on a

towel sunbathing in this tiny black bikini. She was five foot nine and 130 pounds; she had a pretty face, an athletic tone body, a bronzed tan and brown curly hair. She was absolutely gorgeous and I remember Brenda jokingly saying something to the effect of down boy, but it was too late as I was enthralled by this woman.

I ran into Stacey a couple of more times as she liked to party it up and would hang out with Patricia on a semi regular basis and we would all congregate and whoop it up from time to time. I had quit smoking drugs but I still drank as I have never felt that I had a problem when it comes to controlling my consumption of alcohol. It was during this period in my life that I was working at my crappy job at the restaurant but there was one perk to having that job; I had the keys to the place and I could pretty well come and go in the middle of the night as I pleased. And I did, usually with a bunch of my friends, on a pretty regular basis. It was a lot of fun, we would crank the stereo up and drink and be merry till all hours of the night playing pool. It came about that Patricia and her husband Travis joined us one night and enjoyed themselves and soon after that so did Stacey. The night Stacey was to come I was quite excited about it because it was just going to be the four of us.

Did we ever have fun that night and during the course of the night it became apparent that Stacey was interested in me. At one point I remember her pressing her body up against me while I was shooting pool to check if I was lining up my shot correctly. I've never been any good at picking up signs from women, god knows I am not, but this was as blatant as could be and I had to be an idiot not to realize that she was interested. Stacey went bonkers that night and I remember her running around the restaurant and passing out on one of the tables not long afterwards. I ended up carrying her to the car and then again after the drive home, into a bed at Patricia and Travis's, once we retired there later. The bar at Patricia's was once again open for business that night and did we ever tie one on while playing some darts.

Later that night after we had our fill of drinking and everyone
was crashing out; I was lying on the couch in the den directly next
to the bedroom where Stacey was sleeping, watching a little TV
before I passed out. Then all of the sudden Stacey emerges from
the bedroom; enters the room where I am and says that it's sooo
cold in the bedroom and that's it, not another word. She then went
into the washroom and then returned to the bedroom. Inside I said
to myself; is that an invitation to join her in the bedroom? I wrestled with that idea for a little while and then I just said what the hell
go for it Charlie; and I did. I walked into the bedroom and she said
hi so I proceeded to lie down on top of her, and started kissing her
to which she kissed me back. Unfortunately at this point there's a
blur in my memory and I can't remember it all; but I do remember
performing oral sex on her and slamming it into her from behind
until I just couldn't go anymore. Sadly I never did ejaculate that
night due to how drunk I was and for that matter I remember Stacey
asking me to stop because she had had multiple orgasms and her
head was spinning.

After it was all done and over with I did not go to sleep; I sat
there very upset with myself at what I had done. I didn't want it to
be a one night stand to Stacey as I was now in love with her being
the stupid romantic fool I was, and still am. I wrestled and wrestled
with what I had done and for some reason at that time I came to
think that the best course of action would be to leave and so I did. I
walked home bombed out of my mind at 5 in the morning in the
middle of winter all the while very upset with myself and the situation I had put myself into. Once I got home and sobered up more I
had a change of heart, well it actually became a panic and I didn't
go to sleep that morning. I paced around my room just replaying
everything that happened over and over again, blown away at my
own stupid decision. Once the time came that I knew everyone
would be awake at Patricia and Travis's, as Stacey had to go to her
second job that morning, I called up and convinced Patricia to let
me talk on the phone to Stacey. Stacey's first question was of
course why did you leave? Somehow I came up with some sort of
an excuse, without telling her that I loved her, and she bought it,
somewhat and we agreed to see each other in the near future.

One of my greatest attractions to Stacey was the way she smelled; she would wear some sort of Calvin Klein perfume and it just drove me wild. She had been wearing my sweatshirt that night after she passed out and her perfume just coated the sweatshirt. I remember not washing that sweatshirt for weeks afterwards because the scent was embedded into it and I would smell it periodically just to recover the mindset of that night with her. We went on one date after that but things didn't work out. We had a few beers at her place prior to going out and I tried to impress her by showing her how I could down an entire beer in one shot from a glass; I don't think it worked though and it probably made me look foolish actually. We went and saw the movie In the Name of the Father with Daniel Day Lewis in it; the movie which I now consider to be my favourite of all time. That movie honestly made me cry twice during the course of it, and had my arm hairs standing up on end and my heart pounding at the ending. In my opinion it's sad that movie lost to Forest Gump at the Oscars and that Daniel Day Lewis lost to Tom Hanks. Don't get me wrong Forest Gump is a good movie, a great movie, but In the Name of the Father is a true classic; absolutely amazing in my opinion.

The date ended and we kissed when she dropped me off at my home. After she left I was on cloud nine; I went to my room in the basement and cranked up my stereo and threw on some romantic music, November Rain by Guns N' Roses is the song that comes to mind. The next thing I did was so foolish, as I called her and left her a message; but that wasn't enough and I called her again. Oh boy if I could only go back in time and speak to that dumb 21 year old kid, DUMMY! What a dummy I was, I was just so pathetic! I sent flowers to her work but it actually might have been before the date, I'm not sure but I know I did send her flowers.

The end result though, was that she dumped me. I don't even think she gave me that much respect. She was 25, a woman and was career and goal oriented and I was 21 and was still just a kid. Sometime later Patricia, Travis, Stacey and I all went to a Phil

Collins concert together and Stacey seemed to be interested in me that night too, but that really bothered me and I ditched them before the night was over, as being around Stacey made me a little crazy.

Years later I'm pretty sure that Stacey regretted her decision to "dump" me after catching a vibe during a conversation between us at a party; that was once again held at Patricia's. By this time in my life I was all cleaned up and had become somewhat of a respectable family man; Stacey flat out asked me how much my income was and I remember hearing a little sigh when I told her what it was. I was also made privy to a story by Brenda, about the conversation that took place when Stacey was told by Patricia that I had become engaged to Laura; Stacey's reaction was priceless. She replied to Patricia after Patricia told her the news that I was engaged; that she was not surprised by it because I was so good in bed. Yes men love their egos stroked too ladies, especially me.

The one bad thing that came out of my experience with Stacey was that I was so upset when Stacey "dumped" me that I did do drugs one last time. Even though I had quit doing drugs for 5 months I had not broken free from or lost all of my party friends. In time they all slowly faded away, but for the first year or so they were still coming around my place and still smoking and partying on a pretty regular basis. The most common way we smoked back then was doing bottle tokes or BT's as we all called them. We would role little tiny bundles of hash up, and well I don't want to tell anyone reading this how to smoke dope, but anyways every once in a while a BT would fall from the table onto the brown carpet I had in my room and would become lost. It actually became a game over the years who could find the BT's on the carpet and Hawkeye would be the assigned moniker of someone who could locate at BT.

I became quite good at doing this myself and developed a great system at one point, especially to use after parties. The brown carpet was very flat; almost an outdoor carpet and I could use a broom to sweep it up and then put everything into one pile and sift through the pile to retrieve the hash. Clarice has never let me live down to this day that I did my system at her place this one time when I was craving hash and was fresh out. I then I found what looked to be a piece of hash and bit into it to check if it was hash or not and it was a rabbit turd I believe. Clarice laughed so hard and she still references it to this day, grrr.

After being dumped by Stacey I was depressed, very depressed. I wanted my old life back and I retrieved from the carpet what was referred to as a session, which was about 5 BT's. That was enough to get me a little high or so I thought and I smoked it. When that initial feeling of being high hit, I freaked, I was so scared I thought I was going to die and I thought I had thrown it all away. After being clean for 5 months and then smoking some strong hash it got me so high that I panicked, I didn't know what to do. I ended up in the shower and let the water hit me in the face until the feeling subsided and I came back down. I knew from that day forward that I never wanted to get high from recreational drugs ever again, and I never have.

I can honestly say that after all this that I am not a recovering addict, I am a recovered addict. I was so mentally addicted to being high but not physically. Nowadays I can sit in a room with a bunch of guys that are smoking huge joints all night long while playing poker and even roll up those joints for them, which I enjoy doing. I can smell it, breath it, whatever; it does not bother me one single bit; except the fact that they are doing it in the first place. I am recovered I tell you; although some clinical people would probably disagree, but who cares what they think, it's what I think that matters. Smoking dope is not for me, it never was and I should have realized it a lot sooner than I did.

Chapter 4

<u>No Longer Dedicated</u>

Sunshine lights it so real,
darkness then blinds the zeal.
Conceived into everything,
believed onto not a thing.
Ancient words slowly drift on by,
in the end only man's complicated lie.
Long is this journey so far so wide,
all the hatred shames the world outside.
Live in a prayer,
lo a hope.
Live in a dream,
lo a wish.
Dreaming existence is not a crime,
praying for patience in the moments of time.
Long I weep,
lo the sorrow.
Long I cry,
lo the wail.
Crying souls surrounding me,
weeping for evil gripping we.
Forced conformity masks identity,
teetering insanity burns longevity.
Immersed in tears streaming flow,
are these trials leading to anywhere
besides down below.

I met my first fiancée Laura when she came down to my new apartment in Milton on Halloween night to complain about loud the music that was playing while a buddy of mine and I were drinking some beers. Laura lived in the apartment directly above mine and I find the way in which we met to be funny. Here is this attractive woman at the door all dressed up as a genie to complain about the music; realizes the music is not that loud after all, that it's just echoing and then proceeds to accept our invitation to join us and sits down and drinks with us all night until all the alcohol is consumed. I became smitten with Laura almost immediately; she was gorgeous, drop dead gorgeous at 5 feet 2, 110 pounds. She was half Filipino, half Caucasian and she had this long black flowing hair and a great body. After some intense courting and romancing she gave into me and we soon became a couple. I learned she was a poet and an aspiring actress and she was in actuality the first person who ever inspired me to write. After reading her works one night and falling madly in love with her when I felt a certain piece speak to me, I was inspired to write my own poetry. Looking back I don't think anything I wrote at that time was anything of significance, but it is at that moment where the writing started.

The intimate part of Laura's and my relationship started out slowly at first with just a little kissing and fondling. A house warming party we had at the apartment the month after we moved in was the first time I had any carnal knowledge of Laura. After everyone left that night and we were still quite inebriated Laura allowed me to perform oral sex on her in my bedroom, and this was even though I didn't have a bed yet. The love making between Laura and me soon became very intense, unbelievable actually as she was a complete animal in the bedroom. Things continued on like that for the first couple of months of our relationship. It was all very exciting and I fell madly in love with her although I don't think she felt the same way about me until a few months later.

A problem arose early on though outside of our relationship and was out of Laura's and my control but it affected us directly. Somewhat by accident, I found out when thumbing through a letter that my roommate Jessica had written to her cousin that she and Janine had had a lesbian experience together. I was shocked and very upset about this as Jessica and I had a friend relationship that was just a little more than a friendship. I can remember us almost having sex at one point while parked in a car drunk about a year before we decided to become roommates. Jessica always said when referring to our friendship that it was like we were married without the sex. I was furious at the repercussions of what my possible involvement with Jessica could have led to. It was outrageous that she could have done this, and I was beyond furious with her. What! Was she trying to land a brother and sister combination as a notch in her belt of sexual conquest, being that she was bi-sexual. I went into a rage about this to which Laura was witness to and it caused serious issues between us. Laura demanded that I forgive Jessica as she had become friends with Jessica and wanted to maintain the friendship as she didn't have many female friends. I begrudgingly accepted and confronted Jessica and pretended to forgive her, but inside I now despised Jessica with all of my being. I maintained that ruse of forgiveness for months for the sake of Laura's and my relationship.

Janine and I was a different story. I was furious with her as well, although I never really explained why. This situation caused turmoil between my mother and I as well as mom wanted me to forgive Janine for whatever reason I was angry and then used my grandmother's name while trying to convince me to do so. That really upset me, pissed me right off, literally enraged me. It was very close to Christmas when all this happened, so I was so upset that I decided to head to Syracuse, New York to spend the holidays with my father's cousins who lived there. It wasn't a pleasant holiday that year especially since I spent it away from Laura who I was very much in love with, but I did what I did to get through.

When I returned from Syracuse, Laura and I continued our relationship and it was pretty status quo for a long time until she developed a cyst on her vagina for which she required day surgery. It was quite painful for her and she was bed ridden for a week or so while she recovered. Well maybe she milked it looking back because I waited on her hand and foot, but I do remember her crying about the pain which really tugged on my heart strings. Once she recovered from the surgery our relationship began to go to the next level.

Laura was a pure animal when it came to the bedroom; she embraced my every fantasy, every single one. She especially embraced my catholic school girl outfit fetish; since I had gone to a catholic high school myself and spent 5 years of my life chasing girls in that outfit and trying to look up their kilts every chance I got. The love making between Laura and I was so intense at times that I would feel dehydrated. Laura was a "Squirtter", a condition that exists in 10% of women; that when she would ejaculate there would be a large discharge, sometimes a very large discharge, and I would always try my best to swallow it all. Sometimes it was so much that it would even choke me, no word of a lie. We would joke at times that we would need a never ending supply of linens because my bed was always soaked.

I can clearly remember one time while in the crowd at a concert in a club in Toronto, while Don was standing right next to me, that she gave me a hand job with her body pressed right up against me to shield anyone's view. Another time I remember her performing oral sex on me on the train and then us having intercourse in the washroom of that same train while returning home from seeing a musical. Laura's appetite for sex was just as ferocious as mine and she was always ready and willing. Sometimes it would be 2 or 3 or even more times than that a day and it was almost every single day during our relationship. At one point I even developed blisters on my penis from over use and even started getting migraine headaches when I would ejaculate. At then end of our relationship I had even lost 20% of my body weight and I hadn't been that light since I was 13 years old.

Laura was a real sweetheart too, very kind and very romantic. She was an epileptic and my sympathy and help with her condition also brought us closer together. She wrote me love letters and poems. I remember this one time while at the movies she returned from going to the restroom in a full length dress that I had bought for her and wanted to and we did, dance outside in the parking lot in the moonlight. And I was quite the romantic too; after having a Valentine's week, let alone just one day; the week culminated with me giving her a diamond ring while in her room that was lit by 50 candles or so, wearing my suit lying on her bed that was covered in rose petals and flowers. The ring itself was a very simple nice look-ing ring but was not supposed to be an engagement ring as I just thought it suited her when I purchased it.

Later on in our relationship; one night after making love she told me that she actually wished that the ring was an engagement ring out of the blue. So that immediately prompted me to; imagine this, get us out of bed, stark naked in the middle of the night. Then I get down on one knee; told her how much I loved her and proposed to her right there at that moment, to which she then accepted and off we went into all the bliss that accompanies an engagement.

It was all so romantic our time together; but then when things went bad, they went really bad really fast. I found out that Laura was carrying on a love letter campaign with this guy Herbert in Ireland that she had met in a Shakespeare chatroom online. While accidentally snooping again, I was looking for a cd honestly; I found a love letter written to Herbert and it devastated me. Laura had included a poem she said she had written for me in the letter to Herbert. It was never the same for Laura and I after finding that letter to Herbert and my neurotic and erratic behaviour went through the roof after that.

It was also around this same time that I let it be known that I had fraudulently forgiven Jessica for her discretion with Janine as Jessica was becoming closer with Laura and I did not trust Jessica one bit. Plus Jessica was making it clear just how jealous she was of Laura's and my relationship and she was angering me to no end. I found out later on that Jessica was also at this time in love with me as well; man did I ever have it going on at that time. Eventually Laura could no longer handle my erratic behaviour and insecurity and she mercilessly dumped me.

I remember sitting in my bedroom watching Jessica, another girlfriend and Laura, as they goofed around in the parking lot, taking pictures and joking around after a woman's day out together. Then Laura proceeded to enter the apartment and ask me to go out for a walk to talk. Soon after we left the apartment I noticed she wasn't wearing my engagement ring and I told her so. She produced the ring from her pocket and just flat out told me it was over. I started to cry and I begged and pleaded with her not to leave me; but she was stone cold and was not going to relent. I somewhat knew it was coming; we had had discussions to this extent in the not so distant past, but I didn't want to believe it. I was obliterated and destroyed.

Laura wanted to return to my apartment to retrieve her belongings, but I snapped out of my obliteration and told her to get the hell away from me. She wouldn't go; so I screamed at her and shoved this tiny little thing and scared her away. When I returned to the apartment Jessica had already bolted as she knew what was about to happen and I walked around the apartment in a daze. I decided right then and there to start packing as I was moving out of there. I called my mom balling and told her I was coming to stay with her and then called Don to come help me gather my belongings which he did. I remember throwing on Peter Gabriel's album So and listening to the song Don't Give Up and it calmed me somewhat. Don arrived and we grabbed what we could fit in his little Honda Civic and took off. The excruciating howls of my cat Mittens made me cry again as Mittens did not like to travel one bit. I returned to the apartment a few weeks later for my furniture and got through things the best I could with the help of some good friends.

Later on Laura and I met up one more time and I gave her back her belongings and we almost started things back up after a couple of drinks and the promise of a weekend away together. I even sang the song Amanda by Boston to her on the train before parting ways because that had always gotten to her, but she became aloof afterwards. The play she was in at the time was going to a festival and she didn't seem like anything between us mattered. So I wrote her a letter accepting our fate and said my goodbye to her and proceeded on with life as best I could.

After I became somewhat relieved of the sorrow of the rejection by Laura, I then became angry with her, very evil angry after I thought about things from a different perspective. Laura had been so dishonest with me and so very cruel that I wanted to hurt her just like she had hurt me. So I thought and I thought what would hurt Laura, how could I hurt Laura emotionally? I came up with a plan; a plan that I mapped out in my mind and then set out on the course of revenge. This guy I worked with at the time and talked out the whole plan with one night said I was an evil genius and he was dying to see how the plan played out in the future.

Laura had a roommate while we were together named Carol and they had a vicious falling out, it was so bad that physical violence was even involved. I sensed that Carol had a crush on me while I was in my relationship with Laura; well asking someone to have a threesome with them is a pretty obvious sign if you ask me. So I decided to make contact with Carol through a letter addressed to her that I sent to a neighbour across the hall from my old apartment. I knew that the neighbour and Carol were friends and that the neighbour would pass the letter along to Carol. In the letter I fully apologized to Carol for any wrong doing that she might have thought I had done to her during the course of Laura's and my relationship. I further said I wanted to be friends with Carol again, giving her my phone number in the letter.

Carol called me and she was very angry with me. I don't remember what the exact issues were, but I apologized and plead innocence and ignorance to it all and slowly but surely I wore Carol down and we became friends again. Carol was an attractive woman, 5 foot 5, 150 pounds, brown curly hair and had a very large posterior which I was intrigued by. Her voice was a little rough to take at times and she could be a little annoying with her goody goody attitude, but I found her to be attractive nonetheless.

In a few weeks time it came about that she invited me to join her at this re-enactment festival in Orillia. I agreed to go and spent the weekend doing this pioneer re-enactment with her and however corny I found it to be, I did it. Man I would never do that again, I hated it, but I was brimming with self confidence from my time with Laura and used this time together with Carol to romance her. We went skinny dipping in the bay; we walked through the festival shopping, I played the hurt sensitive guy when some old boyfriend of hers showed up and I really tugged at her emotions so that by the end of the weekend I was performing oral sex on her and then having sex. Carol was great in bed and very wild and uninhibited. She screamed a blue streak, she was aggressive in bed and I liked that and she liked to be in control and on top and I had no problem with that. In the shower, in the kitchen, when I was sick, it didn't matter; and that posterior I spoke of, well whoa I loved it and she could work it too, grinding me to death. Happy times my friend, my appetite was full again. It was so funny that by the end of the first time we had sex in the tent at the campsite; when we exited the tent the campsite was completely empty and everyone had left.

So now that I had bedded Carol and was continuing to do so; I put my plan of revenge into full action. I had Janine contact Jessica my old roommate and the confidant of Laura; pretending that things were not that good between Janine and me even though they now were as Janine quickly set aside our issues and supported me when things ended with Laura. Janine then purposely "accidentally" dropped the bomb that my new roommate at the time, Stan; was complaining to Janine when she supposedly was at my home for some reason or other. She said that Carol and I were keeping Stan up till all hours of the night because Carol would be screaming so loud during intercourse. And Janine played it to a T; she played ignorant to everything and that she was not ok with me and was loyal to Jessica. Janine pretended to drop the story totally by accident to Jessica and even sort of got Carol's name wrong, Kara, someone named Carrie, when she told Jessica about it.

Janine told me Jessica's reaction was priceless, CAROL she exclaimed and with that Jessica's jaw literally dropped to the floor and she couldn't believe it, she was absolutely shocked. Unfortunately I will never know what happened next; but I do believe the next chain of events would have been Jessica running straight to Laura and telling her, or freaking out to her, about what she had just heard from Janine and how authentic sounding it was. Well it didn't matter if it sounded authentic or not because I had made it authentic. I honestly did like Carol a lot; she was very hot in her own way and the sex was amazing. I'll never to this day know what Laura's reaction was when Jessica told her about Carol and I, but I believe that somewhere deep down inside of Laura that she did love me in someway in spite of however dishonest and cold she might have been to me during our relationship and when she dumped me. If that was so, which I believed it was, this would have hurt Laura because of her absolute disgust towards Carol. That was enough for me to believe that Laura would have been hurt emotionally in my revenge upon her. The plan played out perfectly, right down to every last detail just as I had foreseen it.

After everything finished up with Laura and Carol, Clarice was still around. She would come to visit me or come to parties and we would talk and once again we developed our connection. She always gave me so much respect and made me feel special. Once again though there was another man in her life and this time it was Steve. I wasn't pursuing Clarice too hard at this point like I had before because the heartbreak from Laura was just too devastating to me. Things changed in Clarice's and my relationship at this time; she was the one helping me out, being my friend, and giving me support and respect. She cared for me so much and treated me so well, and that really helped make me feel like living again. I did finally snap out of the Laura heartbreak after a while and went on with life however hard it was because I had a new purpose. I decided that what would make me happiest in life would be to have a family and going forward I was determined that I was going to have one.

Chapter 5

<u>Reflection</u>

Surprise at discovering vanished perspective,
look to comprise some thoughts of retrospective.
Degradation from a deceitful beauty,
translates to infatuation in the pursuit of family.
Romantic writer,
I condemn your spirit into domestic gloom.
Erratic soul,
I command you slowly fade into quiet doom.
A bond develops into the sublime.
Questions easily answered,
a time in the rays of sunshine.
Higher than the past this simple purity.
Inspire it no longer,
that all encompassing insecurity.
Dominate each day with soothing relief.
Desecrate myself gradually,
to the disbelief.
Trust inevitably broken by yawning complacency,
lust for comfort now just another fond memory.
Find the focus
Find the center
Found the peace

One night in the not too distant future after things ended with Carol I was at this club with a large group of my friends; including Clarice and some of her girlfriends. My soon to be future wife Carrie and her brother Chris also joined us that night after I made a call to Chris inviting him to come out and inquiring as to the status of his sister Carrie whom I called the hottie. Chris was my friend separately from Carrie for years, knowing him through work and other mutual friends. Oddly enough Chris would later become involved with Janine, and there was a relationship for a time that produced a child, my niece Kimberley. So unbelievably my children and their cousin Kimberley are truly the closest of cousins, as close as you can get without being brother and sister.

So the story goes that I was up dancing with Clarice and her girlfriends and then every once and a while I would leave them to go buy Carrie drinks. This continued on for much of the night until at one point when I was leaving Carrie to head back to Clarice, that was when Carrie grabbed me and kissed me. Well that was it, that was all the motivation I needed and Carrie and I started a drunken make out at the bar; that eventually lead to the drunken bedroom sex at my place, and the hung over bedroom sex the next morning and then days and days of intercourse after that. After a while I realized what was going on with Carrie and I knew that I couldn't have Clarice around anymore because of how deeply I felt for Clarice and how that might cause problems in my budding relationship with Carrie. So I told Clarice I couldn't be friends with her anymore, and I was as nice and as vague as possible about it but she got the message. Slowly but surely Clarice faded away.

Carrie was a girl for whom I had a crush on when I was a teenager. I'd see her around the neighbourhood and found her to be very attractive. She was a rocker chick, and I LIKED rocker chicks; Charlene also being a rocker chick. Carrie was a heavier girl, but that appealed to me. I actually love women any way they look as long as the have a pretty face and a nice personality; it doesn't really matter to me what their body looks like. Bring em on I always say I love them all. Carrie was about 5 foot 6, and weighed around 200 pounds and she was very pretty, with blond hair and while being heavy, she still had a nice figure.

So every once in a while I would see Carrie around; and I thought she was hot! I thought she was smoking hot! Brenda used to poke fun at me about it and say down boy. Carrie would later say that at the time when I was crushing on her as a teenager that she was not interested in me because of all the drugs I was constant-ly doing. She didn't like people who were stoners; but odd, the funny thing was that during the course of our marriage I was always the one that was clean and every once and a while she would be the one to smoke drugs with my friends.

Things with Carrie moved fast, really fast. It was like we had been together for years. We grew up in the same neighbourhood; we had many of the same friends and we knew the same people. It just felt so right and so comfortable with Carrie. I got along great with her dad Mark and he and I used to watch baseball games together all the time. Carrie and I sure were in sync and our rela-tionship escalated very quickly. I remember her slipping early on about her and I getting married and actually saying oh I crap I can't believe I just said that and me saying don't worry I am thinking the same thing and that's when I knew I had her. We shared our hopes and dreams and they were very similar. I told her how I wanted a family and so did she and the next thing you know we are deciding together after only less than 3 months into our relationship that we are going to try and have a baby. I still remember her holding her legs up in the air after intercourse trying to hold in my sperm. I proposed to her on Christmas Eve using a ring that my mom gave to me and we moved into my mom's apartment after the New Year for financial reasons.

There was never any turmoil between Carrie and me until we lived with my mom as mom and Carrie did not see eye-to-eye. There was always tension between them. Right around the time when Carrie and I moved in with mom there was a huge falling out between Janine, Chris, Carrie and I that would motivate us all not to talk for many years. Janine became pregnant with Kimberly and Carrie and I were told about it and told not to tell anyone. However I told Larry about it as Janine being pregnant was a crisis in my mind and I always spoke to Larry about crisis. Unfortunately, I don't know if I forgot to tell Larry it was a secret or that I did and he forgot but the next time Larry saw Janine and Chris in the neighbourhood he said congratulations to them. This then sent Janine and Chris into a rage. So Chris comes into their family home where Carrie and I happen to be and a barrage of yelling starts to the point where fuck you were the only words that were left. Carrie stood right beside me for the whole confrontation as she and Chris had their own issues and they also surfaced at this time and we were all done for many many years after that scene. Janine and Chris did not come to Carrie's and my wedding and I did not go to the hospital when Kimberley was born. Things did not change until I sent Janine an invitation to my home for Christmas about three years ago.

This also brought a lot of tension into the new apartment too; as this all transpired not too long after Carrie and I had just moved in with mom. This was just on top of the issues with mom in our living arrangement relating to housework and respect; of which mom seemed to do little of and have little for with regards to Carrie and I. Things were always tense during the time we lived with mom and it almost broke Carrie and I up on more than one occasion. I remember one instance where Carrie was crying while we were in the car parked somewhere and she was saying how she couldn't believe that she was going to be a single mother. Yes Carrie became pregnant with our son Charles Thomas. And what mom said after she was told about the pregnancy motivated me not to talk to her for almost 2 years. I couldn't believe my ears when she said to me how dare you decide to have a child in my home without consulting me first. Soooooo yeah Carrie and I moved out of mom's place and got our own apartment very quickly and what a relief that was for us.

We started being the happy couple again and got ready for the birth of our 1st child and I was ecstatic when Charles was born. I still remember having my head down between Carrie's legs to watch as he came out as we did not know the sex of the baby. When he came out a boy I yelled YES IT'S A BOY and every nurse on the ward heard me and many of them would joke with me about it when I saw them over the next two days. Carrie went through a full day of labour to deliver Charles and she really gave me a lot of grief that I had fallen asleep in the waiting room at 4 am when she was getting an epidural. I slept in the hospital room with her while she was going through the labour and she would wake me up every ten minutes to hold her hand when ever a contraction happened; it felt like she nearly broke my hand during the course of delivering Charles.

Janine, mom and Chris came to the hospital when Charles was born and I was not at all happy that they were there. It felt so very awkward when they arrived and they couldn't have left soon enough for me. I didn't talk to mom again after Charles was born for nearly a year right up until when she called me crying over the phone that she wanted to see her grandson. I relented after giving her a lot of grief for everything that had transpired between her and I and with regards to the living at her apartment.

Once Charles was born, Carrie started becoming more focused on her and I actually getting married and started to begin with the planning. I had gotten myself the best paying job I ever had and she soon got herself into working for the government so we were now financially stable and had the money to start the planning. Carrie took care of most of the work as I really wasn't that interested in the wedding details except to make sure that the music was going to be good as I wanted to make sure it was a great party. I look back and think that's very strange that I wasn't more involved in the wedding as I love talking about weddings; Larry & Brenda's, Don & Connie's, Carlos & Elizabeth's and now starting to just possibly think about Janine and her boyfriend Phil's in the future. I was still carrying around the memory of Laura in my heart and I knew it the whole time; even on the day of the wedding I remember wishing that she would show up and stop the wedding, but I still went through with the whole thing.

Not too long before the wedding a problem arose with Carrie's father Mark that would really be an undertone for Carrie's and my entire marriage. Mark was a very kind, funny man and I liked him a lot but he was schizophrenic and he had a diminished mental capacity so that would cause issues at times because he would have good days and bad days. For many years Carrie had taken advantage of Mark always borrowing money from him when she was broke, as did her brother Chris. Over time Mark had gotten himself very far into debt especially after he and Carrie's mom Susan had split up. Mark was just terrible with money.

Not too long after Carrie and I got together, Mark became involved with this women Wendy and Wendy became very involved in our lives. Once Carrie got a part time job to help with the bills Wendy became Charles's babysitter and watched over him, but she was always late and was very critical of Carrie for her past history with Mark. Mark had explained to Wendy that carrying his children was one of the reasons he was so far into debt. After a while we had to begrudgingly fire Wendy as Charles's babysitter and got Susan to take over the job.

Carrie and I were standing on our own two feet though and we were paying for the whole wedding ourselves. Mark offered to help so we asked him to pay for the wedding dress as his contribution to the wedding and he said he would. Right before we were to pay for the wedding dress, Mark told Carrie that he had decided not to pay for the wedding dress after all and that he was going to make his contribution to the wedding paying for some bag pipers. A wedding is stressful enough as it is and Carrie and I were very upset about all this and knew that Wendy was heavily involved in Mark's decision. She was now controlling his every move and was running his life attempting to get him out of debt. She manipulated the fact that Mark resented Carrie for all the years she had taken advantage of him financially, to get him to change his mind.

This lead to a huge blowup between Mark, Carrie and I and Carrie told Mark that if he was not going to pay for the dress as he had promised that he was not welcome at the wedding. Mark said he was going to get his brother and come to the wedding whether we liked it or not and his brother called us up threatening us to which I invited him to come see me whenever he wanted to, but not that nicely. The crisis expanded and I went to Larry to tell him of the situation and what could possibly happen at the wedding. Larry did not immediately take my side and expressed sympathy and understanding for Mark's situation which almost motivated me to remove Larry as my best man. I warned Don that I might have to institute him as best man because of what Larry had said. Luckily Larry stepped up and had a change of heart and supported me fully through the entire process, but I never did forgive Larry for his initial reaction to the crisis. Mark and his brother never came to the wedding and Carrie would only see him a handful of times again until he passed 6 years later.

My bachelor party was a night of drunken madness that exceeded that what had happened at Larry's bachelor party. We started out that night at my apartment drinking a few beers to get primed up for the night ahead as we were going to strip bar hop the entire night. It was the guys in my wedding party and I and we started the journey at the bar that my friend Cliff and I frequented when we worked together at an auto body shop a few years prior. I was ready to and played along with all the gags of the night and was pulled up on stage more than once as one of the guys was always quick to run to the DJ and tell him that there was a bachelor party going on in their mix. The first time I got on stage that night I got stripped down and had my underwear ripped and a pair of women's underwear shoved in my mouth like I was her dog. The guys had quite the laugh at my expense but I didn't mind as that's what happens on those nights. The night continued on and I was peppered with beers and shots and shooters all night long and by the time we arrived at the last bar of the night I was a total mess.

Of course at the last bar I was once again pulled on stage and this time it was with a feature dancer that really had an act prepared for a guy that was getting married. At first she had me pretend to have intercourse with her using a giant inflatable penis but the problem was I could barely stand and the dancer knew it. So she then got me down on the stage and lied on top of me like we were in a 69 position and then really started to have fun. She had a special dildo and inserted it into my pants and pulled it out of my fly so that it actually looked like my penis was there and then proceeded to give that fake penis a blow job making it look like we were having a 69 right on stage. One problem though, while I was lying there bombed out of my skull I fell asleep right there on the stage and started snoring. The dancer made this known, as there wasn't that many people in the club as it was a Thursday night, and then the DJ came over the sound system talking about what was happening on stage and everyone had a huge laugh. She gave me a smack and looked at me crossly jokingly and proceeded to continue on with her business of performing the felatio on the fake penis. Then after she was done she had this pump attached to the penis and used it to pump out all this liquid to make it look like I had ejaculated all over the stage and all the guys went wild over that as they were also drunk and possibly didn't realize what was happening until after when I told them it was a fake penis. Oh what a night and what a hangover I had the next day.

Carrie and I were married and began our life as a real family; a few months later we decided to buy a home after our rent was raised to the price where I felt it would be just as easy to have a mortgage. So we bought a reasonably priced house in a nice part of town and settled into married life. Everything went pretty smoothly for many years as I am good with money and set up RRSP's, mutual funds and a RESP for Charles. We bought a van and just went on about our daily lives happy for a while. There were issues as there are with any marriage such as household chores, mothers in law, finances, as Carrie wanted to be involved more with the money decisions, and intimacy but nothing that was the end of the world at that point.

The first real time that I ever became absolutely totally furious with Carrie with regards directly to the marriage happened after a couple of years in the home. In my mind it really set the tone for everything that would go wrong for the many years to come. One day out of the blue Carrie began asking about having more children which I guess every couple obviously discusses and I guess she was starting to get a case of baby fever. So I said I still wanted to wait for us to have our second child for a few more years and that's when Carrie replied that if we did not have all of our children before she had turned 30 that we were not going to have anymore children and she meant it as she said it very firmly. She said the reason was that Charles's pregnancy had taken a huge toll on her body and that she wanted to get having children over with early so that she didn't have to keep experiencing those body issues with a great deal of time in between each pregnancy. She wanted to get all of that out of the way before she was 30. I debated with her that what if I wanted to have another child when I was say 40 or something and she said no that this was her decision as it was her body and that this was the way it was going to be.

Well I wasn't about to accept that Carrie was the only one making the decisions as to what the family planning was going to be, it might be her body that would carry the children but I had a part in it too and she was not going to control my family life. I became furious with her and left. I went and stayed with Larry for two days and thought about if I was going to leave Carrie or not and told her so. I did not return to the home until she called me up crying and apologizing for what she had said but in the end this was a sign for what was to come. Carrie wanted to run the show and slowly but surely she did. She took over the finances and made a mess of them, as we were never in any serious debt until Carrie started playing with the money. When the time came that we separated we had made 100K in equity built up over 8 years in the home and almost the whole amount went to paying off debts. I was no angel in the accumulation of debt either and I went along for the ride but the money troubles of our marriage surely should rest on her shoulders as she always has and continues to live outside of her means and can not accept a meager lifestyle. The control in our marriage became a constant tug of war between Carrie and I, especially over money, but also among other issues in the raising the of the children as I am very stern with the children. It got to the point that by the end of our marriage we couldn't compromise or work together in any conflict situation and only harboured resentment towards each other for every single thing that came along.

We had two more children, first Paige 4 years later and then Jack after 3 more years. I made the decision to have Paige after visiting a friend one day after she had a baby and I got a case of baby fever myself. Soon there after I did not pull out of Carrie when having intercourse and she asked what I was doing and I said you want to have another one right; well I'm ready and that's how Paige was conceived. Jack I believe was a more of the save the marriage baby as the emotional troubles were escalating between Carrie and I and we had already been to counseling once before. I'm not really sure how the decision was arrived to have Jack but that decision was made together and so we conceived him.

Carrie and my intimacy problems ran very deep and it was seed-ed in that I was never in love with her when we were married. Don't get me wrong there are many points in the marriage where I felt a great deal of love towards Carrie; at the birth of our children, when we got married, while on our first two trips to the Caribbean, while on some of our sex getaways to Niagara Falls; but I never had that click on moment with Carrie that I could just describe like I had with Laura or Clarice. I always knew something was wrong between Carrie and me especially during the first few years of mar-riage when I would always think about Laura. Pornography became heavily involved in Carrie's and my sexual relationship during the first 4 years of our marriage; whenever we had sex I was always watching pornography and it became a habit and a base of our sexu-al relationship.

Carrie was adventurous though and she would try and satisfy all my desires and fantasies but I never felt the same way that I did when Laura did the same things for me. I always felt that Carrie was such a selfish lover, it always sounded like it was such a chore for her to perform felatio on me or that she had to get on top or just to have sex in general. I knew Carrie liked sex because she did those kinky things like letting me take naked pictures of her 3 times while on vacation and also letting me shoot a pornographic video of her early in the relationship. She never once destroyed those things or took them away when she would get angry at me until near the end. So the selfish behaviour that Carrie exhibited in the bedroom bothered me a great deal as it made me feel unimportant and unattractive.

One of my most personally satisfying moments of the marriage happened one Valentine's Day when I bought Carrie makeup as a gift. I went to the drug store and picked out lipsticks, eye shadows and blush for her and gave it to her as a present because she was running low on makeup and for a time seldom spent money on herself. When she opened the present she actually became upset because she felt that it was a waste of money and the makeup would be useless to her, as I had no clue how to pick makeup. She asked for the receipt so that she could return the makeup to the store and purchase the correct items. What a surprise she got when she took the makeup to the cosmetician and explained the situation because the cosmetician said to her your husband picked this stuff? What a lucky woman you are as he picked all your correct colors and not many men can do that. Women actually pay to have their colors selected; I know this because I remember when my mom did it years ago. So Carrie had to eat crow and apologize to me, although I don't even think she did really. I guess my love of all things women has given me a talent and a friend of mine Andrea was actually shocked recently when she was going for a job interview and I told her exactly what to wear and how to do her makeup and then told her this same story.

As our relationship started to deteriorate and the struggle for control became more aggressive, Carrie began to start to use sex as a weapon to gain control over me. At times she flat out admitted it; she knew what she was doing and I would always cave to her as my appetite for sex is huge and I would probably have it everyday if I could. I love it and I especially loved having sex with Carrie, it just felt so good, better than I had ever had before. There was just something about Carrie's weight that made the sensations feel so good and she knew how to use her weight. We were totally compatible when having sex and Carrie admitted early on in our relationship that she had seldom if ever had a real orgasm up until the point that she became involved with me; let alone the multiple orgasms that she was having with me on a regular basis. We took our sexual relationship to all kinds of levels as long as it always stayed between us as Carrie refused to have any kind of group sex whenever I would suggest the possibility. Looking back I totally regretted not agreeing to the threesome with Laura and Carol years prior after what the end result was with Laura; the threesome would have probably been mind blowing and would have deserved a chapter all on its own in this book.

Carrie and I always seemed to pull through all of our issues though, whatever came along we always got through it and believe me I can really be difficult to deal with especially when I get angry. My temper can be something else and when I start really yelling, well watch out. Carrie always said my anger really scared her especially early on in our relationship when I had little to no control over my temper and blew up a lot with all that was going on with mom, Janine and Larry. Luckily at my job I had one of the best communicators I have ever known as my boss, Dave and he recognized my intelligence and promoted me to leadership positions. Dave, however, also recognized my temper and would always be on top of me about professionalism and how I approached and came off to people. So over time I was able to apply this to my entire life and Carrie recognized that my anger and temper became more controlled, but it would still rear its' ugly head on a somewhat regular basis and she hated it. It got to the point that when a conflict would arise and I would get upset that Carrie would immediately go into defense mode because my anger became an anger-trigger mechanism for Carrie and it just became a vicious circle. Carrie became unable to apologize or admit fault in anything in the marriage and I can count how many times that I can recall her saying sorry to me for something she did wrong. It made it all the worse that she was so strong willed and had a dominant personality. Even though she recognized her inability to apologize and admit fault she did very little to change it and that only infuriated me further.

The last two years of our marriage involved so much conflict that we weren't able to survive as a couple. Probably the most important thing that happened during that time was the passing of her father which affected Carrie greatly. We heard Mark was having a hard time dealing with Wendy and after a while and I know he missed Carrie as they were very close. Carrie ate her pride and saw him a few times when he ended up in the hospital due to depression. It was this depression that was to kill him.

Mark's doctor was a good one and whenever Mark felt out of sorts he would get his medications adjusted so that he would feel ok enough to function. Carrie had always been heavily involved in ensuring how Mark was feeling and making sure that the adjustments were being made and she really took care of him up until Wendy came along. Wendy did not take care of Mark like Carrie did and he was a mess most of the time.

Mark always had a habit of wandering off for long walks once his condition developed, the hopelessness he felt made him want to go I guess. For years everything was ok since he was under control because of his meds. He had hard times but he could function. But once Carrie was out of his life and Wendy was in control, the wandering walks started again and we would be contacted by Carrie's brothers or sometimes even the police whenever this occurred. Carrie was still loyal to her father and would jump to help if she could even though everything was bad between her brothers, her dad and her.

Then one day after Carrie had gone to work I received a phone call from Wendy; Mark was dead. He had wandered off in the early spring and had been gone for a couple of days and had fallen asleep outside, had a heart attack and died. I called Carrie back home on her cell phone as she had left to go work a night shift. I told her there was an emergency and then sat her down once she returned

home and told her that her father had died. She told me that she
knew that was what I was going to say and she started to cry and I
held her to try and be as supportive as I could over the initial shock.
The necessary calls were made and family and friends started to filter in and out of our home and it was during this time that Carrie
and Chris were able to put aside their differences and face Mark's
death as a family. I stayed at Carrie's side through it all and did
everything I could for her and I vividly remember holding her in
bed while she was balling to comfort her and she said that if I ever
died that she would kill me. I felt so much sympathy and love for
Carrie at that moment and in my mind we actually made love for
the first time in who knows how long, probably for one of the only
times ever in our marriage.

The funeral was very tough on Carrie and we got through it
together as best as we could. Although that didn't stop Wendy from
causing issues. I was so disgusted with Wendy at that funeral and
how she said she wanted us to all be friends and still to this day I
would love to inflict some sort of damage upon her for what she did
to Mark and Carrie. One day she will receive her just deserts for
her selfish actions and how her actions destroyed a family. Carrie
was never the same after her father passed and she became very
cold with me as the problems of our marriage returned after not too
long.

One good thing came from Mark's passing though and that was
that Carrie, Chris, her other brother Paul and their mom were once
again a family. It was especially Carrie and Chris's relationship that
I believe that Carrie missed the most as her and Chris were once
very close. Chris had been living with Mark and Wendy when
Mark passed and was not really financially stable and he was going
to need somewhere to go. So he ended up staying with us on a tem-
porary and then later on full time basis. I made a very big sacrifice
so that Chris could live with us. I gave up the man cave in 4th bedroom in the basement so that Chris could have his own room. In
my man cave I had all my collectibles; baseball cards, cd's, beer
glasses, sports memorabilia and just all kinds of general memorabil-

ia. I can be quite the pack rat and collector, but I gave up my room so that Chris would have a place to live and so that Carrie could once again be close to her brother. Unfortunately instead of seeing giving up my room for Chris as the truly positive thing it was; Carrie only believed I did it for the money and further more when Chris was having financial difficulties she decided to lower his rent by $200 without even consulting me. It was just another example of Carrie doing whatever she wanted to. Having Chris in the home also had another negative effect as Carrie started using him as her confidant and her friend inside the home instead of me. Slowly but surely she didn't have to talk to me anymore because she had Chris there and the distance between us only grew with each day.

The true end of our marriage was signaled by my actions though as I was the one who broke the bond of trust between us. I had made a friend through facebook who was an old neighbour of mine Sarah. Sarah lived down the street growing up and we went to Kindergarten though grade 2 together until when mom switched me to a Catholic school to start grade 3. We used to play together as kids and I think she had a crush on me as a teenager as she said she had pictures of me during Larry's and my times at the arena chasing girls and when Larry was with Chrissie, but I had no recollection of Sarah being around. We sent messages back and forth and started to become friends and I found her now to be a very attractive as a woman. She had a beautiful face and long brown hair and was a full figured woman that I now found very attractive after my time with Carrie. She had also been an usher at the Rogers center and was a huge baseball fan which appealed to me. Carrie had been into baseball when we first became a couple but had grown to almost despise it because I was so engrossed with watching baseball, my baseball pool and that I had started collecting baseball cards fanatically. I was spending huge amounts of money on building my collection as I had become addicted to them. I was just as addicted to baseball as I was to sex and I know Carrie really resented me for my love of all things baseball.

So one night I was up late at 2 am as I was on an off night from working night shifts and up pops a message from Sarah which started a chain of messages:

(S) How are you?

(C) I'm cool, up late are you?

(S) Yeah very bored.

(C) Gotta a MSN messenger account?

(S) Good day today?

(C) Yeah, just chilled mostly. I'm working nights this week, so I'm always bagged on nights. You? Whatcha doing up so late, can't sleep?

(S) Yup no sleep and looking for something to do.

(C) What about your hubby? lol

(S) You're right that is funny; I'm looking for something that takes longer than 5 mins. lol

(C) Why? Is he not up for that? lol

(S) Never is, sigh. lol

(C) Yeah, mine too, kids do that to marriages or so I've heard.

(S) But dont guys want it all the time?

(C) Well up to a certain age, guys peak at like 18 and then its gone by like 40 or so, just when women start peaking.

(S) I just NEEEEEEEEEEEEEEEEEED him to want it quickly. lol

(C) lol

(S) So are you saying that it's gone for you too? The sleepy

old bear is poker, poker, poker. Doesn't he know that i neeeeeeeed to be poked.

(C) No way, I have always been; well had quite the appetite for everything. Carrie gets mad at me cause I'm always grop-ing her and grabbing her and she's so straightforward when it comes to relations. Most of the time it's just hurry up and get it over with on her part.

(S) Wow how unfortunate for you. lol But i know where your comming from or not CUMMING from. lol And she gets mad at you, wow you must be doing something wrong. lol

(C) What is he a poker player?

(S) All the time.

(C) I like playing too, but I play once every 2 weeks on Friday, if that. It's just a fun game, we play 2 hands at $10 per hand. My card game used to be euchre, but I've switched. Poker is so fun, so strategic, but not at the expense of my family. I skipped a lot of games this summer for going to the drive in or just staying home. With my work schedule, especially when I'm on nights, we miss each other sometimes.

(S) Awwwww Carrie is very lucky and I hope she takes care of you.

(C) Oh come on, yeah she cooks for me and cleans; but I'm lucky if I get it once a week. Marriage and kids don't make for a good sex life.

(S) Is that all Englishmen like to do, is play cards.

(C) I think so, my father and grandparents sure did; I remem-ber them playing euchre all the time when I was a kid on Saturday nights, it was dinner and cards.

(S) So Carrie gets it from you 4 times a month, WOW you have no idea how lucky she is compared to me.

(C) More if I had it my way. How long you been married?

(S) 3 very long years. Why how many times would you if you had it your way.

(C) Every other day is the way I feel right now, it would probably be every day until I get my fill. A pretty girl like you should get it way more, you gotta do something to snap him out of it. Have you done the Niagara Falls sex o rama.

(S) What is that but it sounds GREEEEAAAAAAAAAAAAAT. I WOULD LOVE everyday or every other day for a while.

(C) Nothing special, just leave the kids with whomever you normally would, rent a hotel room. Do it twice before you even unpack, have a nice dinner, then do it again in the hot tub, and once in the middle of the night and then again in the morning. Ok so that was what we did 2 summers ago. You gotta wear something kinky too, remember La Senza is your friend.

(S) I don't think hes interested in me anymore and I also think he's cheating and maybe I should do the same.

(C) I can't believe that I think you're gorgeous, excuse me for that; there's gotta be something else, does it work? He looks a little older and heavy.

(S) Why thank you and don't apologize, it feels good getting compliments. Hmmmmmmmmmmm now what else do i need that feels good, sorry for that.

(C) Maybe you could double click your mouse. lol

(S) I've been clicking it for so long now that I'm getting fed up and how sad is that.

(C) Does he watch, that's one of my favourites; that would do the trick for me in a split second.

(S) He plays poker but I COULD ALWAYS USE MORE FANS like

the Blue Jays.

(C) Oh the fool, the fool. Just talking like this has got my heart racing; and you're offering it to him on a silver platter.

(S) Funny I was thinking the same, only I'm pulsing somewhere else. Sorry for that. I might have to change my jammies after this.

And with that my heart started to pound as I was already very excited and very aroused and since I was so lonely and felt very unattractive I just went with it:

(C) Wow I'm there, oh my god.

(S) I wish you were. Sorry for that.

(C) I honestly have never done anything like this, online or in person. I keep looking at your pictures and they are fantastic.

(S) That's what feels weird, that it doesn't feel weird. Although if you kept going on the way you were, I'd need a wipe. Wow I wish I had a computer camera so that I could show you something else.

(C) Are you kidding, Tuesday night I totally told my buddy at work about you. I said oh man this girl who used to be my neighbour when I was a kid, she has long brown hair, a big chest, and curves, just how I like it, and now we're talking like this. I am very excited down below seriously excited. One of my favourite things to do is give a woman oral pleasure and I'm quite good at it.

(S) I so wish I had a camera. Do you know how long it's been since I've seen or even held a seriously excited one, how is yours describe.

(C) I thought about you the first 6 hours of my shift, and none of this was even in the realm of possibility in my mind.

(S) I've been thinking about you since we started talking and I can't stop.

(C) Its 8 inches and it curves down so when I'm doing it doggy style it rubs the G spot. It's thick and I keep my balls shaved mostly as I love getting them licked. Ok that's it it's out and it's soaked, wow I'm excited.

(S) I love giving blow jobs. 8 INCHES REALLY 8 INCHES OH MY GOD YOU WOULD TEAR ME UP I THINK, but I'm open WIDE OPEN to the possibility.

(C) What are you wearing?

(S) White cotton stretchy pants and I'm commando bra and panties, swinging free.

(C) I wish I could see.

(S) OMG IM SO HORNY RIGHT NOW IM SOAKING.

(C) I can tell your tits are huge, but how big, what r your nipples like?

(S) 34 d, medium nipples that are very hard right now. How long do you last and are you cut?

(C) Oh I'd have to build up my tolerance, it'd be fast the first time, so I'd have to make up for that by eating you, but by the 3rd time I'd last a good 20 mins. Yes I'm circumcised, I believe so anyways, I've seen ones not done and mine looks like one that has. You've got to rub yourself and penetrate yourself for me.

(S) OH MY GOD PLEASE PLEASE, I WOULD LOVE TO HOLD YOUR COCK AND SUCK TILL YOU CAME AND THEN LAY BACK AND LET YOUR TONGUE MAKE ME WRITHE IN PLEASURE AND THEN FEEL THAT THICK 8 INCHES SLIDE INSIDE. OH MY GOD IM SO HORNY RIGHT NOW AND I AM ABSOLUTLY SOAKED.

(C) Touch yourself for me, massage your tits, and clamp your

thighs around your hand while you stroke your clit. I LOVE A WOMAN WHO DRINKS EVERY DROP OF MY CUM.

(S) Instead of me penetrating myself maybe you could help me out with that?

(C) Of course who am I to deny a lady her pleasure?

(S) I could put a little drop of spit on the top of your cock and then rub with my finger tip till it drove you crazy. WHEN WHEN WHEN WHEN WHEN WHEN? LOL

(C) You already have, this is ecstasy and I don't know which picture to do it to. They don't seem appropriate; I do like your leaf jersey one though, very hot.

(S) IF YOU LIKE, YOU COULD IN PERSON. I like Niagara Falls.

(C) I guess that's the question isn't it?

(S) What's the answer? Hell if I thought I could get away with it tonight I'd have you over now.

(C) I'm not sure, I love my family and if I was caught it'd be over. She told me that before, but man you are smoking hot and I am totally a man with needs. This is very tough like I said; I've never done anything like this before. I've thought about it though and I'm really thinking about you.

(S) I'm looking for someone to help in the bedroom dept PART TIME not looking for another floor manager. lol When the boss is away the employees can PLAY and now all I can think about is the number 8. lol

(C) Yeah but I'm a total romantic, besides what just went on, I'd probably fall hard for a beautiful woman like you. Maybe we just should meet. lol #8.

(S) I'd probably be staring at your crotch all night, but ok ill meet. I'm supposed to be going to a Raptor game next week and my birthday is soon. It could be my present. lol.

(C) Well I'm working 12 hour nights Friday through Monday and I'm off Tuesday and working Wednesday and then going to the Police Thursday; and then off all weekend starting with, and don't hate me, poker Friday. Wow that was amazing; I haven't felt like that in years, I need a smoke.

(S) WHERE DO YOU WANT TO MEET AND WHEN? I'LL TAKE CARE OF MY END; IT'S WAY TOO EASY FOR ME.

(C)It's tough for me, I'm a total homebody, and she's smart. So it would probably have to be Friday.

(S) That's perfect; hubby will be playing poker all weekend starting Friday at noon. He leaves the house around 10 am. I'll leave my jammies on for you.

(C) Whoa careful, a week from Friday.

(S) Every weekend he's gone.

(C) That's bad.

(S) Not for you or me if were meeting up.

(C) Honestly I'm not sure I feel really really guilty. I don't mean to jerk you around and I'd like to see you and be friends and over time who knows; but to just jump up and say I'm going to do this after a couple of hours, when we haven't even seen each other in 15 years or more, it's pretty crazy. I think we might be in different places; you seem very ready for this so maybe it's time you did something with your marriage. Me, while being frustrated and wanting something like this at times, I still love my wife and family very much and couldn't hurt them. You are sooo gorgeous and I'd like to play cat and mouse with you and feel attractive and desired, and you've totally done that, my heart pounded so hard, but I can't just say I'm going to do that on the drop of a dime. You've domi-nated my thoughts for a couple of days, but... and Carrie even called you my girlfriend jokingly because she saw me looking at your profile repeatedly.

And after waiting a while for a response that did not come I went to bed to sleep as best as I could. I honestly did feel guilty about what I had done and still was a little curious as to what might happen with Sarah in the future but the response that was waiting for me on the computer when I awoke the next morning would signal the downward spiral in my marriage that Carrie and I never recovered from:

Just to let you know I was in bed by 12. You were talking to my husband early this morning. He was probably trying to prove a point about why guys contact girls from their past on the computer. I guess he was right. I have no idea how all this started but IT was never going to happen.

I flipped out, oh my god, I woke up from what I was doing and started doing the right thing at the end of it all, but now there was going to be a good chance I was going to get burned. I flipped out, I paced the house trying to think of what to do and in the end I thought the best course of action was honesty so I decided to tell Carrie about it. And Carrie was furious, beyond furious; she told me I was now like every one of her past boyfriends that had cheated on her. After that she just stopped talking to me at all as I found out later that she had decided the marriage was over. I ran down the scenario to many of my friends at work over the next couple of days and each time they told me how stupid I was for telling Carrie what I had done and that I should have waited until I was caught. This story just blew them all away and rightfully so and the debate over whether it was Sarah or her husband doing the messaging raged for weeks; it was all just another example of my horrible luck over the years. Who else could tell a story like this I ask you honestly? But it wasn't over yet as another message came from Sarah four days later:

It's me. Promise. I changed my password so only I have access to my profile now. What happened? He deleted the majority of the conversation so I only got the last few. Enough to get the jist of it. Is that the reason you contacted me in the first place?

And so I replied and believe me I was and still am to this day; absolutely furious that I was made out to be such a fool. Either Sarah or her husband toyed with me without any regard to the consequences; and if it was her husband, what a sick twisted person he is. If it was her, which I do believe it was all along; so what she couldn't take the rejection from me so she decided to mess with me. I guess I got my own just deserts for my role of dishonesty in my marriage and after a while my lust totally consumed me and that I was masturbating to pornography on the internet all the time; but did I deserve that? Well maybe I did maybe I didn't and so my response to her was:

No this was not even in the relm of possibilty for me and was not what I was looking for at all. I felt pretty trapped and goaded into it all, but I'm not at all innocent. I'm sorry but your husband is a pretty twisted person and I am embarassed, upset and extremely angry about this, beyond angry. Evil angry! I've told my wife everything and it's caused major problems bewteen us. I don't know why I did what I did, but it's not going to happen again. I'm sorry for your trouble but please DO NOT contact me again.

But the damage was done and Carrie and I never recovered from this episode, it was the straw that broke the camel's back and the love was gone from us forever. I couldn't forgive that she couldn't forgive me for this and every little thing that I did just enraged her more. I tried to repair things but I didn't have much left in the way of love for motivation. We did get back on track at one point after our second time in counselling but there was no love left between us so when we started having sex again it was based purely on lust. An argument right in the middle of having sex in which I told her to just lie there and let me do my thing ended things again and they only got progressively worse over time.

Carrie resented my baseball card collection, and my playing poker, and that I slept on the couch for the better part of our marriage, and the giant sectional couch that I purchased itself. That she said I made her feel like a whore most of the time grabbing her

chest all the time, and that I didn't do enough housework although
it did seem that all the crappy jobs in the house were mine such as
cleaning toilets and the cat litter box. For that matter she also wanted to get rid of my cat Mittens and I wouldn't let her, and that we
took my mother on a trip to Hawaii for her 70th birthday, and that
she wanted to replace the carpet in the living room and I didn't care.
And above all else; it was my anger and that she felt I didn't support her in her endevours especially her budding Insurance career
that she resented the most. I tried and tried to make things better
but all I could see was disrespect from her and that she was someone who would never admit to any faults and would never say I'm
sorry for anything. Things just got worse and worse and Carrie did
whatever she wanted to; she spent us right into the ground, especially whenever she got mad at me. That would always be her first
reaction whenever she got mad at me, well screw him I'll do what I
want and buy what I want. She had fast food almost everyday or
every other day for either lunch or dinner when she was off work
for her knee injury and when she did work she never brought a
lunch to work. She would never eat leftovers and almost always
turned her nose up at any meal I made and worst of all she was
totally addicted to Pepsi Cola and drank it constantly. It got to the
point that every little thing was resented or an argument and those
arguments would always lead to the talk of divorce.

Then one day in mid November while everything had been quiet
for a little while and I was hopfeul that things were going to
change; she came to me and said are we going to continue pretending that everything is ok? I aksed her if we could go to counselling
again and she said that she didn't see the point and with that the
plan for a new year divorce was put into place. I also told her that I
wanted Charles to live with me as I felt that a 10 year old boy needs
his father more than his mother but she flat out refused. Nothing
really changed between us from that point going forward and Carrie
grew more distant and deceitful as the days went on. She continued
to spend money hand over fist, even though I made double what she
did. She had actually been off work for a knee injury for most of

the previous two years and was even making less. The entitlement
she felt towards my money was ridiculous and I threatened to cut
her off many times as all our money was in joint accounts.

Once the holidays passed and the reality of what was going to
happen set in; I was going through a wide range of emotions all the
time; anger, resentment, embarassment and saddness. It was one
after the other and sometimes a combination of more than one and
sometimes it was all at once. I started to lash out at Carrie more
and more because I wasn't holding things back anymore as I was
beginning to accept the end. I still made attempts at saving things
for the sake of my children and the thought that I was becoming my
father was very hard to think about. Carrie stood strong against my
outbursts and really worked hard at preparing the home to be sold;
but still she was spending money hand over fist and that infuriated
me to no end. She also arranged to and had a real estate agent prepare to list the home and view it without my knowledge which infuriated me as well and we were at a stalemate about listing the home
for a very long time.

I did not wait until the home was listed to leave though and the
day I left was a horrible experience. Carrie and I had taken out a
loan to get by for the few months until the home was sold; as no
matter how many times I told her she would not change her spending habits and the debt was becoming insurmountable. So from the
loan I took 4K with Carrie's knowledge and approval and opened
up a new bank account to keep the money aside for minor renovations and as a emergency fund if we needed it. We had gotten the
flooring done in the house and I had given her the ATM pin number
for the bank card for my new account so that she could buy some
supplies for the repairs. Well after I awoke from sleeping that day
after a night shift and we had an argument about packing boxes to
prepare for the move; here's Carrie with a printout of the transaction
history of my bank account. She says where's the money as a thou-
sand dollars or more was missing in her opinion. I had spent $200
on some new sneakers, some groceries and a day out with Paige;
but she was mistaken in her calculations and all the money was still
there after paying for the floor renovations.

She further went on to say that she had removed $500 from my bank account to create her own bank account to be prepared for the future. That immediately got me angry and I told her to give the money back as she had no right to go into my bank account without my consent or knowledge and to that she said no and stormed off upstairs. I saw red and my blood began to boil and I thought of what I would do; when I saw her purse sitting on the counter I thought if she was going to take my bank card while I was sleeping well then turnabout is fair play.

So I went into her purse and into her wallet and took two of her credit cards and her bank card and headed upstairs after her. She was in our daughters's room by herself and I entered the room and closed the door behind me. I proceeded to show her that I had her cards and said if she wanted to play I could play too and that I wanted the money back and she would have to give me the money back if she wanted her cards back. Well that's when she really lost it and yelled at me to give the cards back and when I said no only if you give the money back; she started grabbing, clawing at me and wrestling with me to try and get the cards back. But there was no way that I was going to allow that to happen and she yelled and screamed and claimed forcible confinement. This, went on for a while and I just plain out laughed at her and her attempts.

I left the room and headed back downstairs and sat in the living room. Not too long afterwards she entered the room and started trying to get her cards again by clawing and grabbing at me, but it was not going to happen. She threw a phone in the direction of my head and called me every name you can think of as her rage was full blown and out of control. While this was going on Paige and Jack entered the room and the look of fear on their faces was evident as I saw them, I said it's ok kids just go back upstairs. That's when Carrie said the most disgusting thing that I had ever or will ever hear come out of a mother's mouth. It's not ok your father is a fucking asshole; and with that she grabbed her purse and stormed out of the house and drove away. I called after her as she left reiterating that if she wanted the cards all she had to do was return the money but she slammed the door behind her and did not acknowledge if she heard me.

I looked around at the aftermath and saw the blood streaming from my arms as she had scratched me so badly that I was bleeding. That was it for me and I knew at that moment that I was leaving the home and called my mom to tell her I was coming to her house, but mom had her cell phone turned off and it took about 5 attempts to finally contact her. While waiting to speak to my mom I started to pack a bag to stay at my mom's apartment but then something came over me. I thought about mom and Bill and where Carrie and I were headed to now that violence had been brought into the marriage and I knew that I would never forgive Carrie for what she had done or said. That was it; I started to pack all of my clothes as I knew I was leaving for good.

I thought about the whole big picture from outside of how I felt and I realized that in order to protect myself I needed to call the police to report that Carrie had assaulted me. The cuts from the scratches she had inflicted upon me were deep and there was no way I was going to allow her to get away with this, especially not after what I had grown up with. So I called the police and reported the assault. The police showed up at my door and took down a report for the complaint and asked me what my plans were and after they left. I finally got a hold of mom and got Chris, who was in the basement, but had no clue as to what had happened until I knocked on his door to tell him that the police were coming as he had his stereo on; to watch the kids until Carrie returned. And with that I got into my car and drove away only to be called back to the house by Chris to get my cell phone charger. The sense of relief I felt as I drove away from the house for the second time was beyond anything I can describe; it was just like the feeling I had when I threw Bill out of the family home. It was over, it was finally over and not one tear did I shed for my marriage as I drove away; actually I can't remember the last time I shed a tear for my marriage. All my tears that I shed towards the end of my marriage were for my children.

Telling my children that the marriage was over and I wouldn't be living with them any longer was the hardest thing I've ever had to do in my life. Carrie had been pestering me about telling the children that we were divorcing but I kept telling her that I did not want to hurt them until it was absolutely necessary as I knew that they were oblivious to what was going on. Carrie and I never fought in front of the children and always kept up appearances. We kept up appearances everywhere for that matter. So many of my friends that didn't know that Carrie and I were having problems were shocked when I told them of the split as Carrie is very funny and friendly if she likes you, and almost all my friends thought we were a great couple together. Well the children were no different and they had no clue what was going to happen as much as Carrie kept saying that they did. After another argument between her and I a couple of weeks prior to me leaving, I just decided to up and tell them.

I told them as nicely as I could and laid no blame or grudge against Carrie while telling them. I just said that mommy and daddy can't be friends anymore and that when you move to your new house that daddy will not be moving there with you. Jack was too young to understand any of this, not yet being three but Charles and Paige knew what I was saying and their reactions just broke my heart into two. Charles blamed himself since he had heard Carrie and I disagree about him many times about how I disciplined him and how she felt that I was ruining him. Paige was just flat out heart broken. She honestly is daddy's little girl and it was so excriutiatinly hard to experience the total look of sorrow on her. The children cried and wailed horrifically and Carrie and I both embraced them repeatedly as the questions continued on about living arrangements and assuring them that none of this was in any way their fault.

After the initial shock was over; first I took Charles upstairs to my bedroom to talk one-on-one with him to reinforce my love for him and that I was not going to abandon him. Things went ok with him if you could call it that; he still continued to cry as did I. He blamed himself and said he knew that this was going to happen one day as he was a bad child and it was his fault. I told him that he should never ever blame himself and he should never hate his mother either and I repeated that it was because his mother and I could no longer be friends. After Charles and I hugged for a while I then retrieved Paige to talk. The conversation with Paige was more than I was prepared for or able to handle as she cried uncontrollably to the point where she was hyper ventatlating and all I could do was hold her in my arms on the bed to try and calm her.

My heart was obliterated as I was doing this and I could honestly feel physical pain in my chest listening to her wail while I held her. The only way I could calm her was by replaying a father daughter moment from our vacation to Hawaii where her and I were floating in the ocean way out from the beach. She was in my arms as the sun was beginning to set and we spoke of our lives together and how happy we were at that moment in time and how much we loved each other. I told Paige that we would have more times like that and this was not the end for us. That things were just going to be different and that I would always be her daddy and she would always be my little girl. Later that day I called in a vaction day at work and we all went for a walk and Charles went skating on a pond near our home but it was the first step to ending the marriage and there was no going back after it.

The night I left the home for good I got Charles and Paige together just before I left and told them I was sorry but I was leaving at that moment instead of when the house was sold because mommy had hurt me. I told the kids not to hate mommy as she was angry and didn't know what she was doing. Paige of course started to cry but what happened next made me feel as good as I possibly could at that moment with what was transpiring. Charles instead of crying, took it upon himself to console Paige and tell her that everything would be ok. That they would see dad, talk to dad, and that dad would always be there for them. I was so proud of my son at that moment as he was showing the first signs of being an emotionally strong man thankfully. I had never ever made a promise to my children that I couldn't keep and so when I told my son something, he beleieved me and he believed in me at that moment. As angry,

irrational and violent as Carrie had been I had kept my cool at this
time and Charles recognized it and said he believed in me and knew
that everything was going to be ok. I did my best to conceal my
sorrow at that time and hugged my children and said I would see
them soon and I left.

When I arrived at mom's apartment she was understandably concerned but I was ok; I was just angry but not sad and just sat around
telling mom what went on. There wasn't much to say as mom and I
had started to grow close over the last couple of years and she knew
that my marriage was over and that I had predominantly been staying for the sake of the children. I had told her many times that if it
was not for the children there was no way that Carrie and I would
have lasted out even a year. Mom and I would email each other all
the time so she was well informed of all the developments in my
marriage and there wasn't much to say other than I'm here and this
is what happened today to get me here.

The next day Carrie texted me, as that was now how we commu-
nicated after the separation and she said that if I chose to pursue the
police action any further that she would report my car stolen as the
ownership was in her name and further said that she had reported
her 3 bank cards stolen. I didn't care what she said, the relief I now
felt was unbelievable, and to be out of that house was such a release
of negative emotion. I was immediately so happy and the only
regret I had about the whole thing was the children. I took some
time off work just to get accustomed to things and to get myself
mentally stable and rested, and I was able to sleep. For the first
time in years I was able to regularly sleep through the night. The
sleepless nights that I had so often experienced during the course of
my marriage became a thing of the : past. I always thought they
were caused by shift work I did, but I now know it was because of
the stress and anxeity suffered during my marriage. I spent those
early days cleaning mom's apartment as it really needed some TLC.
Mom's work days consisted of her leaving the home by 7:30 and
returning home around the same time in the evening; so she didn't
have much time for housework.

I also threw myself into basketball during these days playing anywhere between 2 to 4 times a week and I just loved it. I started taking the children for visits almost immediately and I spoiled them at first just so that they would feel comfortable. We did fun stuff like going to Chuckie Cheese, bowling, playing at the park and visiting Raymond and his family. Things were at their worst but I was just so happy to be removed from Carrie and all the misery that she directed at me and still tries to direct at me.

Once I started telling people what had happened, they would sometimes say, "well you guys were so great together maybe you can work things out" and my answer always was and always will be the same, that I am never going back, EVER! I could never allow myself to be pulled back into that life just like I couldn't allow Larry to pull me back to when I was 18 years old and I was ready to kill myself. I've been released from it all and I will continue to fly free forever more from the anger and sorrow that held me in my marriage.

Chapter 6

Context

Abandoned to despair,
left with only what is fair.
The prophecy saw now true,
the crimson flame frozen ice blue.
Enveloped in layers of shame,
only one really to blame.
Embrace the anguish,
the agony.
My dear sweet agony.
Return oh passionate lover!
Come dance in the moonlight of sorrow,
blind to the sunrise of tomorrow.
Broken wings that have soared so high,
crash my soul to where I lie,
knowing only the path to cry.
My dear sweet agony.

    I was living with mom now and trying to make the best of things and we were. Mom and I had become very close again bonding over the breakup of my marriage and issues that were taking place between her and her boyfriend Peter. Peter and mom had been together for 2 years and were always on the rocks; Peter was emotionally unstable as was mom at times and they had many disagreements. Peter was mom's first love back when they were teenagers and had found mom again later in life in the strangest and most romantic of ways. After Peter's wife had passed a few years prior he decided he wanted to find mom as he had always wondered what had became of her, but mom had changed her name two times since they last were together and he could not find mom under her maiden or original married name. So Peter remembered which cemetery mom's father had been buried at and Peter went there to find the grave. When he did he left a note attached to the headstone for mom which she found when she visited the grave on Mother's day. Mom was shocked and excited at finding the note from Peter and contacted him and they began dating and became a couple.

Peter wanted to marry mom and lavished gifts upon her and he totally became her life as mom fell in love with Peter again. Peter was a very generous man and freely gave mom a large sum of money as a gift to get her out of debt and for her to buy a new car. Mom basically lived at Peter's house as they were preparing to wed. Mom's motivation to be with Peter was love but it helped a lot that he had money and told her that he was going to leave everything to mom in his will when he died as he had no family whatsoever.

The big problem in their relationship was that Peter had serious anger issues as does mom at times and mom and him would have serious arguments repeatedly as time went on. Mom would cry to Janine and me about issues from time to time. Peter's sister in law who lived with Peter went as far to advise mom to leave Peter as he was not a good man; and she alluded to that his ways had sent her sister to an early grave.

Just before I moved in with mom, I helped her move her possessions out of Peter's home as she decided to break up with him after another episode. Peter was driving erratically one night as he always did as mom said and he had a bit to drink. He had lost his glasses and was wearing mom's so that he could see to drive and mom was really scared to be in the car with him. So after a couple of near misses and her getting startled by his driving and kind of flinching, Peter became upset with mom and started yelling at her to which she yelled back and the fight escalated and they were finished. They were on again off again a couple of more times until one day he called her up verbally abusing her on the phone after going out with one of his friends that I assumed told him he had done nothing wrong. So he let mom have it, mom fought back and it was over again.

Mom ignored Peter and screened his calls and cut off all contact but still the letters and postcards came and it was a good one followed by a bad one followed by a good one and so on. Peter was a classic manipulator molded in my own likeness and it got so bad and funny in a way that I could predict his every move which astounded mom. I could predict when the next letter or postcard would arrive and what they might say or what he was saying in his voice messages before she would even tell me what they were. Mom consistently sought out my counsel about her relationship with Peter and after watching the pattern for a long time I advised her to end the relationship for various reasons.

Mom's health was deteriorating while she was with Peter as she had taken back up smoking after giving it up for many years and she was smoking far too much. Peter was a chain smoker and mom was going along for the ride whenever she was around him. Mom had also lost a great deal of weight during her time with Peter and was not looking very healthy. Mom also seemed to be very depressed at times and told me on more than one occasion that she was losing her will to live as Janine lived in Belleville and her visits with my family were understandably very limited due to the problems within my marriage and between her and I. So she didn't see much of her family and rested her existence on Peter; who did not treat her all that well except for taking care of her financially.

So once everything was done with Peter; mom and I decided that we were going to live together permanently and once she got older that I would take care of her. There was no way mom was going to be able to afford to live in a retirement community, as she was not prepared with a nest egg for retirement. At first mom and I decided that we were going to rent something together but that thnking soon turned to the idea of buying a condo or town home as the real estate market was a buyers market and interest rates were at an all time low. Mom was very nervous about the idea but also excited as it had been almost 15 years since she was a homeowner and she craved having a large space to live in again.

Mom knew a lady from church who was a real estate agent and with that we got the ball rolling and got the financing approved and began to search for our new home. It took about a month, but we found our home and did what was needed to be done and prepared for the closing of the deal on the home. One step was to have an inspection done on the home and we arranged to have the agent, the inspector and mom and I to meet there one night, but a lot more was to happen than just an inspection that night.

As much as I had tried to keep the peace with mom things were not always so good between us for those three months that we were together in that little one bedroom apartment and issues arose. The issues were not that monumental as it was mom not helping with the housework enough, mom complaining when I would go to bas-ketball too much, a lack of privacy for me and mom becoming too overly involved in my life and getting offended whenever I would say something about it to her. But there was a bigger problem, mom's time with Peter had left her bitter and very negative about life and she was quick to snap at me about anything she didn't like with either little digs or flat out anger. It was this behaviour that would trigger the many of the memories of yesteryear for me with her and provoke a huge argument on the night of the inspection.

Before mom and I agreed to the purchase of the home together I was sure to lay out some ground rules for the home and the pur-chase so that I would be sure that everything would go as smoothly as possible. One of the big points was to be that I was going to have the master bedroom in whatever home we purchased. The rea-sons for this were threefold; one because I was going to need the space because of the children's visits; two because I would feel embarrassed if I ever was to bring a woman into my home and was not the person in the master bedroom making me feel like the child and three because I was to be the head of the family and the head of the family has the master bedroom. Mom agreed to the conditions grudgingly, but she did agree; on more than one occasion, joking, while viewing a home she made comments to me with the real estate agent present about why was there this rule again about the master bedroom.

Well on the night of the inspection mom caught me in a bad mood and she once again made comments about the need to discuss the matter of the master bedroom further and by this point the offer had been made on the home and accepted and we were in the process of completing the sale of the home. Then mom hit me with one of my anger trigger mechanisms with regards to her after I became upset with her because she had once again brought up the issue of the master bedroom. Mom would always infuriate me whenever she would say I AM YOUR MOTHER in a way like saying not to disrespect her and that she could say whatever she wanted to me. Mom used that phrase on me all the time and it was her means to treat me any way she saw fit or that she did not have to treat me as an equal or as an adult.

That did it and I was angry and the car ride from the town home to the apartment was just brutal. I expressed to mom how cross I was with her in a calm but somewhat loud manner as I am always loud period, but then mom absolutely lost it and shrieked, yelled at me and screamed at me to shut up on more than one occasion. That, made me stop the car in the middle of the road as I honestly wanted to hit her and it took all of my self restraint and control not to do so. But that was it! There was no way that I was going to go through with this move as all I saw was the woman, who had condoned and gone along with the abuse me by Bill and had even mentally abused me herself all those years ago.

I told her this was all a mistake and there was no way that I was going to go through the plan that we had in place and I meant it. I had no where to go and I started to weigh my options but living with mom was not going to happen; that was for sure. But she wasn't done yet and started with her guilt and mom is good at laying guilt trips. She spoke about how she had given me a place to live and that I hadn't paid her any rent and how she was there for me through all the troubles with Carrie.

That was it, it was on and I blasted her all over; I brought out everything, every last thing that I had forgiven or forgotten or let go over the years because it was all still there and it had never gone away. I am truly my mother's son and I know how to hold a grudge with the best of them. I started to blast her with everything I could think of; starting with how I had scrubbed and cleaned her apartment from top to bottom with little to no help from her even though I constantly asked her to do so. Since I had moved in with her I had basically bought all the groceries as mom barely ever shopped or ate for that matter and I had to have food in the house for my kids when they came over and further more that I had pretty well done all the cooking too. And when I asked her to specifically cook for me my favourite meal that she made; it just so happened that she got cross with me on that day for some reason and out of pure spite and disobedience she made a different meal.

Mom continued to argue away with me but then I brought out the big guns and really tattooed her with why Carrie did not like her so much while Carrie and I had been together and why she resented the trip to Jamaica so much. It was because of the effect my mother had upon me with her verbal abuse and guilt trips, especially while Carrie and I lived with her. Mom would send me into absolute rages on a regular basis to the point where I had to choose Carrie over mom because I couldn't stand to have mom around any longer and neither could Carrie. Add in all the disrespect and negativity that mom showed towards me and Carrie for that matter with her comments and lack of contributions to the apartment and Carrie justifiably came to hate mom and mom did nothing but expect to be forgiven because of who she was.

And that's when mom said it again about being my mother and that's when I really started to scream and by this point I was out of control and was crying. That's when I brought up the subject of Bill, Janine and my grandparents into the argument and I began to purge it all. The abuse that she condoned; helped and ignored from Bill and that it was I that had to throw him out of the house instead of her. Which, it should have been after the time he punched me in the face let alone intimidating me on a regular basis and making me walk on egg shells for years. Then there was Janine and that mom had never really stuck up for me during all those years that I was mortgage. Although she did give me the mortgage money back she never gave me the respect that went along with paying the mortgage and allowed Janine to run wild even though she knew that I was very upset by the lack of respect my sister showed me. And then it was my grandparents and the grudges she held against them for their actions during her divorce from my father and how she would try and use their names to guilt me into forgiving my sister at times when I knew that they would actually be mad at mom for letting Janine run wild all those years ago. I was a bad teenager yes, very bad but Janine went completely out of control when she was 12 years old and instead of focusing all her energies on raising Janine and I for that matter; mom's energies went to the men in her life and they always came first on the priorities list before Janine and I.

Luckily one man Carl made Janine and I a priority for a couple of years so there was some stability in our home for a time. But mom left Carl for Bill as Bill looked like a cross between Robert Redford and Nick Nolte. Mom was very attracted to Bill and his idealisms rather than stable Carl who mom was not that attracted to because of his somewhat goody goody lifestyle. And that was it at the basis of it all, mom had put so many before me for so very long and still to this very day would not treat me with the respect I deserved even though I had let so much fade away. I was not going to put up with it any longer and I told her you can no longer say I am your mother to me, just because you gave birth to me and gave me a home as a child does not mean you own me. WE ARE EVEN, DO YOU HEAR ME EVEN!

And she heard me and she apologized and she cried and cried. Of course I accepted her apology; I had to, she was my mom and I loved her so. I wanted everything to work out with her and for us to have a family again and for my children to be close to her. Slowly but surely things did get better, not great but she made me my favourite meal in the not too distant future. She gave me a free reign over almost everything without much debate anymore as I told her she needed to get used to me making the decisions as I wasn't going to be able to function when she was in her 80's and still debating and fighting me all the way for every inch. She now accepted that I was the head of the family and that her place was now behind me as support and counsel just like it was the day I threw Bill out of our lives for good and like it should have been ever since that monumental day.

Mom still continued to discuss Peter on a regular basis though as the letters and post cards still arrived periodically even after mom was sure that it was going to stop after she changed her phone number. Peter had a hold over mom just like Bill had years earlier and it was going to be very hard to break her out of her inability to be without a man cycle in her life. Mom's need for a man came from her very low self esteem developed during her childhood years as her father was an abusive man and treated both my mom and her mother poorly from an emotional standpoint.

One particular story involved the purchase of the first television for their family home when mom was sick in bed around the age of ten. Mom of course wanted a TV just like everyone did back then and mom was one of if not the last of her friends to not have one. You could imagine how her friends treated her and how she felt about that and mom would cry to her mother about it and of course her mother felt badly for her. At this time mom was so very sick and to raise her spirits her mother used her own money to purchase a TV for her. Her father upon learning about the TV became incensed as he had forbade a TV in the home as he felt that it would take mom away from her school work. He screamed and yelled about how he was going to smash the TV and directed his full anger at mom and her mother over this. After a while her father's anger subsided and mom always resented that after all the fuss he raised over the TV, he became addicted to watching it especially pro wrestling from the old Maple Leaf Gardens.

Mom's father also slapped her in front of all her friends on her 21st birthday for what he felt was a show of disrespect towards him. Mom said he was lecturing her girlfriend about makeup and eating right and all kinds of things and mom turned to him and said I'm sure she doesn't want to be hearing that right now and with that he slapped mom right across the face. She was so embarrassed that he would do that to her on her 21st birthday in front of her friends no less.

Mom's absolute worst childhood memory was the passing of her aunt, her mother's sister and every time I hear that story it upsets me about how her father treated mom and her mother in this situation. My mother's parents were Ukrainian immigrants and they both still had family back home, in particular was mom's aunt who her mother wanted to move to Canada above all else. Mom's father agreed to sponsor his sister-in-law but the process got held up because mom's aunt got tuberculosis and couldn't and wasn't allowed to make the journey. Once she recovered and was ready to come, my mother's father up and changed his mind and it broke my grandmother's heart to have to tell her sister that she couldn't come. So she didn't and sponsored her sister anyway and brought her to Canada. My grandmother stretched her household budget to the limit and mom still remembers riding her bike with the basket full of meals to her aunt's place because they couldn't afford to give her grocery money so my grandmother would just make extra portions and mom would deliver them.

In the summer when mom was 15 her family took a vacation to Parry Sound for a week and while they were gone mom's aunt was killed in a tragic accident while crossing the Gardiner expressway to get to the CNE. She did not know the city very well and spoke little to no English and was heading to the CNE as Princess Margaret was there for the opening. The police were unable to contact mom's parents because they were away and mom and her parents did not find out about the accident until they returned home and a neighbour took mom's father aside and told him what happened. So instead of dealing with grief, my mother and grandmother had to deal with the rage of mom's father who only then found out that his sister-in-law was living in Canada. My grandmother passed later after many illnesses, 2 months after mom married my father. Mom always believed her mother passed because of the broken heart she suffered because of the death of her sister.

Mom was also the victim of physical abuse at the hands of her father from time to time and I will share what I believe to be the most brutal story I have ever heard from my mother that even eclipses any of my own. Her mother became ill from time to time after the passing of her sister and one time she was in very bad shape with a high fever and mom was very worried about her and pleaded with her father to take her mother to the doctor which he refused to do. So mom took it upon herself to drive her mother to the doctor and they were late returning home, arriving only just before her father did and when he entered the home he realized that mom had taken my grandmother to the doctor. For disobeying him, he grabbed mom and raised his arm over her and smashed her on the head with his elbow knocking her to the ground and sending her mother crying to her room in absolute fear.

Mom lived in total fear of her father as he was all about the image he projected and keeping total control of the household. It was so bad for mom that she married my father to escape her family home after only knowing my father for under a year. Once they were married mom was welcomed into my father's family and came to call my father's mother and father, mom and dad and as the years progressed my grandparents and my uncle and his wife were at our home constantly until my grandparents moved back to England to retire when I was With that the tight knit family that she knew was gone and so was the pride she felt about our family and the self esteem that she had garnered from that.

Once my father left and we became almost paupers, as mom was only a part time secretary caring a household, mom began a pattern of clinging to men. Luckily mom's father had left her a sum of money that she could buy out my father's portion of the home with, so that we could continue to live there as my father wanted us to move to an apartment and to sell the home. Mom felt a lot of pride in being a homeowner and was the one who pushed my father to buy the home in the first place and saved her paychecks for five years for the down payment on the family home.

I can almost never remember mom being without a man in her life and there were six significant boyfriends in the 30 years since my father left. Involvement with three of those boyfriends (one husband) were disastrous relationships that literally took years off mom's life and ruined or put a major strain on many of her relationships and friendships including that with her immediate and extended family.

Peter was no different than this possibly being the worst of the bunch being boyfriend number six; and whoa guess what? By total coincidence what is the chapter number that belongs to mom? And just for good measure, guess how many women I have had sex with in my life, yup you guessed it, my number is six. There's one woman I have not spoken of in the book as it was basically just a one night stand where I ended up looking pathetic in love again and I think I've already made that point abundantly clear enough already in this book; so OH BOY!

Going forward from here I know that mom needs some professional counseling to address her self esteem issues and the demons from her past. I hope one day that she will actually do so because I can not help much more then I have as I will be biased by my own heavy involvement, observations and insights into her life. I love my mom oh so much and I have come to try and understand her as best as I can, although she sure can, has and will continue to make me oh so crazy and neurotic almost every day of my life. Moving forward though at least now we can exist together as a family again and I can feel nothing but love for her for the rest of my life and that's all I have ever wanted with her.

Chapter 7

<u>Blessed Peril</u>

I break into the frenzy of the calling.
Oh sensuous muse help me,
I'm falling.
Silence drives me to the point of madness.
Tears stream through my,
revolving sadness.
I'm begging to evoke even just a miniscule glimpse.
Nothing has or ever will be the,
same since.
My mind races to the furthest reaches.
I'm dying to bask inside of what,
she teaches.
I'm left with a reflection so repulsive
Questioning to understand her disgust at what,
was impulsive.
So golden were her smiles.
So spectacular were her styles.
Such kindness were her praises.
So uplifting were her phrases.
So cluttered was my mind.
Epiphany!
I'm focused now to the affection,
that I long,
and I dream,
to find.

I miss you

Four days after my epiphany about self esteem and respect at work I sat down at the computer in the morning ready to write poem number 14. I had just spent the last 2 hours working myself into frenzy by listening to some Coldplay; the albums, a Rush of Blood to the Head and Viva la Vida, which I wasn't too particularly fond of previously in comparison to the Parachutes and X&Y albums; or so I had thought. I had found so many hidden gems on those albums that I had forgotten about while my music collection was packed away during my transitional time; going through a divorce as I was. The music had worked me up so high and for some reason I decided to write a poem about this woman I had become very interested in the most recent past but didn't find the love with her I was searching for.

Roberta was this gorgeous woman who was the commissioner of the softball league I had transferred the team I captained to. I honestly love playing softball so much; I consider it a passion just like basketball. The league was called the Cross West Slo Pitch softball league and the name of the league still makes me smile every time I say it. I believe it to be such a creative name and Roberta being the commissioner of this league was so fitting as she is an absolutely brilliant woman. The first time I met her I was shocked to see how attractive she was as she was not at all what I was expecting when I visited their league tournament that past summer. I went to their league tournament to gauge what their league was like before possibly transferring my team there.

Roberta had long beautiful blond hair, blue eyes, and a gorgeous pearly white smile. She stood about five foot three inches tall, had a slim build, but was curvy and she wore a fitting black track suit. I could tell she was a little older than I, but that didn't matter as she truly is a gorgeous woman. She looked like the singer Taylor Swift if you added 20 years to her age, so basically just a knockout. And

Roberta was so friendly too, very touchy feely; as the first time I approached her she hugged me more than once and while conversing with me she stood next to me stroking my arm, not sexually, but as a nice gesture.

When the guys on the softball team asked of her I remember hearing so is she hot from them to which I replied actually yeah, she's a little older but man you can tell that when she was 25 she was smoking hot. Oh please that didn't even matter she was still smoking hot. Later on when those same guys saw her at a softball game for the first time it was said to me if you looked up the term cougar in the dictionary; her picture would be posted right there. I laughed so hard because little did they know by that time I had already somewhat developed a special bond with Roberta and was looking for romance with her. But thinking back I didn't really give her a second thought at that tournament as I was still married; a marriage in shambles, but married nonetheless.

The second time I met Roberta was at the league captain's meeting for set softball league, as I had decided upon the transfer of my team to the league. Again she was very warm with me and very attentive. I was very impressed with the way she conducted the meeting as there seemed to be some unruly characters present that were quite boisterous. The meeting was like any other really and at the end as I prepared to leave, I stopped to say goodbye to her. Roberta attentively asked questions about small talk and then brought up the subject of my son Charles whom she had met when I had brought him to the tournament to sell some charity chocolates for his school. She went on about his industrious spirit and as she talked I realized that she didn't know I also had another son and a daughter, so I told her so. Her eyes lit up and she asked to see pictures and I had some saved in my cell phone so I proceeded to show them to her. She commented on how beautiful my children are; Charles and Jack being blond and Paige being the redhead; they are very adorable, if you ask my opinion. So I bid her adieu and proceeded back to my home and my hum drum existence. My separation was in full effect by this time and I spent my time at my factory job, hanging out with my friends and playing basketball.

About a week later Roberta emailed me a receipt for the cheque I had written for the initial deposit for the softball league fee. She attached a note and in it specifically made mention to thank me for sharing the pictures of my children, how beautiful they were and how lucky I was to have such a wonderful family. I had felt a little uncomfortable about having the face of this family man at the meeting while talking to her when inside I knew that everything had fallen apart. I had now developed some curiosity about Roberta from a romantic stand point; so I decided to tell her about the separation from Carrie and how uncomfortable I was about all the happy family talk when that was not the case. She responded very kindly offering to talk if I needed to and how she respected my candor and honesty about the situation.

That was all the motivation I needed and I took that kindness as a starting point to begin an email writing campaign about everything and anything. Each time Roberta wrote me she said the most brilliant and kind things to me; so I would push further and further ahead offering more information about myself and my feelings about life. Slowly through the emails we negotiated a meeting for coffee and that initial meeting was supposed to be to deliver a captain's kit for the softball league but once that delivery was done at an actual softball game and the talk of coffee continued and that spurred me on with my romantic intentions. The day Roberta delivered that captain's kit to me; it set my heart on fire when I saw her for the first time not wearing a track suit and a baseball cap.

The way Roberta was dressed was spectacular, fabulous, breath taking; god I need to use every adjective I can think of when describing that beauty, because that was what Roberta defined for me at that moment, beauty. She wore a British style cap, with her hair in a pony tail draped over her shoulder. Her makeup was beautifully done and she had on these large stylish sunglasses, Gucci possibly. She wore a brown leather jacket with boots to match that had 2 inch heals and then this amazing long flowing black summery dress. Wow, I thought she looked like Stevie Nicks with what she was wearing and told her so as subtly as I could. Roberta did nothing but apologize for canceling our first meeting for coffee as something had come up in her. This, life and I tried to calm her but this time when she hugged me she also kissed me on the cheek which just sent my heart pounding. So when I was telling her it was ok to relax, I leaned in and kissed her on the cheek too, it seemed she was a little caught off guard by the kiss but she allowed me to anyway. Roberta had made a little mix up and had gotten my team's schedule wrong and as she arrived I had to leave and head to work; so I apologized and left. I was so giddy inside at what had just happened and once I got to work I sent her another email because I just couldn't stop thinking how gorgeous she looked that night and I felt the need to tell her again.

Roberta would always hold back personal information about herself in her emails saying she would tell me about herself at a later time or that her life was not too exciting. She was a career woman working for this very large renewable energy company, in the office of the CEO in a legal capacity no less so I found that in itself to be quite impressive. The softball league has its' own website and on it was a picture of Roberta which was stunning. I copied it and kept it on my computer at home and at work and would look at it from time to time or show it to those I was close to, when I was describing who she was.

The email writing developed my excitement with regards to Roberta. I felt myself starting to develop strong romantic feelings about her and continued to push hard with what I was writing, trying to impress her as much as she had impressed me. Each time though we were to meet for coffee she cancelled; this happened 3 times in all. It also happened that twice during the emailing she did not respond to me for a week or longer. So I always felt a little insecure about Roberta but she always seemed to calm and excite me with her emails as they were so intelligent and well written. I continued on with my pursuit of Roberta with little or no motivation at times.

I then decided to send her some roses by delivery trying to push our relationship to the romantic phase. The response I received sent me soaring inside, it started with words can not describe and she thanked me. She even made a point to say that she didn't want to disturb my time with my children on a weekend as she knew that was when I was doing visitations with them; but she said she just couldn't wait another day to thank me for the beautiful roses; you really shouldn't have she continued. I began to feel myself losing control of my emotions with regards to Roberta at what I perceived to be the initial stages of love. I began to fantasize about intercourse with her, living with her and even marrying her. Crazy I know, but it's something I do with almost every woman I find romantic interest in; I'm soooo stupid sometimes and I can't control my self talk at all. I remember listening to the song Little Jeanie by Elton John over and over again, singing it in the car like I was singing to her directly in a way. I was definitely falling for Roberta; there was no question about it.

Then it happened, she cancelled on me for the 3rd time for our coffee date, she said she was ill; but once again she offered to reschedule the date, just like she had done on 2 previous occasions. I was heartbroken at the cancellation; angry even. I had been excitedly waiting to find out everything about her on this date for a couple of months and I had even suggested drinks or dinner but she said she preferred the idea of coffee because of her time being so occupied between her career and being the commissioner of the softball league. I wondered about her thoughts about me and more specifically about an email she had sent me very early on about how she had the distinction of being hurt by those she loved and that were closest to her. With all her time being so heavily occupied by work and softball I hypothesized that possibly she was throwing herself into those activities rather than getting romantically involved with anyone as you can't get hurt if you don't open up to someone and allow them inside your heart. I also thought there was the distinct possibility that she could be involved with someone because as beautiful and gorgeous as she is, how could this woman possibly be single?

I wrote her an email including 4 poems I had written for her; which looking back were not all that good; and pretty well begged her to tell me about herself. I tried to write it as classy as I could; throwing in compliments, plays on words and every possible subtle manipulation I could think of. But in the end this only brought silence, nothing but silence. Day after day of silence, I constantly checked my email waiting for a reply from her to which one never came.

Mom and I moved into our new home during this exact time frame and I even drove to check my email at an internet café during a 2 day span when I didn't have access to a computer; but the silence continued. I soon realized that it was quite possible that I had made a huge mistake writing that email to Roberta. It was the same mistake that I had made so many times before with so many other women by showing that I had fallen too hard too fast; or at least that is what I believed. Maybe I had offended her but I don't know what happened to be precise; still to this day she has never said a word about anything.

So five days later I sent another email; this time apologizing for scaring her, offending her or going too far with my writings. I told her that I would leave her alone and would not cause any problems for her in the softball league. I sincerely meant what I said although I was honestly hoping for a reply telling me how ridiculous I was and that she had also developed feelings for me because of my writing and the romantic gesture I had made to her with the delivery of flowers. A response never came though and slowly I began to close the book on Roberta, or Bertie as she told me to call her as that was what she was called by her friends. When she told me that I laughed so hard as I would say Charlie and Bertie or Bertie and Charlie together, thinking in the sense of us becoming a couple one day.

I honestly had believed that some higher power had been bringing Roberta and I together, by a few coincidences that had occurred during the course of emailing. The first coincidence was that each of our mothers are the same age and that we had both decided to live with them and begin the process of caring for them. Weird I thought that both our mothers were the same age, hmmm oh well. The second coincidence had to do with some emailing between Connie and I. When describing my marital situation in an email to Connie; I told her that I felt that the person that you are in love with should inspire you to challenge yourself to become a better person; and for that matter I did not feel that Carrie had ever made me feel that way. Well within exactly one week of that email being written to Connie; Roberta said in one of her emails to me that I was an inspiration for being able to see the positives when looking at the situation of the break up of my marriage. Once the word inspiration was said by Roberta, it only added to my growing crush on her.

The last and what I feel to be the most profound coincidence had to again do with an email I wrote to Roberta. She had once again apologized for appearing to be aloof with her tardiness in responding to emails and as such was promising accessibility in the future once the zaniness of the start of softball season was completed. She talked of working 12 hour days and not being able to have lunch, or a coffee; or any free time whatsoever for that matter. Apparently her firm was in the process of closing a big deal or something and it was monopolizing all her time which was understandable in my opinion. I wrote her a long email thanking her for her apologies, told her not to worry and expounded on her positive qualities trying to be as romantic as I could.

At that point in time I was listening a lot to Genesis, Paul McCartney, Rod Stewart, Elton John and Peter Gabriel as there were only a few discs I had access to in my cd collection with me being in my transition period and my cd collection being packed away. I was really in the mood for some good classic rock n' roll that really spoke to me; music that I felt in my heart and soul. I was specifically listening to Peter Gabriel that day specifically the songs Don't Give Up, I Have the Touch and Red Rain over and over again. To this day the song Don't Give Up still helps me emotionally whenever I feel helpless and sometimes it even makes me feel better.

So I had those 3 songs rotating over and over again in the car whenever I was driving or when I would sit outside on my break at work. I then decided to take what I felt to be a relevant line from the song Red Rain and use it in that email to Roberta. It said, "I come to you, defenses down, with the trust of a child". I thought it fit because I was being very honest with everything I was saying to Roberta and I wanted her to comfort me more than she already was; um yeah, I wanted her to comfort me a lot more.

Her response really sent me soaring; she said that Peter Gabriel was her all time favourite singer and that she had actually traveled to his birthplace in England, Bath I believe she said, while on a trip to her hometown. Further to that she had a concert DVD of his that she would lend to me if I wanted it. I replied that I had already attended one of his concerts and that I couldn't believe the coincidence that I chosen to quote him in that email. While also being a large fan of his; the song In Your Eyes is actually one of my all time favourites, he was in no way my favourite singer or artist. My favourite band of all time is either Black Sabbath or Tool. I pondered as to why oh why had I quoted Mr. Gabriel, I was so amazed that I had done that and I told many of my friends about the coincidence and they were also very surprised.

After a week of silence email-wise had passed I believed that things were over with Roberta and I had blown it. I sadly deleted all the email history between us on both my work and home computers. I longed to hear from her but knew that I could not contact her again for the reasons of both self respect and also not to cause problems for the softball team and league. One thing I took from my time writing emails to Roberta was that it started me writing poetry again.

During my time with Laura 11 years prior I had started writing and at the time I developed a real flair and passion for it. But slowly during the course of my failed marriage I lost that passion for writing. I was never sure why I lost the passion and deep down inside it always bothered me very much. I thought maybe it was because I wasn't miserable in romance and that inspiration for writing comes from the misery and pain of romance. I thought maybe it was because I was lazy about it, just like I had become lazy in almost every facet of my life. Looking back I think it's possible that it was because I didn't think I was any good at writing at all. But I decided during my time writing emails to Roberta, to give writing another go. I had shared a couple of my favourite pieces from my past with Roberta and she seemed to like them; as her responses seemed to be positive. Responses from Connie and another friend at work Deidre were also somewhat positive. There weren't too many people in my life by this time that knew or remembered that there was a point in my life that I used to write like gangbusters. One of my favourite poems from back then that I shared was this piece I wrote about falling out of the boat at this monster wave while white water rafting:

The Coliseum

Courage and fear at the same moment,
the point of no return approaches rapidly.
My heart pounds so fast,
and I push myself ahead.
The wall hits me,
throwing me into chaos.
I've lost all control,

it encompasses my entire being.
Throwing me in every direction,
and yet I am not afraid.
I find my oasis,
the place where I'll be safe,
But I let go.
I have to experience this fully,
so when it's over,
I'll know,
I gave everything I have.

So while writing all those emails to Roberta I began to take some notes; notes about looking back on my marriage and believing that I had been living a life dominated by the 7 deadly sins: sloth, gluttony, wrath, envy, lust, greed and pride. I could see all those qualities in myself, some very much so at times and I was now fully in the process of trying to change all that. I had thrown myself into playing an excessive amount of basketball. I was playing once a week at first but gradually grew to the point of playing 3 sometimes 4 times a week, playing between 2 and 4 hours at a time. I changed my diet. I threw myself into doing housework around mom's apartment. I really felt things were changing for me. I started to reconnect with friends long gone; ones who I had perceived had wronged me in some way and I felt very good about where my life was going. So while things were heating up with Roberta; or what I perceived to be heating up; that is when Clarice full blown returned and my attention started to focus on writing about a love lost long ago.

But right now I was thinking of Roberta and that I missed her so; I missed emailing her, I missed hearing her words and being inspired by them. So two days previous to that I had sent the ten poems I had written up until that point in which I had changed my style to a more rhyming structure and to which I felt I was garnering amazing results. But still there was the maddening silence, always the maddening silence from Roberta. So I had written 4 more poems since those 10 and decided to send those four to her as well. I entitled the email an invitation to look into the eyes of my soul and just pasted the 4 poems onto the email without saying anything else and sent it; I felt the poems would hopefully speak for themselves especially the one called Blessed Peril that I had written specifically for and about her.

I felt at this point that Blessed Peril was the best poem I had ever written and declared it as my masterpiece. I had comprised the name from the shared admiration that Roberta and I both had for the Monty Python comedy troupe; and based the title from the quotes that we were sending back and forth to each other by email. It developed the movies Life of Brian (my favourite) and the Holy Grail (hers). I then after sending the email; read the 4 poems consecutively over and something came over me; a feeling that was very powerful. I guess it was because of where those 4 poems came from deep inside the heart of my soul, where great pain existed and was hiding. And I started to cry and cry and cry, and I was balling and I couldn't stop for a couple of minutes; I was happy but the crying was uncontrollable.

I was so proud of all these poems and I loved them so; they were like my children in a way. I had come to believe that writing was my calling and the words would just ring out of me again and again; washing over me, cleansing me, filling my soul. Finally I regained some semblance of composure and headed to my stereo; I needed some heavy music to regain my balance and my center. This had worked for me in the days leading up to this day; as I had already cried a couple of times previously while writing poetry. This emotional unbalance was something I knew I had to be careful of and even my friend Billy had warned me of the same idea when I shared a few pieces with him. That is losing control of your emotions when you open up that door inside of you and then not being able to close it afterwards.

So I threw on some Tool and asked the lead singer Maynard James Keenan to speak to me and to please relieve me of this state I was in. I blasted the album Enema and faced the speakers together, I turned up the stereo as loud I as I could play it; but it just wasn't enough to give me the relief I sought. I sat between the speakers and just did some sort of meditation and then after three songs I finally started to feel a little relieved. I then ran down in my head what I had to do that day, the most important being that I had to visit my lawyer to give him the final documents to finish my financial statement for the separation agreement from Carrie. So off I went and got a shower and afterwards I felt even better. I got myself dressed and put on a pair of pants that I hadn't worn in ages; and what a shock I got! Oh my god I thought as I looked in the mirror, look at how much weight I've lost! I could actually fit into these pants at my natural waist as opposed to barely being able to get them around below my belly previously when last I had tried. Well the starvation and exercise was working I guess, I thought to myself and I patted myself on the back.

So I got myselfready, got into my car, put it in gear, looked at the seat beside me and realized that I had forgotten the financial documents that I had gathered for my lawyer. Oh god what was happening to me I thought, I'm losing my mind and I started to get that feeling of being upset again. I went and retrieved the documents from the house and returned to the car, put the cd Lateralus by Tool (in my opinion their best) in the stereo, cranked it up and off I went. I tried once again to find some relief in the music I was listening to and once I hit the freeway and got the speed of the car up to 130 km/h that's when I started feeling fine. Unfortunately the highway driving only lasted for a couple of minutes as I only had to pass one interchange. As I exited the highway the urge to get back on again was so overpowering and I realized that I needed to go for a long drive somewhere; but where to go, where to go? I decided that I wanted it to be mainly highway driving as I always felt most relaxed cruising at 130 km/h with the music blaring to keep me company. So where to go, where to go?

The first idea I got was to travel to Windsor to possibly visit my friends Willy and Greg; who are gay. I have made close friends with them over the years through contact through Don. Honestly a person's sexuality does not bother me in the least; nor for that matter does a person's personal beliefs as long as they don't try to enforce them upon me if I don't happen to agree with them or if those beliefs involve anger, hatred or violence.

I remember when Don first told me about discovering that Willy was gay; as Willy was his good friend of his from his college days. Willy never tried to make any sort of pass at Don in any way and always for some reason kept quiet about his sexual preference; maybe it's quite possible that for a long time he didn't even know he was gay. To be quite honest, it never even dawned on me that when I would see Willy around before he came out that it was even a possibility that he was gay. But the way Don found out that Willy was gay was a little shocking for him and he called me when he realized it. He had seen a picture of Willy and Greg together in an embrace in a bedroom that Don was staying in and it caught him off guard, maybe he was even shocked.

So when Don called me and told me about Willy being gay in a concerned manner; after thinking it through for a minute and processing the information in my mind I replied, ok so what? It's still Willy right Don, he's still the same guy who you went to college with and he's still the same guy who has gone to all these concerts with us. He hasn't done anything to you or to me; so what's the big deal? Are you going to disown him now because he's gay; well of course not I hope? There are lots of good people in the world that are gay, so what? Willy's a good guy and I don't care about him being gay and neither should you.

I don't think Don was being a homophobe with his concerns; well maybe just a little as he and I in our lives up until that point had had very little contact with people who were gay. I guess you never really know how you really feel about hot morality topics; such as homosexuality, abortion or the death penalty right up until it actually directly affects your life in some way.

And since then nothing has ever changed between Willy, Greg, Don and I and now Connie in our friendship together. If anything it has actually made us all a lot closer over the years since we were able speak freely on the subject and for a long time (well between Greg the old queen and I, who are the talkers) it was actually a good conversation topic. Greg at one point spoke about how much he had admired the way I had handled the situation with Don when it occurred and he really appreciated my honesty on my views on the subject. I'm not so sure that it's morally ethical to be gay, I've never been able to decide my position on that subject, but I will never condemn anyone for being gay and I really don't see a point in deciding any of that.

I have however always been a firm believer in the death penalty and it bothers me that the death penalty has been abolished in Canada. Let me make it clear that I only believe that the death penalty should only be used in the most extreme cases of violent murder where guilt is proven beyond any possible doubt whatsoever. Obviously I believe in the relief of revenge and so sympathize with all those victims and families of victims out there who have suffered because of a violent crime.

I think back to my OAC Law course that I took in high school where the teacher I had really tried to put the entire class's beliefs to the test. He started out by polling the class as to see how many of us were in favour or against the death penalty and the class was almost split down the middle with maybe the against side just having a few more people on it. He then proceeded to show an actual graphic video of someone being executed in an electric chair as he was using shock value to influence our decisions as I soon found out that he was dead set against the death penalty. The video was very brutal and hard to watch as the prisoner's eyes were popping out against the tape that had been placed over them and he was shaking so violently. Afterwards when he was dead he was smoldering from being cooked.

After the video the teacher once again polled the class to see what the result was now and the vote had drastically changed as it was now twenty some odd against three; with me being one of the three. The discussion in the class was heated and the other students and the teacher ganged up on the other 2 students and myself; questioning just how we could still be in favour of the death penalty after the brutal video we had just viewed. After much debate, I was allowed to speak and my point was simple; yes the video was brutal and it was horrible to see that happen to a human being, but there was one major part missing. There was no video of the crime that the criminal had committed to show why he had been given the death penalty. Had he raped and murdered a child or children or was he a serial killer? We didn't know; there was no video of the extreme torture and agony that his victims had suffered and what effect that crime had had on their families. That is, what I wanted shown because if there was a video of the actual crime itself and the class had viewed it then maybe the vote would have been the complete opposite.

This is why I was and still am in favour of the death penalty to this day and will always be, for the rights of the victims. A person who commits a brutal violent murder has forfeited his rights as a part of society and in my mind and should be removed from this earth if his or her victim(s) family so desire. But that's my opinion and yours may differ from mine and that's ok; I would just like things to be different.

And since you might be wondering I do consider myself pro choice in the area of abortion as there is too huge a grey area to discuss when it comes to the subject. No one should be able to tell a woman what she can do with her body, no one. I am a firm believer in freedoms of every kind and if a woman terminates a pregnancy for the wrong reason then that is a choice that she will have to live with; she and she alone. And that choice is not for anyone else in this world to decide except for the individual woman, no one. Again your opinion may differ from mine and that's fine because that is your right, I respect that and your freedom of choice to disagree with me.

However at this specific moment in time when I was deciding where to travel to, to clear my head; I thought to myself that Willy would probably be sleeping when I arrived as he worked afternoons. Willy was the friend who I had known longer and felt I was closer to and that would leave me with Greg to speak with, who was the older of the two. That previous Christmas at another one of Don's DX parties, while discussing the problems of my marriage with Greg I had told him how unattractive Carrie had made me feel at times by repeatedly rejecting me sexually.

It was both funny and a little awkward that then Greg piped up with somewhat of a compliment, well it was; and told me that he would suck my penis until my eyes rolled back in my head under the right circumstances. Well maybe he didn't say it as nicely as that, but it was a compliment taken in the right context. So even though Greg was a good friend and I had no problem with him at all; I just thought because of the state of mind I was in and how he had made me feel just ever so slightly uncomfortable over the holidays; that it wasn't a good idea to head there for a pop in visit at that exact time. I feel bad at times as I just don't see those guys enough as they live down in Windsor which is about 3 hours away, and I only ever see them at parties and concerts.

After some more thought the idea came to me; I would drive to Cobourg to visit my Foster grand parent's gravesite which was about a 2 hour drive away. I estimated that I hadn't been there to visit in five years, so it would be a nice idea to head there. I then thought that it also might be pleasant to retrieve Janine and Kimberly and take them along to the cemetery as Janine only lived 30 minutes from Cobourg and to the best of my knowledge had only been to our grandparent's grave once before when I had taken her there. So now how to get in touch with Janine? She was in a transitional phase in her life and unfortunately for me; she did not have a phone at the moment. I really wanted her to join me in Cobourg; so I called my mom and cryptically told her what I wanted to do. I couldn't get the words out to tell her what was going on. I actually almost started crying again when I attempted to start telling her about the writing. So I told mom to please just get a hold of Janine as best she could either by email or by messaging her boyfriend Phil and told her I would call her back to find out the results.

I went about my business of the day first visiting my lawyer and finally delivering all the information needed to complete my financial statement for my separation agreement. I handed the stuff to him personally and tried to leave but he wanted to sit down and go over it; to which I told him I'd rather not, it's all there and I can't afford for you to charge me another $350 for a sit down. He said don't worry this one will be free of charge; and now let's get all this straight. I've always believed lawyers are supposed to be so smart but during the course of my separation I've been dumfounded that this lawyer could not understand how my first time home buyers RRSP loan repayment schedule worked and spent another 20 minutes for the third time in person trying to get him to figure it out.

After I left the lawyer it was off to the truck rental place I had used during the move to retrieve the voucher for Blue Jays tickets they owed me as they were out of vouchers the day I returned the truck. Then it was onto a retail wholesalers store to buy the MP3 player for Clarice so I could give it to her as a gift before she left for the visit with her dad. Of course I just couldn't buy the one item and ended up buying a second MP3 player for myself, an office chair as I didn't have one and a Sony DVD/VCR combo for the house. Geez Charlie and you still haven't put any of that stuff to use yet, what a waste of money.

I hadn't eaten that day yet either and I got it in my mind that it would be fitting to eat at my current favourite restaurant for lunch before I hit the road. Mmmm Burrito Boyz in Port Credit; I'll save you the details of just how great the food is; but if you like Mexican food this place is a must. Get the steak Burrito my absolute favourite thing to eat for the last two years. The lineup that day at the restaurant was huge and it was going to be 30 people prior to me before I got my food. So that's when I decided to call up my buddy Carlos as I was really ready to talk to him about my entire life for the first time and I was going to have lots of time on my hands.

Chapter 8

<u>Unlocked</u>

Ecstasy is your hand holding mine.
Lighting me,
this ray of sunshine.
Whisper to me of hidden desires.
Every word,
ignites countless fires.
Bliss is your head resting on my shoulder.
Heart is now,
beginning to smolder.
Cry to me of sorrow inside.
Nothing that,
I want you to hide.
Rapture is being embraced in your arms.
Project onto me,
all of your charms.
Speak to me of a soul flying.
Without you,
surely I would feel like dying.
Erotic is the kiss of your sweet lips.
My spirit is,
tumbling doing back flips.
Explain to me of days together.
This moment,
I hope,
will last for ever and ever.

Carlos has been one of my closest friends for the last ten years although I've known him since I was in grade 8. We first met playing video games at the old pizzeria in the neighbourhood we grew up in during lunch breaks at school. We actually went to different elementary schools but made friends hanging out playing video games almost every day. We ended up going to the same high school and even though he was in the general courses and I was in the advanced ones our friendship grew during our high school years. I would sleep over at his house all the time and we would listen to music and talk sports till all hours of the night. Carlos was not the party guy I was but he still floated in and out of the crowds I hung out in; joining me at parties from time to time.

Carlos could be quite the lightweight in those early years, and mom didn't like him for a long time after he got smashed off six beers one night and accidentally ripped a sink off the wall in the lower bathroom of our house while he was vomiting. Another hilarious story that repeatedly gets told to this day is when I took his young 1st cousin Jamie, who was 14 at the time, out one night while we were doing a sleepover at Carlos's place. I got Jamie absolutely sloshed on Southern Comfort at this girl's place we ventured out in the middle of the night. Then later on Carlos was calling up demanding that I bring Jamie back as he was worried his mom and dad were going to find out that Jamie and I were gone and would kill Carlos upon discovery of this.

This story gets more complex and funny every time I hear it as it's taken on a life of its own. The story has gotten to the point that Jamie has sex for the first time with the neigbourhood tramp and that I lost him at one point. But all that really happened was that Jamie was smashed and he tripped and fell on the way back to Carlos's house and lost his confirmation cross in the snow. I wonder how the story will next be told the next time it comes up in conversation.

Carlos and I ran into an issue in our senior year of high school
which put a wedge between us for many years until he whole heartedly apologized when we were in our 20's. I had become close
friends with this girl Elizabeth during my last few years of high
school and she would some times be a goody goody when it came
to drugs and alcohol and then at other times she was a wild woman.
I mean geez she got so hammered at my 17th birthday party and
had drunken wild sex with Raymond; and that was soon after scold-
ing me for catching me smoking a joint with Larry earlier in the
night.

Elizabeth, her friend Glenda and her boyfriend Jas and I used to
frequent this bar called Hot Rocks when we were 17 & 18 as they
never asked for identification. It was awesome; we always used to
go on jam night on Sundays as Jas was an accomplished drummer
and he'd get up and play with the band every time. I believe they
almost always would kick out Paranoid by Black Sabbath when
ever Jas would hit the stage; as he could emulate Bill Ward's style
very well. So one night at Hot Rocks Elizabeth starts getting on
Jas's case about drinking and driving after he had like 4 beers or
something. It was the goody goody in her coming out and she really
nagged him to death at that time.

The next week or soon thereafter we went to Hot Rocks again
and this time Jas was sure to only have 2 beers that night. After the
night ended and we were in his Mustang getting ready to head out, I
piped up from the back seat, hey Jas you've had 2 beers are you
sure you are ok to drive man, are you sure you are not too hammered? I was very sarcastic and Jas and I laughed whole heartedly;
but I guess this burned Elizabeth really bad and the next morning in
Finite math class Elizabeth and Glenda wouldn't even talk to me.
After class I got an earful about how dare you and you jerk about
her concerns about drinking and driving and so on. Well it's like
9:30 am and I'm hung-over and just sat through math class instead
of skipping it or just staying home and sleeping. Soooo out came
go fuck yourself hypocrite or bitch or whatever I said and that was
the last I ever spoke to Elizabeth until this year actually; when she

approached me on facebook. I missed her though as we were really close and shared a lot in high school and I immediately attempted to reconnect with her.

So not too long after the issue with Elizabeth occurred, Elizabeth and Carlos became a couple. Elizabeth now hated me so Carlos and a couple of other mutual friends went along for the ride and with that my senior year at high school really sucked. It was horrible; I didn't go to grad because of that stuff and the time I spent at school after the incident was not pleasant at all as all my partying buddies went to the public high school in the neighbourhood and I was getting bused to the Catholic high school. Later on after Carlos broke up with Elizabeth and he came to the realization of the gravity of his actions towards me, he gave me a heartfelt in person apology over some beers which I accepted and we have been close buds again ever since. I think when we both became family men it really strengthened our bond and we shared things like playing softball, going to baseball, hockey and football games, being baseball poolies and going to countless rock concerts. In general just being the best of buds.

When the split was decided between Carrie and I; that's when Carlos really stepped up and showed me what kind of friend he really was. He knew we were having marriage problems the whole while as I never hid it from him that I wasn't happy in my marriage and he hung out with me and we chatted whenever there was time. When I told him that it was over between Carrie and I, just before we were going to a Chris Cornell concert together, he offered to help in anyway he could; primarily with moving and emotional support, which he did. He was there at every moment I needed him and helped me move stuff three times after the separation; always acting the part of the good guy friend; calling Carrie a bitch and such.

Only four weeks before this important telephone conversation was to take place with Carlos while I was at Burrito Boyz there was a quick passing conversation between he and I that really stuck with me. I was at the flea market with my kids buying some new cd's

144

and up pops Carlos and his family out of the blue. Usually Carlos and I go to the flea market together from time to time to buy cd's, but this time I was on my own. My taste in music hasn't always appealed to Carlos at times, especially my love of retro new wave 80's music which I grew up on, while he was listening mostly to glam hair metal. I remember him complaining incessantly recently when I purchased a Pet Shop Boys anthology album, saying have I taught you nothing? And this time I had the Bee Gees greatest hits, Annie Lennox's greatest hits, the Beach Boys greatest hits and Jackson Browne's greatest hits amongst my selections.

So Carlos smacked me in the shoulder and said hey what's up man and grabbed my stack of cd's to see what I was buying; but before he even said one word, I told him I didn't want to hear it man and don't even start with me. He flipped through the discs and I knew what was coming and what he said afterwards really stuck to me; he said dude I don't even know you. He meant it from a musical standpoint, as Carlos loves everything heavy metal with some classic rock mixed in, but my thinking of that statement was from the overall picture. He was right he didn't know me at all, the real me; how I felt inside and there was a lot of stories that I had held back from him. So I called him up and this time I was ready to talk:

Hey there cheesy Farley what's up buddy? Oh nothing man just down at Burrito Boyz getting some lunch, mmm burrito. Yeah man everything is cool, just going to head out to Cobourg in a bit, which is about 30 minutes outside Oshawa. Yeah I'm going to visit my grandparent's grave, I haven't been there in about 5 years and I feel like going for a drive today. Yeah man it will take me about 2 hours or so, just getting some lunch first. So hey man listen; do you remember when we bumped into each other at the flea market a few weeks ago and once you looked through my cd's you said to me that you didn't even know me. Well that statement meant a lot more to me than you think it did; I was discussing it over with Connie the other day and you were totally right Carlos you really don't know me. Now don't worry man I'm not about to tell you I'm gay or any-

*thing. That would never happen. No it's different man, it's like that
there's this whole other side to me that I have never really shared
with you. Well Carlos truthfully I'm a poet and a writer. Yup that's
what I said man. And I don't want to sound arrogant or anything
but I'm really good at it, really good. Yeah man; I showed my stuff
to this guy Vince at my work; and he's a serious successful accomplished artist who makes bank from his paintings, like serious bank;
and he really liked it and he's agreed to become my mentor and I
think I'm going to pursue publishing and actually become a professional writer. Yeah man; Connie joked that you would probably
make some sort of sarcastic comment and call me gay or something.
Well I'm sorry man; you gotta understand I didn't mean to leave
you out of this and that this was in no way meant to be a slight on
you. I in no way meant to disrespect you, I only really just got
started back on this stuff in the last month or so and it was only in
the last week that it really all clicked for me. Yeah I actually started
writing like about 11 years ago when I was living in Milton but lost
the interest or inspiration during my marriage. You've got to
understand man you've always been my guy friend; my sports
buddy, my concert buddy and my beer drinking buddy and I need
that type of relationship in my life; you know what I mean man ha-
ha. And if I was to bring in this other persona inside of our friendship, well I wouldn't want to lose the type of friendship that we have
now. Look at how you reacted when I bought those cd's at the flea
market that time or when I speak of 80's new wave music or of liking Coldplay. Yeah yeah I know Depeche Mode is cool and that you
grew to appreciate U2; but it's like that scene from the 40 year old
virgin man; the you know how I know you're gay and stuff. Alright
man alright, cool, I'll share some stuff with you in the near future,
I'll print the poems off and bring them to our next softball game.
Alright man take it easy, I'll talk to you soon.*

And with that I finally got my burrito and devoured it, mmm. I
got in my car and headed for the highway to begin my journey to
Cobourg. When I first wrote an outline for this book I thought this
was where I would tell all my historical stories and give all the back
information as to who everyone was and how I had gotten to this

point in my life, but the actual traveling out of Toronto was quite frustrating because even at 1:30 pm that damn 401 highway is jammed always. So I cranked up the Tool and alternated between them and Coldplay, Tom Petty, Metallica and A Perfect Circle and slowly went on my way until I got out past Oshawa, where is when I really started to cruise.

I thought of Clarice almost the entire way there, all of our history also time to time I would think of my mom, sister or grandparents and memories of them as well. Mom called just as I got to the Peterborough cut off and said Janine and Kimberly weren't feeling well and that I shouldn't go by there; which was fine by me as I was going to Cobourg anyways alone or not. Like I said it had been a long time since I had been there and I actually missed the cut off from the 401 and had to double back 10 km when exiting the highway; oh man I still wasn't quite right in the head just yet I thought. While traveling north from the 401 highway I stopped at a convenience store to purchase some flowers for my grandparent's grave. They charged me $12.99 for a bunch of carnations and daisies which was ridiculous but I didn't feel like haggling and paid for them and left. I thought to myself, damn Grandma and Grandpa would be so pissed with me for spending so much on the flowers.

It was only 10 minutes more to the cemetery and I grew excited at visiting that place again. I remembered the route to the cemetery quite easily and as I arrived at the cemetery I turned off the stereo and drove up slowly taking in all that was around me. I drove along the path leading to where I knew I had to park and I thought it was just so beautiful there. I parked and turned off the engine and the blare of a garden trimmer filled the air, oh damn I thought I was hoping for some peace and tranquility. The thought of Clarice continued to fill my head and I thought of her personality and how even with the faults she had that they only just added to her and made her a real person. I knew that I loved every little quirk or imperfection about her, both the good and the bad and I really wished she was there with me right then. I pulled out my cell phone and just began to message her, writing whatever I felt and it just flowed out:

As I prepare to approach my grand parent's grave my thoughts are about you and everything you mean to me and the strength that that has given me to face everything I am. Whatever happens I love you. Don't worry; no need for all the good heart stuff, no promises right? I'm finally free.

I then unwrapped the flowers I had bought, opened the door and got out. I started the walk up the incline to the site and as I did the noise from the trimmer stopped, I guess they're instructed to stop if someone is visiting or something. I looked at the headstone and thought wow grandpa was 5 years older than grandma, I never knew that before. I counted the months between their passing and yes it was 6 months just as I remembered. Grandma had passed at 62 after her 2nd stroke and then grandpa lost the will to live and smoked himself to death.

I was told by a few family members that grandpa was smoking around 3 packs a day at the time and he then succumbed to a heart attack at my cousin's house in her bathroom. It was very sad, he loved grandma that much, she was his whole world and he couldn't go on living without her, I think very romantic in a way though. Although knowing grandma and her stern, prim and proper personality, she would have wanted him to go on.

I laid down the flowers and I took one white daisy for myself as a memento of the day and then proceeded to sit down on top of my grandparents with my legs crossed. I told them if they were out there they probably knew why I was there. I had such a deep connection to them, they loved me and my sister so and I felt closer to them than anyone else ever in my entire life. I took in the ambiance of the entire scene and breathed deeply but I then felt the need for a cigarette and said I'm going to go have a smoke over there because I don't want you to see me smoke as I know that is what killed you both so early.

One of my favourite childhood memories was helping grandpa run his cigarette rolling machine and it's unfortunate isn't it that that's the favourite memory. I still look back over old pictures of the family and see everyone holding or smoking a cigarette, even with children, including me, in their arms. How the times have changed though; we can't even smoke in the car nowadays if a minor is in the car with us, but that's a good thing I think.

I stared out over the river from the top of the valley and it was just a gorgeous view I thought to myself and when I die I would like to be buried here with my grandparents. There were fully mature trees lining the river banks and it looked more like a lake actually as the river was probably 500 meters across at that spot. There was a houseboat sailing down river slowly and I saw a stork gliding across the water looking for fish. I called mom to tell her I was ok as I knew she was very concerned about my motivation for the trip to Cobourg:

Yes mom I'm ok, yes mom I know, I'm sorry I just wanted to be here today, I needed to go somewhere. I know I didn't mean to scare you, I'm sorry. I can understand why you would be so worried; if I wanted to commit suicide this would probably be the place I would do it. I'm sorry I know I shouldn't joke about that, but this would be the place don't you think? Ok well I'm going to go now. No I'm going to stay for a while longer it's so beautiful here.

After the phone call ended I returned to the gravesite and lied down on top of my grandparents with my head at the headstone. It was very morbid I know but I just wanted to feel as close to them as best I could. I stared up at the sky and it was such a clear day and the sun was burning so hot. There were a few white clouds in the sky; but there were these two clouds that were almost directly above me in the sky. I watched them closely and saw them swirl around and it seemed like they were alive. They just seemed to be suspended directly above me not moving at all and I had this strange feeling like I was not alone? I'm not sure what I believe in when it comes to the spirit world and such, but on that day at that time I felt like I belonged.

The sun continued to beat down upon me heating me up to the point of irritability. I tried to deflect the sun out of my eyes with my ball cap but it was to no avail and so I said if you are out there, couldn't you move to block that sun for me; referring to my grand-parent's spirits. I didn't care what I said as I was all alone and the place was deserted as the gardener had moved to the far other side of the cemetery. So I got up after I couldn't take the sun anymore and luckily there was a 15 foot tree 5 feet behind their gravesite, so I decided to sit under the shade there.

Just then Don called to talk about the Tool concert I had just purchased tickets for the other day to verify the money situation for the tickets. The conversation headed into a work discussion and at that point I had to cut him off and told him I couldn't talk about work right now as I couldn't take the negativity that our jobs brought into our lives at that moment in time. I told him I wanted to talk to him but just not about work. I said let's talk about some-thing else and so he proceeded to tell me about his surprise plans for his one year wedding anniversary celebration.

He was going to have a limousine pick Connie and him up from their home, drive them to the airport and then fly to Quebec City for dinner, stay over and then fly back the next day. I honestly was impressed with his plans and told him so. I said you know who you are talking to when it comes to this stuff; you know I'm a romantic and I honestly I am impressed, good job man. I told him to make sure that there was champagne around and flowers. I told him that I would tell Connie not to snoop about his plans as it would be a very nice surprise and then continued to tell him where I was. He asked if I was ok and I told him yes that I just wanted to be here today. We said our goodbye pleasantries and hung up.

I then realized it had been 5 days since I had talked to my son as he had not been home when I had, I spoken to my other children on the previous day. It was 4 pm so he should be home I thought and I called and spoke to him. I asked the usual questions of how is school and such and he spoke to me about Transformers as that was his big interest at this time. I told him he needed to speak to Donnie about that as Don is a big kid at heart and an expert on all kids' toys from the 80's. I gave Charles a little inkling as to where I was but I didn't tell him what I was doing as he is still very young. I told him I loved him and I would see him on the weekend.

I then called Vince and left him a message telling him all was well and I looked forward to talking to him soon; I was still just so excited about my writing from earlier in the day. Vince is a guy I met through my job and he is like I said a very accomplished artist and very successful. It is odd that he works a factory job, but he uses the income to supplant his lifestyle and to help make ends meet. If he was single he wouldn't need the job and for that matter he might not even really need it anyway but a cottage and new cars and a big house in the suburbs cost money. Our job pays pretty well; so a part time job for him turned into a full time income that he has grown accustomed to.

When I first realized just how good I thought my poems were, I approached him one day at shift change asking for his guidance and the next day gave him the first nine poems I had completed. He read them over and said that they were much better than he had anticipated and starting giving me advice about submitting them to magazines and going to poetry readings. He then asked me to read aloud Don't Ever Go to see how I would present myself and I read aloud one of my poems to a person for the first time. He said I needed to work on how I presented myself but that he liked what he saw.

I then asked him if he would become my mentor even though he was a painter and I was a writer; I knew I was going to need his help in dealing with people from the world of the arts as I was totally ignorant to that entire world. He accepted and then gave me his first exceptional piece of advice which was for me to continually read aloud my pieces to make sure they sounded and flowed right when they were heard. I thanked him for everything and we shook hands and continued on with our jobs.

Some cloud cover was now rolling in at the cemetery and it was blocking out the sun so I returned to sit with my grandparents again. Almost just as I sat down the phone rang again and it was mom again:

Yes mom. Did you know grandpa was 5 years older than grandma? Yes she passed in 1985 and he in 1986, it was 6 months apart like I said. Grandma was only 62 years old; I know I know that is younger than we thought. I'm glad you called mom as I know the problem you had with grandma, with what she said to you when you called there after my father left. I know, I know grandpa said you could call for any reason at any time and when you did she said I'm sure he didn't mean 5000 miles away. But I need you to understand why these people are so important to me. If not for them I might not be here right now. They gave me a connection to the Foster side of the family that I didn't have because my father abandoned me. They gave me the unconditional love that no one else did, no one. When their son abandoned me they still came to take Janine and me for visits no matter what he thought. They didn't care, they were going to see us whether he liked it or not, or whether you liked it or not. I miss them so and I wish that instead of sitting on top of them that I was sitting in their laps again. Yes it was one of my favourite things to do. Had they not came to take us for visits, things may have been a lot worse for me; I just might have killed myself when I was younger. We don't know how things might have been different if I didn't have that connection with them, it more than likely would have been worse for me. And when they passed and my father told you when you called him, about grandpa's death; that he did not want to see the children under these circum-stances. Well that was devastating to me, absolutely devastating that I no longer had any connection to the family for which the name I bore. Yes mom they were that important to me and now I hope you truly truly realize it. I'm still so sad that grandpa didn't make it to our home on his return from Linda's wedding in Syracuse and that he died while stopping in Hamilton at Stephanie's before he could get to our home. I still think it bothers his spirit too. I don't think I had seen them in a year or two before they died because grandma was so ill from her stroke. I still can remember the dream when I was in Syracuse for the small family reunion years after his passing; where I was with him walking and talking and all of the sudden I became aware of the reality of the situation. I stopped and said to him wait a moment you are dead, I know you are and then he then turned to me and looked at me in the face and started to cry. Almost in an instant I awoke with the strangest of feelings that grandpa and grandma were in some way watching over me always. Yes mom when we were in Syracuse, yeah I told you about it before but it has stayed with me always. Yes I'm almost done here I'll be home later.

I then went to the car and retrieved a black magic marker and returned to the grave. On the grave marker I wrote Charles Christopher Foster was here and drew a big black heart on it. I said goodbye to them and returned to the car and started the engine. I put the car into gear, beeped the horn twice and prepared to leave. Just then I realized something and put the car in reverse and pulled up close to the headstone. I reached into my pocket to retrieve my wallet, got back out of the car and walked over to the headstone one more time. Out of my wallet I pulled the copy of the family portrait that had been taken earlier in the year and I faced the picture to the headstone and said you know who these people are on the top refer-ring to mom, Janine and I; but down below we have Charles Gordon Foster, Kimberly Kayla Foster, Paige Irene Foster and Jack Peter Foster. Charles is the 5th Charles Foster and Irene is after you grandma and Jack is after your brother grandpa. I then crouched down and moved the flowers to proceed to try my best to dig up some grass at the headstone. I put the picture into the spot and buried it a bit and returned the flowers to their spot. I rose to leave and turned to head to the car and I looked back and my voice cracked a little as I said I love you both very much and I miss you and with that I got into the car. I drove away.

As I headed through Cobourg I looked back fondly on the mem-ories I had of spending time there with my grandparents and felt happy. I phoned my mom and told her I was on my way home and said that I was going to have enough new material for a few poems and then as I said it hit me. That this wasn't material for poems; this was a book, my book. I was going to write a book about my life. I saw the whole day play out as a movie and I fantasized about how the movie would look for the entire time I drove for the next two hours on my way home.

When I arrived home and said all my pleasantries to my mom I headed up to my office and began to furiously write what I thought was the beginning of the book at that moment in time; which was by starting to describe Roberta. I pushed myself to start churning out the words and it was easy to describe Roberta as the feelings I had for her were not yet gone, but I only got through about 4 pages as it was late in the evening and I was tired and mentally drained. So after about 3 hours I gave up and noticed my friend Mary online and started to chat with her.

Mary was an old friend from way back that I knew through Brenda; when I had initially met Brenda when I was 13 years old and Mary was one of her best friends at the time. Mary and I had in the last couple of years made friends chatting online about small talk. We talked about Larry & Brenda; that Mary's oldest child's father was married to a friend of mine at work and about the few old times we had together. Mary did not know about my marital situation up until just recently and when I told her she was very supportive of me. She had also been giving me wonderful feedback about my poetry that I was sharing with her as she absolutely loved my poems. She went so far to say that she felt there was no question that my poems were going to be published and that furthermore I was going to have my choice of publishers when it came time. I loved Mary's reactions to my writing and we chatted for a while.

After a little small talk about my poems I asked Mary if she would be interested in reading a short story I had written and she said yes. I then asked her if she was offended by pornography, because of the nature of the story and she said no not at all. I said ok I'm going to let you read this as Clarice said it was not for her as she was not a reader. I told Mary that she had to stay online with me after she was done reading it, as it was 12:30 am, and tell me

absolutely honestly every emotion and feeling it provoked in her.
She said she was intrigued by everything I was saying and promised
to do so and I sent her the short story about Clarice and I:

You ring the doorbell and I answer. You're surprised to see that
I'm wearing a suit at 10am for a lunch date. From behind my back
I produce a single red rose and pass it to you. You giggle and I put
my finger to your lips gesturing for you to be quiet. I take you by
the hand and lead you into my home.

There you find many candles lighting the room. I lead you to
the center of the room and as I pass the stereo I push play. Never
Tear Us Apart by INXS comes on and I open my arms inviting you
to dance with me. We sway gently back and forth to the song that
ignited me nearly 2 decades earlier. You rest your head on my chest
hoping the moment will never end. The song seems to last forever
and as the final note plays I lean back and look into your eyes with
so much intensity and then lean into you kissing you deeply.

The next song starts to blare and we laugh and I quickly stumble
over to the stereo turning my back to you; after I stop it I turn
around and you are right in front of me. You through your arms
around my shoulders; smile and we kiss again and again. Deeper
and harder each time. I sweep you from your feet and proceed to
carry you up the stairs looking into your eyes smiling. I stumble a
little on the second flight and you giggle; we kiss a little more and
you ask if you're too heavy and I re-adjust you a little and say no.

I carry you into my bedroom and you're aghast to see so many
more candles lighting the room. You look into my eyes and smile
and we kiss again. I lay you down on the bed and take my jacket
off and lie down beside you. We embrace holding each other. I
pull back and brush my hand against your face and run my fingers
through your hair, "you look so beautiful" I say. "I've been waiting
for this for half my life". "Are you ever old" you say and we giggle
again.

I kiss you again and this time we roll our tongues into each other. The kissing lasts forever and I reach behind you and squeeze your bum; my strong hands feel so good on your body. You playfully reach over and squeeze my bum as well; we look at each other and smile. You lie back now and I slowly move away from your lips to your neck and ears, you giggle once more. I slowly slide my hand from your hips up to your chest caressing your body along the way. I return to kissing you on the mouth and start to massage your right breast through your shirt. You sigh as it feels so good.

The kissing becomes more furious and I slowly reach back down and put my hand up under your blouse. I reach up and fondle both your breasts, firmly but gently. Each of us is kissing the other so hard. I reach back down and grab your hip pulling you back to your side. Then my hand starts to travel back along your back to your strap. I fiddle with the strap for a little while and you giggle, "having trouble are you, just wait a moment" and you sit up reaching down to your waist and pulling your top over your head. I gasp at the sight of you in your bra and lean in kissing you on your neck and chest. You put your hand on my head stroking my hair, the sensation feels so nice and you lie back down guiding my head into your chest.

I kiss your chest even more and begin to lick you as well. You continue to stroke my hair. I then reach up and slowly slide your straps down your arms one at a time. You again sit up and say "just let me take it off" and I move back as you reach behind undoing the clasps. You then reach around holding the cups in place at first and then let it go. My eyes open so wide as I see you topless for the first time and I lean in and you stop me with an extended arm.

You then reach down and grab at the bottom of my shirt pulling it out of my pants. You then begin to unbutton my shirt, smiling along the way. You then gesture for me to stand; sitting up in front of me and undo my belt, my button and pull down my zipper. You yank down on the sides of my pants, revealing as they come down the huge bulge in my underwear. The sight opens your eyes wide. I step out of my pants and reach down pulling off my socks.

I then look at you again smiling and lean in to kiss you again pushing you backwards on to the bed climbing on top of you. We kiss long and hard and I slide my right hand back up your body to your chest cupping your left breast. I kiss and lick my way back down from your mouth to your neck and chest. The sensation feels so good and you put your arms around me stroking my back and head. I then take your left nipple in my mouth sucking it ever so gently rolling my tongue against it. I move my hand back down to your bum squeezing it. My mouth feels so good on your breast and you sigh again. I slide my hand slowly around your waist and begin to caress your thighs. Your heart begins to pound and you can feel mine pounding as well against your skin.

I slide my hand between your legs and you close your thighs on it, you can feel your juices beginning to flow. I rub my hand around stroking you and slowly kiss my way to your right breast. You reach down and unbutton your pants and I look down and see this, I then help with your zipper. You then raise your hips and grab both sides of your pants sliding them down your waist. I grab your pants and help them down and you slide your legs out of them. As you lay your hips back down my hand meets your underwear as your bum hits the bed. I grab you through your underwear caressing you and you're soaked.

I kiss you on the mouth again and you guide my head back to your breasts. I giggle and lick, suck and gently nibble at both your breasts and nipples alternately while still stroking you through your underwear. I then slowly move my hand into your underwear sliding my middle finger between your lips. Your heart is pounding so hard now and you feel your climax start to build. I stroke you passionately, reaching down and penetrating you and then stroking you more with your juices on my finger. I touch your clit and it feels so good, your nipples are so erect and the pleasure is building and building.

You again raise your hips and reach to slide your underwear off. I move down your body and help to pull them down. I then hold your legs apart and look you over and the smile across my face is wide. I reposition myself between your legs and lean back in kissing you on your right inner knee. I slowly make my way up your thigh and just as I approach your pussy and you are getting so excited, I stop and skip over to your left knee. I repeat the same process, but this time when I reach your pussy I lick you up your right lip. I then lick you up your left lip and you feel like you're going to burst. I then lick you up the middle and you moan, "It feels so good".

I giggle and say "and now what you've been waiting for" and I stick my tongue right up your slit and push it to your clit. You tilt your head back into the pillow as I start to lick and kiss you, gentle at first and then with a little more vigor. I reach both my hands up and spread you apart. I put my tongue directly on your clit and use the entire length of my tongue to lick you. Again you say it feels so good and with that I bury my whole face in, licking, kissing and sucking you. You begin to rock your hips and I move my mouth up and down and side to side continually. I reach behind you grabbing your bum with both my hands pulling your pussy to my face. Your climax is building greatly and my every moment takes you higher. I pull back and gasp for air and you giggle and say are you OK, I say yes of course and begin to lean back in.

You reach down and spread your lips apart for me with your fingers and you can see the smile and nasty look on my face as I dive back in pushing my mouth hard against you. I then reach up and fondle your breasts while my tongue and mouth continue to work your pussy; it feels so good and you can feel your orgasm approaching. I'm pushing and licking so hard now. And then every once in a while I pull back and just gently lick your clit a little. This goes on for a bit until you can feel yourself almost there and you grab the back of my head driving my mouth to you and you thrust your hips towards me. I'm licking so hard now and you rock your hips and you can feel it coming and you buck, one two three times and the pleasure travels over your body in waves. I then pull back and kiss both your lips and flick my tongue at your clit and you feel your whole body tingling as the orgasm ends.

You open your eyes and look down at me smiling and gasping for air. You can feel the sweat all over your body and see the sweat beads on my head. I sit up lick my lips and wipe away my mouth. You sit up to meet me and we kiss again deeply for a minute or so and then guide me on to my back sitting astride me. You reach down into my underwear and you can feel that they are very wet from the excitement. You grab my cock from inside my underwear and start to stroke it and then you reach down further and cup my balls rolling them around gently in your hands. You can hear me breathing a little heavy and moaning ever so slightly. I raise my hips and you slide my underwear down, revealing my erection.

You again stroke my cock and I moan again. I reach over and cup your breast fondling it. You lean forward and kiss the head of my cock and then slowly take it into your mouth. I moan again and say yesssssss. You reach over and cup my balls and then start to slide your mouth up and down, rolling your tongue along at the shaft at the same time. You pull it out and lick it up and down the shaft. I reach down and stroke your hair and your back. You can tell I love it so much and it gets you even more excited. You lean down and tongue my balls and then back up and put me back in your mouth. You take it down all the way and then up, and begin to move more rapidly. I put my hand on your head and help you keep the rhythm. This goes on for a bit and just when it's getting so fast, I pull away and stop you.

I sit up and firmly lay you back on the bed, roll gently on top of you and push your legs to the side and push my cock inside of you, leaning down to kiss you in the same motion. We roll our tongues and I slowly begin to thrust back and forth. The motions get stronger and you can feel your climax starting to begin again as I kiss and push and pull in and out of you. It feels so good to have me inside you and it feels like this goes on forever. Sweat starts dripping from my brow onto you and you feel so hot with me pressed up against you, pounding my cock into you.

This continues and soon you can feel me start to go more rapidly and my kissing is becoming harder. This excites you even more

and you can feel your orgasm building again. It soon feels like I'm
pounding into you harder than ever and you can feel another orgasm
rushing. I then jerk and shake and the waves crash over you and I
fall onto you with big groan and you can feel me fill your pussy
with my sperm. It's so warm inside you and I collapse into your
arms, gasping for air.

I lean back up smiling at you and kiss you again while still
inside you and we hold each other, rolling onto our sides. I stroke
your face and tell you how wonderful and beautiful you are and that
I love you and you say the same and we kiss softly and hug each
other. It's so relaxing as we lie there quietly holding each other,
until I say "ok so are you ready to go again?"

So while Mary read the short story I went and got a drink and
had a smoke and came back to the computer to wait for her. When
she came back to the conversation the first word she typed was
wow; and then she asked if that really did happen. And I said nope,
its complete fantasy, every single word of it; although that is me as
lover. For that matter and still actually to this very day I have never
even once kissed Clarice. I then explained further to Mary how
Clarice felt about reading but how she had said that she expected
me to act out every bit of that fantasy line for line.

So I started asking Mary questions about her reaction to the
story and honestly I was looking specifically for one answer. Did it
get her juices flowing? She told me a lot of things that made me
really happy. How completely realistic she felt the story was and
that it was describing what it was like having actual sex not like a
romance novel while still being very romantic. She continued on
that when and if a woman would ever read this they would think to
themselves why I can't find a man like that. She said how I had
described the foreplay so perfectly and that all the giggling and talking was in the exact right spots. That all those parts were her
favourite and it was why she liked the story so much. She then
even gave me some advice that if I wanted to pursue this type of
writing that I should tone down the graphic use of the words such as
cock, pussy and clit and also maybe not be so graphic with the face

160

grinding, oral sex and penetration. I thanked her and further suggested that maybe she could help me with that stuff as I was going
to pursue writing. She got excited about the prospect of helping me
to edit the story, but I stopped her and told her I just wanted her
opinions and that I was not looking forward to having someone edit
me in the future and I didn't want to start now when I was just starting out; she said she understood.

　　There was still a question I wanted answered and that was the
physical part, did Mary get aroused. She replied that she wished
her husband was awake and I said no that's not good enough; come
on you promised and she said you're really going to make me say
this aren't you? I replied yes and she said ok yes I'm very aroused,
like I said I wish my husband was awake and there are things happening down there. And with that I became very happy, I admitted
that what Mary had said had aroused me as well and I thanked her
ever so much for her honesty and we parted ways as it was now 2
am and she was tired and so was I.

Chapter 9
<u>Why</u>

Oh natural statuesque flowing beauty;
how is it that,
the gift of your presence free?
Your gorgeous eyes that just devastate;
oh luscious lips,
kiss me before it's too late.
You have the kindest most beautiful smile;
I sing and I dance,
and turn up that dial.
Your personality ever so kind;
absolutely and truly,
you blow my mind.
I listen intently to each word you say;
they resonate inside me,
each and every day.
Never would you need a sense of fashion;
your every movement,
defines passion.
You have ultimate strength to which I am witness;
a goddess's spirit,
that lights the darkness.
You are a queen ruling the kingdom that is me;
watching you leave now,
can I continue to be?
A complete man I am if I live to please;
live to please,

the breath taking Clarice.

The following day I awoke to a strange feeling and had what was the first of my many morning realizations. I've come to know and understand that it is in the morning when I do my best thinking and best writing. After dropping off mom at the go train station and having a cup of tea I sat down at the computer and just started writing about how I was feeling and what I was thinking rather than continuing on with the Roberta description story. So I wrote the following soliloquy:

I awoke today and I thought it's strange I have not masturbated since my epiphany. Why? I just don't know? The closest I came was last night while chatting with Mary online for instance but I still didn't do it. I shared ideas with her and allowed her to read my pornographic short story about the fantasy of intercourse with Clarice and then prodded Mary to honestly tell me about her reaction. I was ecstatic she admitted that it got her seriously aroused while reading the story and that she wished her husband was awake as it was 1am or so.

While chatting online my motivation was to look for the true reaction that my writing could provoke. What it would make a person feel like deep inside their being; and I got exactly the reaction I wanted to hear. But there was still this person inside me that wanted to use that conversation to masturbate to. In the past I would have poked and prodded Mary and even been dishonest if she didn't go along and even might have masturbated with or without her. Or even after the conversation, it wouldn't have mattered; but before my epiphany I would have masturbated, that is almost for sure. I did actually do that during my marriage, but not exactly in the same way. But not this time; why is that? I felt my genitals start to get erect, how could I not get aroused with what Mary told me? But I still didn't? Why? Have I found god? What happened that I wouldn't do what has been so engrained into me since I was like 13?

Is it because I'm so exhausted with so little sleep that I can't perform? Usually; I only can't perform when I'm drunk; oh I can get erect but I can't have an orgasm most of the time or it's really really hard to do. Hmm, I seem to remember not wanting to masturbate after being destroyed by Laura either. Well if it is god that I have found; and I have come to believe that god is inside each one of us. Doesn't god say do not pray before any false idols besides him? Correct? Is that it? Is it that love is god? Or is love just my god for that matter and before I was living a life of the devil with all the lust I had.

I still have the pornographic Polaroid pictures and home video I took of Carrie; and for the longest time I used them to masturbate to. I found what I did in the act of taking those pictures and making the video was far more erotic than anything someone else could ever do, in the sense of something that I would view. The same principle goes for the pictures of Laura I have that I shot many years ago. I guess what I truly believe is that love is god and that god is love.

I have to be very careful when distinguishing between lust and love. With Carrie; all I believe that I had was lust for her. I found her so ever appealing in the physical sense and that her body felt so amazing when I would have sex with her. The sensations felt better than any I ever had before in the ways of physical pleasure. But where did lust and having intercourse before the building of the bond of love ever get me? A few years into my marriage and I'm fantasizing about being single. And I'm quite sure the lust heavily contributed to all the misery of the last few years of my marriage.

If Clarice ever gave herself to me, would that be true love? Would I find my god? I wonder that if you truly feel the love returned that you give to someone; if then you would be in the presence of god? Is it that it? And for that matter am I in love with Clarice right now? I told her I loved her in the text message I sent to her from the graveyard of my grandparents and I truly meant it. I do love her very deeply.

I masturbated early in the day before Clarice came over for lunch, that day being the one before I had my epiphany. It was to try and prevent pre-mature ejaculation in case we did have inter-course. But then when she was there and she had her feet in my crotch as I rubbed them; to relieve her pain from falling down some stairs a couple of days prior; my penis was still just dripping in pre-cum. There was no controlling myself in that way when it came to Clarice. And then it happened again later on when she squeezed my hand tightly after I grabbed it to hold it; just even for a few minutes before she left to return to her life.

Hmm, I think I am in love with Clarice; I think I always have been since the dance at the wedding, or at least I had the building blocks in place for it. And now our relationship has developed again on my part since she returned to my life. I think there's a dis-tinct possibility I broke Clarice's heart when I rejected her for Laura 11 years ago, just as she had rejected me for Sean a few years prior to that.

When I brought up the subject of rejection a few years back when we first reconnected after 7 years away on facebook; after some small chats I asked her if she remembered the conversation of my rejection of her. She then flat out denied it ever happened but I remember we were in my bedroom in Milton during a huge party at my apartment. She was being very attentive to me that night, sitting in my lap, really affectionate. She then told me in my bedroom how she regretted her decision to stay with Sean and that it was the wrong choice and that she wished she had been with me instead. She then said she wanted to kiss me. I then I said I couldn't as I was in love with Laura. Did I break her heart into pieces? Could she not admit to that conversation because it hurt so much? Did it actually happen? It was a party and I was pretty drunk at the time? But I'm just so sure it happened though, I was there, I know what she said and I know what I was feeling when she said it. I clearly said something to the extent of uh oh, I can't do this I love Laura.

I wonder what might happen the first time I kiss Clarice; will it be everything I've ever searched for in love? While creating the outline of this story by separating my poems into chapters; I found that I was so surprised to learn that Clarice was going to get one chapter all to herself and at the same time family, friends, marriage and children were all one chapter on their own. So what? When looking at what's been significant in my life; what's defined who I am as a person; the bond I have with Clarice defines me just as much as family, friends and being a father put together? Does love define me just as much as those same 3 things combined? If love is then god, then does god define me just as much as those 3 things combined?

Well since I haven't felt what I believe to be a true return of love from Clarice; I'm still unsure. I know she cares very deeply, she always says so and I believe her; but I don't know what holds her back from passion? Does she not truly feel physically attracted to me? I've seen her comment on facebook about old pictures of me; that I was so very handsome then. But is she truly physically attracted to me?

Did her hard drug abuse with Sean and her subsequent momentary relapse partially happen because she was destroyed that she was not mature enough to realize what she could have had with me; and by my subsequent rejection once she had realized and admitted it? I've been saying to myself, or have come to the realization from my epiphany; that if it's not Clarice (but I sure hope it is) then maybe it's someone else. Maybe it's still Roberta; or maybe there's someone else out there for me. There probably is; I just haven't found them yet. Women are looking so appealing to me these days; there were a couple on my spiritual journey that just made my tongue waggle.

I have not yet made the MP3 player for Clarice as a gift for her on her trip to see her father. The songs that I feel feed my soul and that I want to share with her and have them feed her soul as well. Possibly even manipulating her to realize that it's me she should be with instead of Steve. Normally I would have done this in a heart-

beat. Why not now? Why haven't I done this? Do I not want to
manipulate Clarice? Do I want her to come to me just as I have
come to her? Have I found love in Clarice? Have I found god in
her?

Does she feel that I rejected her once and she's so scared that I
will do it again? That maybe she's not good enough for me? I just
don't know. She rejected me first so why would I have thought that
conversation in Milton in my bedroom at the party was a monumental moment for her in admitting to her mistake? Was her one time
hard drug slip up caused by my rejection? I don't have any
answers? Honestly I just don't know? So, hmm, what do I do, oh
my god, do I do it? Oh my god, well...it's off to the phone I go; to
make that call to Clarice; and at which time I will read to her exactly what I just wrote starting from today, no fear of rejection any
longer, only love and god...

This is my life. I will be happy no matter what comes along; no
longer depending on whether I have found love or not. No matter
how much pain I suffer I am strong enough to get through it, I hope.
It's what Red said when traveling to see Andy on the bus in the
Shawshank Redemption and it's what I say to you now. I hope.
There's always hope. Be strong my friend you are or you will be
loved. There's someone out there to love you, always. There is a
god for you and a god for me and a god for everyone. Love in all
its' capacities is god. The devil is to be alone wallowing in whatever
you believe to be evil and allowing that thing to consume you and
accepting it. Live with god my friend, hope, wish and pray to find
love in whatever capacity or form it may be. Wherever you think
you find love and happiness that is where your god is. Now I'm
going to go cry, then crank the stereo and try and come back again
and get centered.

And with that I thought the book ending was finished, I thought
I'd fill the book in with the many many interesting stories of my life
and I'd leave the reader in the end with the question of what happened after I told Clarice all of this? Did she say I love you too and
we went off into the sunset as a couple or did she reject me and I

chased after Roberta or some other woman? Well what was to come after I finally read this to Clarice over the phone was just absolutely mind blowing and completely life altering and I haven't been the same nor will I ever be the same since. This was one of the greatest realizations of my life and it only built up to what was to come and what has now made me firmly believe in every thought I wrote in that soliloquy and for that matter made me a changed man forever. So read on my friend, read on as it's about to really get good. If all that graphic sex has really bothered you, well don't worry it's all clean from here on out and if you liked the graphic sex; well maybe there'll be a story or two in a future book for you as well.

Chapter 10

<u>All With You</u>

Help me,
rescue me,
I'm sinking so fast;
I've fallen,
I'm downtrodden,
I'm encompassed by my past.
It's all ever I wanted,
to, from and with;
it is where I am living,
I have to go through this myth.
I've waited a lifetime,
to capture that beautiful dove;
I'll wait a eon more,
for that soul so full of love.
Always forever,
there will I stand;
patience my friend,
it was all planned.

So I did get up from the computer and phoned Clarice right at that exact moment when I said I was going to; but I got her voice mail and left her a message telling her how badly I wanted to talk to her and then returned to the computer and wrote what I believed to be the first book ending. I continued on writing while I was waiting to hear back from her and got pretty engrossed in what I was doing. A couple of hours later I found it strange that I hadn't heard from Clarice as she was usually very quick on the phone in the morning hours being she was a housewife and usually was just puttering around the house. After a couple of hours I began to believe that she was ignoring me because of the I love you message from the gravesite so I messaged her:

If you don't let me read this to you it will hurt me more than rejecting me ever possibly could. Please listen to your voice mail.

Still there was no reply and I found that to be even stranger as Clarice was always quick on the instant messages during the day. I started to believe that was it for us and she was taking a walk, leaving me in the dust; so off went another message:

Say something, anything. If it's over please tell me so I can live free without regret, just say something please oh please. Just please don't leave me like this, not you.

But still there was nothing and I started to get very upset. I sent off an email to Connie begging her to call me as I needed someone to talk to as Connie was the closest and most knowledgeable person with regards to what was going on. Connie called and we spoke for an hour or so. After fully warning her about what she was going to hear I read the soliloquy to her. She took it all in and said wow Clarice needs to hear that. I know I said but she's not calling back and it's driving me nuts. Connie tried to calm me as best she could, but it wasn't helping; so we discussed the style of the writing and some of the content but not the masturbating part. I said to her it might be best not to talk with Don about this, as I believed if the roles were reversed I wouldn't want some guy discussing masturbation with my wife no matter who it is, even if it was me. She replied, she could see my point and agreed.

I asked Connie if she thought I was crazy and she said she couldn't fully understand my thought process as she is more of an analytical or logical thinker than me. Me being the hopeless romantic, with the logical part usually being quieted in matters of the heart. So I thanked Connie for listening, continued on about my day and off went instant message number three:

I read it to Connie and she said Clarice needs to hear that. Please beautiful it's not another poem.

The day went on and still there was no call or message from Clarice. It was a rough day for me, my mind was racing and I think I slept maybe 4 or 5 hours that night if I was lucky.

The next day began like any other and I started writing again. A few hours into the morning my phone rang and it was Clarice. She said I was being stupid. She said to remember that she had told me that she was going on her son's school trip yesterday and had turned off her phone for the day. Then she continued with how I needed to tone down the contact as she didn't want Steve to get suspicious for what might be no reason. She was upset that when she had turned on her phone that morning it had started beeping like crazy with all the messages I had sent her.

I slowly calmed her and explained that what I was about to read to her to her would probably explain my behaviour a little better. I further said that a one line message after someone says I love you might have also calmed things a little, to which she said she understood. So I asked if I could read her the soliloquy and she agreed. I prepped her very intensely before I started to read it to her telling her that this time I would probably shock her and that there was going to be a lot of information in the piece that she might disagree with and that she might want to stop me to correct but I asked her to please allow me to finish as I really wanted her to hear the whole thing uninterrupted. She agreed and so I read it to her line for line, maybe changing the odd grammatical error along the way. As I read the soliloquy to her I felt so nervous and part of me wanted to stop because of the in love with you part; but I pushed forward and finished reading it to her.

I told her when I was done and she paused and then said so is that how you feel? And I said yes that's exactly how I feel. Then she said wow that's a lot to take in at once and I replied I know. I continued, you don't have to say anything right now and I think I actually would prefer it if you thought about it for a while before you said anything. She commented though that she was happy to hear that a guy exhibited what she felt was the thought patterns of a woman; as women were always wondering if men thought like that and then she joked that I was about one step away from wearing a bra. I told her to be careful as I hadn't met many men who thought like I do and I was in a very small percentile in my opinion.

She agreed that it was a good idea to think about things for a while but I again outlined to her my plan for what might happen if we did ever get together. I had told her after our lunch the previous Thursday that it would be a good idea to keep things quiet to which she responded no promises; but this time I made sure it was clear what I thought. I told her there were two major factors involved if her and I ever were to be together and that was Steve and her daughter Morgan. I explained Steve was a simple one; in my opinion if the roles were reversed and some guy took my woman away from me, well depending on my mindset, there might be a good chance that I might try to kill the guy. Well who knows what might happen as you can't predict the future and know what kind of circumstances might arise; he might just say ok, no problem and that would be the ideal response. But I've always said hope for the best but always prepare for the worst and the violent reaction could also happen. I said to Clarice that I can be as strong and courageous as can be, but when I'm staring down the barrel of a gun or have a knife in my back; well being strong and courageous isn't going to help me one bit.

I then continued on speaking about Morgan and this time I spoke from the experience of growing up in a broken home. I told her that at first if we became a couple that things would probably be fine between Morgan and I as she was just a kid and being that I have three kids of my own I know how to handle kids. It was Morgan's and my future relationship I was worried about. I could foresee that maybe when she was in her teens and evaluating why her parents were not together any longer that she would probably look at me and say it's him; he's the reason that my mom and dad are not together; he broke them up and I hate him. Clarice agreed that it was a very good way of thinking and that if this all possibly came to fruition that it would be best if she got her own place and we just started out dating at first to keep up appearances. She continued that she was somewhat impressed that I had given so much thought to all of this, to which I responded that everything I had wrote in the soliloquy was all true.

We then just started to gab about everything and this is when she detailed for me the beginnings of her hard drug abuse, how it progressed and how she had finally gotten clean. It had to deal with the situation involving her daughter when she was a year old or so with her being taken away by Children's Aid and how she was unable to deal with the pain of the situation. That little bastard Sean made the drugs readily available to her and Clarice quickly and easily got hooked. She then developed her own friends with addictions and it all spiraled out of control from there. Clarice explained that she finally got clean when her best friend made her stand on a scale in a store and her severe weight loss scared her straight and into sobriety.

I then told Clarice the entire story of revenge on Laura and she listened intently to fill in the blanks of the stuff she didn't know from that time in my life. I also started to fill in more of the blanks as to why my marriage had broken up. Up until this time I had told Clarice the major reasons as to why the split had occurred but I always glazed over the little things as they always upset me. I didn't want to be one of those guys who complained and complained it get to the point where Clarice didn't want to talk to me anymore because that would be all she ever heard. That's something I've tried to do with all my friends, just try to stay as positive as I possibly can. I remember when I told Carlos about the split just before we were heading into the Chris Cornell concert and of course he was sympathetic to my situation but he also said he was glad that I was in the frame of mind I was in about the entire thing as his cousin had also gone through a divorce years prior and had been inconsolable at times. It was tough on Carlos at times because he didn't know how to help his cousin because that was all he wanted to do for him.

Clarice became the good friend at this point in the conversation and started criticizing Carrie about the things she had done wrong during our marriage but I wasn't feeling like I was in the same place at that moment. Yeah I had used the what a bitch or whatever swear words you can think of when a man describes a woman in anger, but I wasn't at that place right now. The soliloquy had started a change in me and I was feeling remorse for the dishonesty I had brought into my marriage; specifically that I had never had the click on moment when I decided to marry Carrie. There was love there, but I never fell in love with her or had that one special moment when I knew that I could clearly describe. I always knew that for the entire duration of my marriage.

I felt responsible for the break up of my marriage from an emotional standpoint as I never had that initial spark or bond of falling in love to fall back upon to help repair things when they went wrong. Being in love is what always motivates my romantic tendencies and maybe if I had been able to be more romantic with Carrie when the troubles occurred things might have been easier to repair. Or maybe my eyes wouldn't have wandered during the course of our marriage, yes there was the facebook sex with Sarah, but I also checked out that cheating married person's website, I entertained the slight advances of a woman at my housewarming party for whom I had a very large crush on for years and was ready for sex with Clarice when we went out for coffee a few weeks before I left the house for good. I was never in love with Carrie during the course of our marriage; it was always just lust and friendship.

So wouldn't you know it my cell phone went dead and our conversation was cut off after about 90 minutes into it. I called my mom and asked her to message Clarice the landline phone number that mom had just gotten a few days prior and started thinking about everything Clarice and I had just talked about. I truly became over-whelmed with remorse for my role in the failure of my marriage and then sent the following emails to Carrie with the soliloquy attached to the first one:

I need for you to read this. It doesn't change anything between us, everything has to go forward on the same course it is on now, exactly the same course it is now, no matter what. And I mean everything with the lawyers; absolutely no matter what. I no longer wish to hurt you or anyone else for that matter. The issues between us are far and wide and can never ever be repaired because of my dishonesty from the first moment I met you. We each have our responsibility in what went wrong in the marriage but in the end emotionally this is all honestly and truly my fault, 100%. I'm so sorry for what I have done to you and I don't know if you can ever for-give me. This is the ending to my book, it's called Eat Away at Anything for Redemption and you will obviously play a big part in it. Only in actually speaking to Clarice, Connie and my mom did I realize what I actually I did to you. Again I extend my most sincere apology and ask your forgiveness so that each of us can live without hatred and resentment. There are more poems and maybe one day I will share them with you if you like. I'm so so sorry for all I have done and I don't expect you to forgive me, I probably would not. And I'm so sorry if this hurts you even more, it probably will. I don't want you to hurt anymore. Honestly and truly I do even though you have no reason to believe me. I'm sorry, so sorry.

My mind was going pretty good at this time and I soon came to the realization that not only did I need to repair things with Carrie but it was also time to start working on my sister and Larry as well. And so I sent the following message to Janine:

Janine I need to spend some serious one on one time with you in the near future and I also need you to read the ending of my book. You will play a huge part in it and I need you to be on board with everything. I need to email the ending of the book to you. Please keep your mind wide open when you read it.

And Janine replied:

That sounds very daunting. Is it about our family? This is my email address in case you dont have it saved. I will be in Mississauga for a week in July because Kimberly and I have some important doctors appointments (don't know if Mum told you about it yet) We will likely be there the Sunday till the following Saturday. If the book is going to upset me please prepare me a little.

I called Larry and left a message for him that I wanted to talk to him and see him. I knew now that I was ready to see him and begin to address what had happened between he and I. I went about my business and waited for Clarice to call back and after a couple of hours she did and we continued chatting away. I discussed how strange it was that she had pretty well been out of my life for the last 10 years and even still that when we were together it felt like no time had passed. Inside I knew that was not the case.

She had never even met my children nor had I her youngest daughter and it quickly popped into my mind to say by the way sweetheart what's your middle name? And she answered it's Audrey Kate. I asked her if she wanted the MP3 player after all and she said sure it would keep her company on her trip.

She discussed the upcoming trip to Alberta to visit her dad and her excitement and worries about what was going to happen. I gave her my insight into all that and expressed how excited I was for her as she was going to have the opportunity with her father that Janine and I did not have with ours.

I then told her about what I had just done with Carrie, Janine and Larry and she was speechless, she was shocked. I continued on with how inspired I was at this time and I then discussed the journey to Cobourg to her. I talked about how the book was constantly changing, that I had started to develop an outline for the book and what I was going to do going forward. I had previously thought the book was going to be about me clearing out once and for all these emotions that I had regarding my father and freeing myself from all of the anger that I had towards him and the other negative things in my life. But while I was on the phone with Clarice I realized that I wasn't going to be free unless I freed myself from every negative thing in my life. That meant I also needed to be free from what was between myself and Carrie, myself and Janine and myself and Larry too. The conversation with Clarice left me floating on air and I was so inspired about making things right that I knew what the first step was to freedom and so, I sent the following message to Carrie:

While printing stuff to show to my mentor, I realized that I should show you this poem (Reflection). So again, I am so very very sorry, I will return the pics and video tomorrow; plus I will have your child support cheque. Don't mistake though, everything else goes forward the same. Each of us has our own penance we must deal with.

That night I went off to my softball game and played in the pouring rain, geez we got totally soaked, but we won so that was nice and it was off to work I went. I got my day underway and did my usual tasks but was I ever distracted by everything that was going on. After getting caught up for the night I grabbed a piece of paper and started to write out the outline for the book and it came out very quickly:

Eat Away Anything for Redemption: First Story Outline

Chapter 1: Introduction
Masturbation, love, god, lust, devil, hope

Chapter 2: Clarice phone call part 1
- *being neurotic "don't leave me this way"*
- *reading her the story "Is this how you feel"*
- *Possible vision for the future (Steve & Morgan)*

Chapter 3: Clarice phone call part 1 continued
becoming clean from drugs on both parts

Chapter 4: Clarice phone call part 1 continued 2
- *Destruction by Laura*
- *Revenge on Laura*
- *Remorse for marriage dishonesty*

Chapter 5: Need for Redemption
- *Emails to Carrie*
- *Return of video & pics*
- *Email to Janine*
- *Phone call to Larry*
- *realizing the "finale" written is actually the beginning of the story*

Chapter 6: Clarice phone call part 2
- *The spiritual journey to Cobourg to visit grand parent's gravesite*
- *Honesty with Carlos*
- *Feelings of being pathetic in dealings with relationships with women: Roberta, Stacey, Denise, Carol, Kim, Stella, Laura*

Chapter 7: Mom's story
- *Tom, Carl, Bob*
- *Bill (abuse, Baptist hypocrite, throwing him out)*
- *Fred (mannequin story)*
- *Peter (amateur shrink)*
- *grudges (Florence, Grandma)*
- *The fight over the master bedroom & 1st real redemption*

Chapter 8: Carrie
- *Beginnings*
- *Charles*
- *Wedding*
- *Intercourse*
- *All children by 30*
- *Marital problems (finances, intercourse, housework)*
- *Paige & Jack*

- *Insurance sales*
- *Sarah facebook story*
- *Counseling & Separation*

Chapter 9: Larry

Chapter 10: Janine

Chapter 11: Clarice's story
- *Sean, Burt,*
- *Christina*
- *Maple & Shirkstreet homes*
- *Larry's wedding & Shelburne*

Chapter 12: reconnect with Clarice
- *Coffee w/Clarice 10 years passed*
- *Lunch w/Clarice, Janine & Gene*
- *Missed you in my life*
- *Clarice finds her father & family*
- *Flirting*
- *I can't use what I can't abuse, "Eat Away"*
- *instant messages*

Chapter 13: Falling for Clarice again
- *Lunch with Clarice*
- *Story of my father's death*
- *1st signs of falling in love*

Chapter 14: Pornographic fantasy short story

Chapter 15: The Epiphany

Chapter 16: Clarice returns from Alberta
- *Story ends just as we meet*

Possible Additional Fantasy Chapters:

*Chapter 16: revised, Clarice returns from Alberta, leaves Steve, 1st
kiss*
Chapter 17: the break up with Steve
Chapter 18: Dating, wedding proposal & engagement
Chapter 19: Person of importance dies
Chapter 20: the wedding, Clarice walks the aisle ending

And so the excitement : started; I talked with Francis, my close
friend at work, about everything that was going on and shared the
outline with him. I started to ponder taking the book in a fantasy
direction when it came to Clarice to make the love story portion of
the book end in an appealing way to female readers. I took the idea
in every direction and came up with a couple of scenarios and of
course didn't I just have to call up Clarice to discuss. And then call
her again with a new idea and then messaged her 3 more times with
other ideas; oh Charlie won't you ever learn.

Clarice and I were still supposed to meet up one more time
before she headed on her trip to see her dad and I messaged her to
ask if that meeting could be at my next softball game as I would
like her to meet Carlos, Connie and Don. Just so everyone could put
a face to the names.

As the night progressed; the lack of sleep and the deep chill to
my bones from getting soaked at the softball game caught up with
me and around 2 am I started to feel terrible, really bad; I had shiv-
ers and headaches and I felt like I was going to pass out and told
my backup lead hand that I was going to go home early. It was a
good thing because I left at 4:45 am and during the drive home I
was a total mess. It felt like I was on cheap drugs as the street
lights were looking awful strange and the beams of light were dancing all over the place and flowing into one another. After I finally

got home, my body crashed hard and I slept deeply for 5 hours.

Chapter 11

<u>Anno Domini</u>

Lost in a love,
to forgive the debt;
cost more,
than you are willing to bet.
Atone for that,
which was wrong;
alone now,
encompassed by song.
Delve deep inside,
into trouble;
shelve the rage,
to become humble.
Receive once more,
every memory's toll;
retrieve the light,
for a darkened soul.
Rise above,
the engraved hatred;
wise now,
to blessings understated.
Forgive the existence,
that was rotten;
relive pleasure,
long ago forgotten.
Fade away times,
no longer important;
trade away a cold heart,
never again dormant.

I awoke the next day at around 10 am and slowly got myself into gear with a cup of tea and a smoke. I checked my cell phone and Clarice had replied to my messages from the previous evening. She was sympathetic to my excitement from the book and didn't give me any grief about all the messages I had left her but said she was unable to attend my softball game Monday due to prior commitments. I got started writing and typed out the outline that I had come up with the previous night and then spent the rest of the day working on writing about the cemetery visit to my grandparent's grave. I emailed the outline to Clarice and my sister as they were both to be heavily involved as to where the book was going to go to and I continued typing away for most of the day. I then wrote the following email to Janine that I sent along with my soliloquy and hugs and kisses:

OK so here's what I believed was the ending of my book until I spoke on the phone to Clarice for 2 or 3 hours yesterday. Please be prepared that it involves subject matter of a graphic sexual nature; something probably a sister does not want to hear about her brother. I need you to be involved in my book because of what I will be saying about you in it and I think we finally really need to say some things between us. The book's working title is "Eat Away at Anything for Redemption". Please understand that I don't want to hurt you, I have realized that I don't want to hurt anyone anymore. I have approached Carrie in an email with this story and apologized fully; I am also trying to contact Larry to try and help him in any way I can. Mom and I took care of our stuff about 2 months ago, although I don't think I want her to read this yet, maybe I will when I'm ready, maybe I never will, I'm not sure. So please be prepared, you are not yet mentioned in the book, but you most definitely will be. I only want us to have a real family again, or if not at least I have to try.

Later in the day Janine emailed me that she was having trouble opening the word attachment for the outline as it seems her computer would not open any attachments for some reason. So just before I left for work that night I sent her a 2nd copy of the outline attachment and headed off to work.

When I arrived at work I went and sought out Vince to give him my 5 newest poems and the soliloquy. When I found him we went out to a quiet area and talked. I told him things were going very well and that my book was really starting to take shape. I gave him the new material I had and asked him to read it over when he could as I was very excited at what was going on. He said he would and he quickly skimmed through the new poems and read them over; he had told me over the phone recently that he could already hear my work maturing in the short period of time since my last pieces and then he told me something that really stuck to me and helped get me through the next 24 hours of my life; and also to get through everything else since for that matter. He said Charlie it's very easy to call yourself an artist but it's so much harder to actually live the life of one; honestly truer words I don't think I've ever heard. He once again asked if he could keep the new poems and I said of course they're for you and I've signed them, hopefully one day they will be worth something. Years ago Vince had advised me to always sign my work when I had shared some older pieces with him. Vince and I then parted ways and I went on about my business for the evening putting my 12 hours for the night.

The next morning when I arrived home I wasn't feeling very tired so I decided to stay up for a while and start filling up Clarice's MP3 player. My god I thought, my computer was so slow and how would I ever find the time to fill up 8GB before Clarice left for Alberta in one week. So I continued ripping music like crazy trying to put a dent in the monstrous task I was undertaking. I also found that Janine still had not been able to view the book outline as she once again emailed me and said she could not open it, so I sent it to her again but this time pasting it directly on the email. I continued on with the MP3 player until I received the following email from Janine:

Charles, it sounds like you have included those stories about me regardless of however I may feel about it. You need to understand one thing about me. And that is who I am today, at this very minute, because I am now a mother. It's not my past that shaped me, it's coming to a place where I had to learn to be unselfish, forgive the past, and see the world differently. The only reason I am at a good place now is because I had Kimberly. I do not think I will ever get to a point where I will be comfortable looking back and recognizing that person as myself. I have forgiven myself and chose to try to forget everything else. I am very haunted by things that have happened still and struggle to accept happiness to this day. I do not want you to speak for me in your story. If you need to include me, that's fine. But you truly do not know everything behind all the things that happened to me. No one ever did, and no one ever will. It hurts me to think that my 'chapter' will be all about the things that destroyed me as a child and a teen and not about who I have tried to become as an adult. That is all.

Once I got that email I immediately responded as I recognized that Janine thought that I was just going to write her story as I saw it and that was not what I was trying to do at all. I only wanted to write about repairing the damage that was done between us and the strain that existed in her and my relationship.

You don't get it, it's about our relationship, it's about my relationship with you, and it's about how I feel about you. Not how I see your life or telling the story of your life. And about how our relationship is broken. I can't talk about anything that I don't know about and I don't expect you to tell me about anything I don't know about. You really don't get it. You think because we talk now that everything is forgotten and forgiven. To not talk is stupid and life is too short for that. But do you really think I have forgotten everything that went on in our home. Do you really think that I've forgotten about

how I busted my ass for 4 years working 2 jobs while you par-
tied and manipulated mom. Then the time came and mom
gave me back all the money that I put into the mortgage,
you said where's my money. Do you really think I've forgiven
you for that? No I haven't Janine. That's what I want to do;
I want to be able to forgive you. If you don't want my forgiveness or don't think you've done anything wrong to me,
then we will continue on the path we are on. You must have
things that you are holding about me, whatever they may be,
that I was cruel to you at times. Whatever, I want your forgiveness for things. I don't want to know what sex with
Jessica was like, I don't know what happened, I don't want to
know what happened, but it hurt me a lot that it was hidden
from me. All I would say in that scenario is that I was hurt by
the way I found out. If you don't understand what I want to
talk about then I guess there will only be a chapter with unfulfilled redemption when it comes to you. Unfulfilled forgiveness. I don't want to hurt you at all, I want to talk about the
healing, and that's what it's about. And if we can't heal
ourselves, our relationship then I guess we are not brother and
sister, then I guess I've given you more credit for intelligence
than you have. I forgave mom for allowing Bill to choke me
while she was screaming at me and Charlene was going to
kick the shit out of her. I always resented you for your suicide
attempt, I felt it was the most selfish manipulative thing you
ever did. Do you hate me for that? I always resented that I
worked like a dog and you brought your friends into party
and woke me up. Do you get it, all this is still here, it's not
gone, and it's never been dealt with. I want to deal with it, I
want us to truly be close like we always should have been,
but it wasn't truly our fault, I don't even know if it was even
one bit our fault. We were kids, whom did we have? A
woman who put men in front of us. I have forgiven her for
that. That's the book; I've come to the realization that life's
too short. It's evil to just accept these things and not have
the true love between us. I want to face these things with
you. I wanted you there with me at Grandpa and
Grandma's grave. I want us to truly love each other and forgive each other. If you can't return this to me now. Well
that's all

And what a surprise, instead of hearing what I said, Janine became incensed. I have found over and over again that it's so hard to get my message across to people because of anger trigger mechanisms. They only see one bullet point and get upset and then don't hear a single word I'm saying or what the message really is; so back comes Janine and she's furious with me now.

I was a CHILD. I was abused in ways that you can never understand. If you can't forgive me for being a child that had zero guidance, self esteem or self respect and acted in the only way I knew well then that is on YOU. I had NO ONE to hug me and tell me I was a good person. I had no one to tell me it was okay and I could like myself. EVERYTHING I DID HAD NOTHING TO DO WITH YOU. You can't forgive me for trying to take my own life? I don't ask for your forgiveness and I don't want it. You can call my actions whatever you like and you can say that I am not intelligent NOW; but that little girl I was SCREAMING inside for someone to tell her she was okay. You will never know the extent of what happened to me and I do not seek forgiveness. Our childhood did not just belong to you and your memories. I am forever haunted and trying to protect my own child from those feelings; the feeling of being NOTHING TO NO ONE, and being so worthless that you don't deserve love from anyone. You are struggling to forgive me? Well DON'T! I don't ask for your forgiveness and I don't want it. I am 34 years old and trying to be capable of loving other people unselfishly and accepting love in return. I struggle every day to be able to look myself in the eyes and not still hate that kid inside of me. My memories belong to ME and I don't expect anything from anyone. I do not need someone to tell me I am okay anymore or worthy of being loved. I am trying to love myself and give love back to the people that care about me. If you need more than that from me, I will never be able to give it.

It was at this point that I instant messaged Clarice as it was around 9:30 am or so and I knew that she would be available. I told her that things were off to a very bad start with Janine and that I was very worried that I was doing more damage than good with my

agenda. I asked Clarice if she could come online and chat with me
to help to repair the damage that was now taking place. Clarice
replied and said she would come online and did. I then forwarded
the emails between Janine and I to Clarice as I wrote my next email
to Janine.

What makes you think I want to talk about that Janine?
Honestly. I was hurt you didn't come to my wedding. You
were hurt I didn't come to the hospital when you attempted
suicide or when Kimberly was born. I'm talking about our relationship Janine, yours and I only, yours and I. Nobody else.
Don't you feel these things between us? Well if you don't
then why didn't we talk for 7 years? Did you lose my number? Who was it that invited whom to their home? You still
just don't get what I'm talking about; I wish to know nothing
of your childhood pain unless you wish to share it with me.
What I'm talking about is our teenage years, our adult lives.
As adults, there are still a lot of problems between us especially in those years. Um hence not a word for 7 years I think. So
what now everything is OK? It's not OK and I do want to forgive you so we can have better than we have now. I want
you to tell me what I've done wrong so I can apologize. Yours
and I relationship only, right now, for the last 15 years. I'm so
sorry if I stirred up all that childhood stuff, that was not what I
was looking for. We should have done this in person. I wasn't
there for you when you attempted suicide, DO YOU HATE ME?
I thought you were selfish, DO YOU HATE ME? I don't want
you to hate me, resent me, and hold things inside about me.
Honestly and truly. I'm sorry you were abused. I'm sorry I
couldn't or didn't help you more. I had my own shit to deal
with. I'm sorry that's all and if you can't see that, well what
can I say. That I'll never truly love my sister? That we'll never
be a family? I want to love my sister, I want to forgive her, I
want to hug and kiss her and have her be one of my best
friends in the whole world. This is what this is all leading up to.
This is what it's about, not selling a book at the expense of
your pain. Atoning for that I was so selfish not to talk to you
for 7 years; and to not to come to the hospital when Kimberly
was born. And that I was cruel to you much the time and
even physically violent at times. I want your forgiveness and I

want to forgive you too. That's my epiphany, it's love, happiness and forgiveness; end of story. That's my book. I'm so sorry for everything and everything I've done to you right now; I did not say what I wanted to say the first time. Please oh please forgive me.

And by the time I finished Clarice had read everything and was online and what she said to me only upset me further. She said that I was a bugger and that she totally sympathized with Janine and that she wanted to kick me the next time she saw me. I couldn't believe it and I asked her if she had read the third email and she said yes and I said and you're still mad at me and she said yes. She said Janine is trying to deal with things as best she can and here you are stirring up everything for her again. And now it seemed like I was fighting on two fronts because instead of helping me it felt like all I was getting was criticism from Clarice.

And so we drifted away from that conversation about Janine and I started to question Clarice about how she dealt with pain. I asked her about how she felt about Burt, how he had abused her and how she felt about it in general. My mind was racing as I approached the 24 hour awake mark and I started to ramble as the response she gave me was to just forget about it and go on with life. I told her that society had abandoned her and that he was a bastard and should have gone to jail. I said that I would understand if she was just as mad at the world as I was because the programs society had in place had failed us when we were children. That was it, we were children and no matter how much society nowadays say that the children of today are smarter and more informed than of yesteryear, that does not mean that children are emotionally equipped and prepared to deal with all the violence and hatred of the world. I started to rant about hating society and that Burt should be killed and stuff and with that Clarice said to stop as that was not how she dealt with things. I continued to write my next email to Janine as this all went on and asked Clarice if she would read it as we said goodbye. She said she would and would message me later.

Somehow this all went astray Janine, I never ever wanted to hurt you. I don't know what happened and I guess we can't do anything about those things except forget them. I truly am sorry for any grief I've caused you today as it was not my intention to do so. My only intention was to feel close to you as everything has changed for so much for me over the last week. I didn't mean to be malicious at all and I truly am so sorry; you will have no place in my book. I respect your wishes and hope you can forgive me. I did not want to touch anything from your childhood ever or to tell your story; I just wanted to tell how you related to me, you're a big part of my life. I wanted to atone for not believing your suicide attempt and for not supporting you. And for all the other things that happened too and hoped maybe you would say sorry as well. Again I'm so sorry; I won't involve you in my writing any longer. Please oh please forgive me

And then for the longest time there was silence and I smoked cigarette after cigarette and blared the stereo to try and hold it together. Clarice responded to the email and said that it was better but:

How about: Janine, I'm an asshole for the most part and I'm sorry, I will not put you in my book. Love your bro, Charlie

Short and sweet, not bringing up anything, with no expectations. Then for your rough copy, for your healing purposes like in a journal, you can mention whatever you want. No one has to see it but then in your good copy this is the one you show.

And low and behold Clarice had now hit my anger trigger mechanism by using the word asshole and I now really got upset and emailed her back.

I'm an asshole for the most part? You think of me as an asshole in this situation? I know I didn't go the right way, but I wasn't ever trying to be mean. It's very very hard to hear you reference me as an asshole in any way. Bugger I can take. Asshole no, not coming from you. A lot of people have

called me an asshole. Carrie called me a fucking asshole to
my kids. So please don't use that one on me, ok not you.
Please support me too. You seem to only see her side,
maybe because you are similar or kindred to her? We've all
had a tough life, all of us. What makes her so right and me
so wrong? I need you on my side too. Ok? There's no
hatred here, no anger here. I just said it was all about her, I
wanted it to be all about us. Her and I together. The point
got lost somewhere that a brother wanted to feel closer to his
sister. I didn't mean to hurt her and the lesson has been
learned for sure.

But I didn't stop there as I was going a mile a minute, I now
approached the 26 hour awake mark and started with the messaging:

I tried to do better. Check back when you can. For that
matter I'm not going to talk about stuff about you that is
uncomfortable either, i.e. Christina, Burt or drug abuse.
Another day another chapter, you are the ying to my yang.
Maybe the book is only about you and me and the profound
affect you are having on me. I wouldn't have seen the effect
that this was having on Janine without you. Maybe it's one
big love letter to you. That I want to show to the world, how
truly beautiful you are inside and out. And now the roles are
reversed from all those years ago where you are now protect-
ing me from my own worst enemy, myself. I only wish I had
done a better job back then for you. I should have helped
you and not worried about romancing you. I could have
helped you better. So sorry, forgive me.

And now Clarice was starting to get even angrier and told me
that I had to quit it with the emails, messages and texts as I was
really starting to scare her with my emotional instability. She said
that she was out for lunch and would read my next email when she
got home but I had to stop. I knew how upset she was; as clouded
as my mind was, but there was no controlling my anxiety and emotions on this day.

The next thing I had to do was pick up my children for our visit and that meant it was time to actually take the first real step to redemption and give back the pornographic home video and the disc of scanned pictures that I had of Carrie. Would I actually be able to do that since I had such a deep connection to those items? They were mine and I was in them just as much as Carrie was, but who honestly cares about seeing the guy in pornography? The male body is ugly while a woman is just so appealing, especially to me in this instance with the way that I had displayed Carrie. But my mind was in the right place and I grabbed everything I needed and made the drive to her home. When I entered I immediately handed her the video, the disc and the 1st full child support cheque.

We had already spoken on the phone that day about Paige's sleepover and that was the first time we had spoken more than two words to each other in months. I had so wondered what her reaction was going to be to this and it was so strange as when we were together I felt no negative energy in the room or between us. There was nothing there and she didn't yell at me or scream at me or slap me or anything. She just took the video and disc and then handed me an envelope with some old family pictures of mine in it that she said she had found in a box and I took it and the kids and left. I guess that is the best I could ask for and for that matter it was all that I wanted with Carrie anyways. I had now taken the first step on the path to my redemption with this simple gesture and I replayed it over and over again in my mind while talking to my kids on the drive to my home.

Once I returned home and got the kids settled in; I returned to the computer and an email from Janine was waiting for me and it was more than I could have ever hoped for in my wildest dreams:

Charles today is a bad day for me. I honestly vried more than I have in a little while. I do not deal with my emotions well because I choose not to. This is the thing I want you to under-stand; for everything that has happened, right up until today, I make a CHOICE whether or not to feel my emotions and how I want to deal with them. If it helps me to bury them, then bury them I will. And if I need to talk or deal with things, I think first. Yes I am angry at you. I have been angry with you for our whole lives. Did I need to say it? For you, I guess that's what you want. I am angry at you for so many things. Mostly it's the violence and verbal abuse that you directed at me. You didn't realize the impact it had on me. I wasn't looking for a father figure or a role model in you. I was looking for a brother and protector. I would have given you the respect you wanted at the time if you had been someone I respected and not feared. I did not hold you to a standard because you showed me how a man can intimidate a woman with his voice and fists. I retaliated against you using what I had. I consider you a bully still and that makes me very angry. YES I am angry at your reaction to my suicide attempt. I did not want to wake up that morning and I went to bed every night for MONTHS praying that my life would be over. I would not have taken 50 pills; or written a note and made peace with my decision if had I just wanted some attention. I will never forget the feeling I had waking up that morning and then I remember your voice and what you said. Don't make that an experience about our relationship. I was entirely alone. You talk about your not coming to the hospital during that time and my not coming to your wedding. I absolutely regret and apologize for not coming to your wedding. I was so blinded by everyone's actions at that time and I was always sorry I did not go. I remember so many things that hurt me even now when thinking back. But the biggest feeling I have and strug- gle with is being alone or going through the worst moments of my life by myself. I could have used one person in my corner from my family, it was you and that was all I wanted. But I accepted things a long time ago and deal with it all my own way. I am answering all of this because you asked me too but I really don't feel resentment in my heart. If I did, I would not be who I am. Your writing to me talking about the things you did really stirred up so much anger and pain but tomorrow I will go back to dealing with things as I always do. Am I angry at mom? No; not at all anymore. Mom did not have a clue how to handle her life once our Dad walked out. I will not say she did the best she could, but I will say that she is who she is and I love her for everything she is, the good and the bad. She and I do not look at each other and think back, we look

forward. That is how our relationship has survived. She is the
Grandmother to my daughter that I always hoped for. That is
everything I need to move forward. I can never ask forgiveness for what you are asking. It would not be genuine for me
to say sorry for being a selfish teenager. The only way I can
say sorry (if that's what you need) is by moving forward and
loving you as my brother now. If you can accept that, then
we will continue to work on being a family. I am not even the
same person that I was 5 years ago and am so far gone from
who I was 15 years ago. This is how I am NOW and if you
want to be in my life you have to let go of our past because I
really don't think I can make it if I have to keep reliving it with
you. Love, your sister

In real time with almost no wait time between responses:

I will now thank you, thank you, thank you, thank you ever so
much. I'm crying so much right now as this is all I ever wanted. You've made me so happy and I'm so sorry for all the
things I've done to you, truly I am. I thought of us together, in
the presence of our grandparents, the only people who ever
truly unconditionally loved us, that that was where we could
have done this. I wanted you there with me so very much.
You are just as smart as I've always given you credit for and I
know that you are smarter than I. I've always said so and
that's why your behaviour always bothered me so much, I felt
you wasted everything life had to offer you. I knew you were
a genius from an early age and therapy would be a total
waste on you. Well except maybe for the childhood stuff,
which I don't really know about. I wish we were together for
all of this. Janine I never knew how to deal with anything or
how to be a man, which is what I thought I needed to be.
There would be bursts when I was your protector and then I
would turn around and be total scum. I know what I've done
and I'm trying to make it right and yes I did need you to tell
me that you are angry at me; I needed to hear it. I can't
live these lies anymore. Every day I tell mom to stop being so
neurotic, that she projects it upon me and that I can't function properly at times because of what she has instilled in me.
I even think I am blowing it with Clarice because of it now. I
have to share every thought with Clarice and I can't be

alone just like mom. My book has changed again and it's
now just my voice only, I speak to people but you can't hear
their voice. I know that it's ok to be alone. I can never tell
you my shame that I used physical violence towards you, it
will stay with me forever. I can't even forgive Carrie for just
scratching my arms. The vision of mom egging on Bill while
Charlene yanks at her arm was burned into me for so long
and I couldn't remember specifics, it was a lot of blur and
very painful times when I would remember it. Many of those
times have blurred due to all the drugs I was doing back then
but I do remember specifically once something to do with the
phone and mom's friend Vera being on it and chasing you
around the house. I am ashamed of that right now as I am
ashamed of a lot of things in my life. If you can not offer an
apology for being a selfish teenager that is fine, but can you
offer respect for the fact that I worked 2 jobs to pay the mortgage, recognition is what I need. Yeah your brother needs a
pat on the head please, good job Charles for throwing that
motherfucker out of the house and then still doing what had
to be done when mom wasn't treating you all that good
about it. How about that? You do not have to apologize for
your pain but possibly recognize and understand mine as well.
God you're so fucking smart and you're wasting your life
Janine, would you like to help me with my book when you
come to visit? I 'm being completely honest with everything,
EVERY DAMN THING! I would like to put our conversations in,
with your permission and edited to your liking. I failed you my
sister, just like I failed my wife with my dishonesty as to not
admitting to being in love with someone else. I thought
even now until you wrote me, that you were being selfish; I
never understood the depth of the scars I put into you. I
failed you my sister. I don't want to fail you any longer.
Mom and I have gone through this in our own way and I'm so
glad for what you have told me; it will help me to be a better
person I hope. By the way I've been up for oh 27.5 hours.
Please don't cry too much, I've cried enough for both of us
today. I never want to hurt you again and I love you and
thank you so much from the bottom of my heart. Mom will
be so happy. Clarice was so dead wrong. Do you think
she's right for me Janine, am I clinging to a pipe dream?
She's so strong, probably stronger than either of us and then

of course gorgeous, but she doesn't understand my depths
and what I've put in front of her. If all this means something
to you and I hope it does, help me oh sister. If you believe
Clarice is the one for me, then be a voice in my corner at this
time and I will be one in your corner forever more. Just don't
ask me for money ok unless my book gets published as I'm
broke. You have my love, my gratitude and my respect and I
fall at your feet to beg mercy from my torment. You've
released me, just like Carrie set me free. And now it's onto
Larry and it's going to be oh so tough. Oooh this sounds like
book material :) Oh fuck I need a smoke...I'm smoking way
too much

Charles of course you have my gratitude for getting rid of Bill
and working so hard to help our family. When I think back,
those are important things in my life. Bill made me fearful
everyday and you know this. The older I got, the more he
used his hands with me and I knew it was a matter of time
before I got his full fury too. Mom was blinded at the time and
I can't blame her for it. We all get blinded sometimes and
unfortunately for us, her blindness was at the expense of her
children. I do not believe that this thing with Clarice will have
the outcome you're hoping for. I really wish I could say yeah,
go for it and throw your whole heart into loving her; but I feel
like you might regret it. I know Clarice is strong, she always has
been; but I don't think she is strong enough to walk away
from her life with Steve as it might be too costly a decision to
make. She is someone that has always sought out security
and stability and unless Steve leaves HER, or suggests it; I don't
think it's likely that she will take a chance on something else
and giving all that up. I worry that there isn't what you want
there with her. I think we all need someone to make us feel
like there is one person out there that will really love us and
hear us; but trust me, Clarice isn't that deep. She is smart and
she IS very pretty; and true she is strong; but she is not a poet,
or a writer or someone that expresses herself through creativi-
ty, she is just a regular girl. And if you want her to see your
heart you have to stand back and let her love you as a
friend, because in the end, that's bigger than what you actually want. All I hope is for the best, and I never want to see
you hurt. As for me, I hope I will get to a point in the future

where I FEEL smart. I think a lot of the decisions I have made in my life make me question my capabilities, but sometimes I surprise myself. So; who knows? Maybe I'll have things figured out in a year or two and maybe I will go back to school? We'll see but I will always stand beside you, don't forget that. How you handle this thing with Clarice is on you but my support is unconditional either way. I have a crying headache and poor Phil because I wanted to be pretty and upbeat when I saw him tonight (it's our one year anniversary this weekend) so wish me luck in pulling it together in time. Have a good sleep go GET SOME REST!

I want you to ponder something Janine. OK this will be hard but I never felt loved by you at all when we were kids. It's hard to describe and maybe you felt the same of me. We can go and try to figure out to who threw the first stone, but I think that feeling just escalated into our teenage years. I have never felt we were close ever; just that we were so alike that when things were good it was easy to co-exist. That's why this is so important to me; I don't want to co-exist with you any longer. I co-existed with Carrie. And now maybe you can understand my pain from the destruction by Laura more than ever. If right now we really understand each other you'll know why I am referencing her at this point. If you also have pain, I want to feel your pain and try to help you with your pain. I don't feel any pain right now at all, that's why I'm crying all the time, I'm not used to being happy. I used to cry a lot with Laura, I would look at her and burst into tears. Oh no I'm a chick, ah FUCK! But no there's no pain here inside me at all. Well on second thought actually now I do have pain, thanks a lot eh! FUCK AGAIN! No just kidding I'm released, I love you and I have gotta go. Message me or call me OK, I I want to talk with you, so please oh please. FUCK-ING CALL ME, SERIOUS or I'll be pissed.

: I was completely exhausted and all cried out but the hours passed by with no sleep in sight for me. Thankfully mom came home and watched over the children while this was going on so they wouldn't see the state I was in. I took the whole thread of emails between Janine and I, put them in the correct sequence and printed them off for mom so she could read them. I watched the expressions on her face as all the enormous pain of her children raced through her mind. Every once in a while she would stop to ask me a question if there was a grammatical error that had confused her or if there was some online chat lingo that she didn't understand; but not a cross word came from her mouth. Little did I know that slowly but surely her soul and her faith in god was being restored with every word and every sentence and every paragraph and every page. : I was sitting there with her having a smoke after she finally finished reading all 6 pages and all she could do, was smile; it was one of the happiest smiles I can ever remember seeing on her face. We sat there and talked, and I discussed how I believed that the book was becoming an entity and that a higher power had become involved in our lives.

I returned to the computer and there was an email from Clarice responding to the one I had sent her earlier about calling me an asshole and asking her to support me and it read:

My gosh Charlie; you need to get a handle on your emotions! I never called you an asshole, I simply stated what you should write to your sister to lighten the situation! Now I'm getting mad and I'm going to tell you like it is: I think of you in this situation as harsh and stubborn to see only the way you feel! Your example is in your note, so read it again! I also believe that when you're hearing something you don't like you get all defensive and throw a curve ball to hurt that someone back and that is totally unfair and uncalled for. Please support you? That's all I have been doing, just because I disagree with you doesn't mean I don't support you! I will be on no one's side period, end of story. I simply offered to tell you my point of view, TAKE IT or LEAVE IT! Now I am going to make myself clear, I do not want any drama in my life, no emotional baggage, nor do I want people in my life who are gonna shit on me especially when they ask for help or advice. I have a family and enough problems of my own and do not want to be put in a position to pick and choose sides. I'm too old for BULLSHIT. If you're my friend then be a friend and PLEASE do as I ask about the phoning & messaging & now you have my email; so that too. Steve will think something is about and I don't want him to think anything as I do love him and I'm gonna be gone for awhile and I would hate for us to fight before I left. Honestly I get together with my friends once in awhile and it would be totally out of whack to have everyday contact with my friends. I also believe you have taken something I have said and blown it into something out of proportion; such as my comment if I was single you would be first on my list. Now you're telling me that you love me and you're scaring me Charlie. I care very much for you as a friend but that is all I can offer you. Trust me if I'm going to leave Steve it's because I want too and it will never be for another man. You're allowed to have your hopes and dreams and fantasies but that is all. Please stop putting me in a position in which I feel I'm going to break your heart in the long run. When you grabbed my hand at lunch that day, it was very unlike you to do so, and that is the position I'm talking about. Even though it was nothing it still made me uncomfortable and I was shocked that you would put me there in the first place. I will never offer a man a part of me unless I could give him all of me. All I have to offer you is my friendship. So with that being said, please don't be mad or hate me or never talk to me again, I do not think any different of you, or have any hard feelings. I truly care about you and wish nothing but happiness for you and some emotional healing. You have an amazing heart and truly are a great person and a great friend. I will be there for you when you need me and I will tell you like it is and you may not always like what I say but I will be there. That's what friends are for!

While reading Clarice's response I was still completely overwhelmed by what had transpired with Janine. I was fully convinced of the book's new purpose and at first sent Clarice each email between Janine and I with a note attached but then sent Clarice the entire thread of emails in the correct sequence with the following note attached:

I'm so sorry again Clarice, but read it in one long thread like I did, it's so beautiful. I'm so sorry to put you through this as I wanted you there with me. I guess at the end of the day; I don't know again, I just don't know. But all I do know now is I can't wait to see Janine again and throw my arms around her and kiss her and hold her. I hope it's soon, maybe even on Sunday. May peace and love and god be with you Clarice. I won't go on to tell you how Carrie reacted to me giving her back the video and pictures, but we talked on the phone today for the first time since the separation, so take a guess. There will be no more drama and I will leave you be going forward. I have to live my life and repair what's been broken; I honestly thought you were going to be there with me while I went through this but you have your own life to live to. I will change your name in the book if you want me to.

And after 36 hours the zombie that was me, finally crashed and burned on the couch. When I awoke 4 hours later and I checked the computer I found Janine's latest response:

Charles I had to consider this email for a minute before responding. Not that I didn't know the answer when I read it but because it is hard for me to love anyone and I had to consider if that's just the answer. I don't like being too close to anyone. I like having friends that I really care about and like Clarice said to me recently, you really recognize real friendship as you get older. People will let you down no matter what and it's just easier to forgive the people that you love. The moment I stopped looking up to you as my big brother was when I was about 11 or 12 and you made a bet with your friends about me. It was about at what age I would get pregnant. Do you know that I hadn't even had my first real kiss when you guys decided to make me a slut? It's absolutely true and I remember it more clearly than any fight we've ever had; and yet I was still fiercely protective of you to everybody back then. I could call you an asshole all I wanted to but no one could ever say a bad word about my brother to me; I remember always thinking that no one could ever talk bad about you or Mom. I wouldn't allow it even if I didn't have the voice to speak up and I would be consumed with my hatred if anyone dared to talk shit about MY family. I always felt that you and mom would tear me apart to anyone, especially to each other. Tell me it's not true and I will accept it, but please don't take the time to justify it because I don't believe in not having loyalty to your family. In my heart I always loved you and mom but you never would have known it and I agree with that statement.

It was 2 am but it was morning to me and my mind was as clear as it ever has been in my whole life. So I started typing my reply to Janine as I never felt much of anything for her in my entire life:

Somewhere Janine, an email got lost that I wrote to you and as I was writing things I was so confused and delirious I wasn't able to re-write it out of exhaustion. But know that my mind has been clear and my heart is pure in everything that I have said to you in the past 24 hours. I do love you oh so very very much and I want you to understand the realization that I've come to in all this. It's about how I did not think I was worthy of receiving love, especially romantic love up until I fell in love with Laura. Yes there was Charlene whom I loved dearly with all my heart, but truthfully I did not respect her intelligence much, and I could get her to do almost anything I wanted her to while we were together. I was the greatest of manipulators (am), and I owe her such an apology. The only problem is that over time her mind has deteriorated so much that even though I have apologized to her for hurting her when I broke up with her; I don't really think she could understand why I would be apologizing now. I was never as honest and true with anyone in my life as I was with Laura, absolutely 100% positively true. I used to be able to lie in bed with her and just free up my mind and allow myself to start talking with absolutely no filter and just find out what would come out. It used to scare her and she was unable to do it, I guess now in retrospect, it was because she was so dishonest with me and she was scared what might come out if she did it. Between carrying on in the love letters with that guy in Ireland, actually telling people that she was moving there, to the way she broke up with me, well that was one of if not the most absolute brutal experience of my life. It just slowly but surely shut me down inside. Watching Laura and Jessica bounce around in the parking lot from my bedroom window, joking, laughing, taking pictures and then Laura took me outside and dumped me like it was nothing at all, that our time together meant nothing at all and that I meant nothing at all to her after all we had been through. It almost literally ripped me apart once again, maybe even worse this time than what our father did to me when I was 16 years old by rejecting me (us) again when our grandparents died. I had little if any self esteem whatsoever, probably only just a minute fraction. And due to how I think and what I know, it made it all the worse because all the thoughts were there but I was just never able to put them all into place clearly until I was an adult, until I was with Laura. Well I found a reason somehow to go on living instead of trying to kill myself, the reason was I wanted to have children, I wanted to have a family and I decided that was what I was going to do. I wanted to prove I was not my father. So first there was Carol, you know all about that Janine. Thank you so much for your role in that, if Laura was ever hurt in anyway because of my relationship with Carol, well she deserved to be because she was so dishonest. Easily I could have become a woman hater and violent because of the pain of what she did to me. But Carol could have been easily Carrie, actually she was Carrie, I don't know if you know that. She just up and left me though, never a word or an explanation, she could have my child right now for all I know. I had her agreeing to what I had Carrie agreeing to in under a week. It would have been my ultimate revenge on Laura. It was easier to manipulate Carol than Carrie obviously because I knew Carol very well; I had spent so much time with her and she had a huge crush on me while I was with Laura. At one point she flat out offered to have a three some with Laura and I, to which I refused, yes it's really true. I didn't want anything hurting my relationship with Laura. Not Jessica, not you, no one would I swore. I could never manipulate Laura; she could see right through me, we were just so in sync or so I thought. Obviously this is why I have taken full responsibility in the failure of my marriage from an emotional standpoint, because I was dishonest and manipulative with Carrie too. I have never seen it all as clearly as I have at this moment and now I wonder if I will ever be able to truly love anyone again. Although I did know it; my father broke me in more ways than anyone could ever know,

ever! Oh god haven't I cried enough already yesterday.
Because of trying to deal with the divorce of our parents as a
child; I became unable to give or receive love from anyone
especially with the entire trauma in our home with mom and
Bill. Bill! That motherfucker! He is lucky I never slit his throat in
his sleep; and that I still forgave him later on for all that he did
too me. Fucking bastard; punch me in the fucking face,
choke me, spit in my face, throw me downstairs, fucking asshole fuck you! Burn for what you've done! And for that matter too; Charles James Foster fucking burn in hell for what
you've done to me too! I can never ever forgive you; I can
forget you. Fuck you! GOD, I honestly can't believe I've written this. Janine, I want you to know how truly sorry I am for
what I have done to you.

Carrie, I now have to bring you into this email as well as I want
you to know the same apology. I knew somewhat better
what I was doing to you; but not the full extent until right now,
really and truly not until this exact moment. Please believe
me. Thank god that you learned to resist my manipulations.
You have truly set me free from all the pain that I had inside
with sticking to the plan of divorce. Thank you. My penance
for all of this is I no longer live with my children; I need you to
understand how much that hurts me on a daily basis, a little
bit inside at all times. But I now no longer feel any pain from
the past, I made peace and am at peace. This book has a
life of its own and this email obviously will be a part of it.
What you guys do now is up to you. Carrie I can never go
back; Janine you know what I want with you. I am so sorry to
each of you. I need a smoke, god I need a smoke, I need to
quit smoking. Peace be with each of you. Janine please let
me help you and I hope you understand that Carrie needs to
be apart of this as well.

I then took that email and forwarded it to both Clarice:

Maybe now Clarice you can understand it since now I do.
Live your life be free, I hope you find everything you are looking for in Alberta with your father. The book must be written.

And Larry:

Larry, please read the below email, please I would like to help you in any way I can, and not just for the book I'm writing, I can change your name, it doesn't matter. What matters is I thought of you as a brother and I'm so sorry for everything that has clouded what was between us, please let me help you. You can tell me everything, I don't care, don't be scared my friend I only have love and god in my heart. Not the bullshit god of the lies of man, a true love and a true god. Maybe I can explain to you why I think that or what I wrote. Please call me, as I've called you 3 times this last week. I almost came to your house yesterday when I was in the area but I don't want to scare you. Relax, it's me. I'm not going to hurt you.

And I copied Janine and Carrie each time I forwarded the email:

Janine & Carrie: Ladies just so you know with regards to Larry I am dead serious about all this. How could you not know that? The book must be . If we can help others at all, truly just one person in the world, then maybe it will ease our pains as well.

Mom, mom, wake up. Please wake up. Please, please wake up. I need you to read something, please after everything that happened yesterday I need you to read this. I know I know its 4am but I woke up, please come and read this, I am a writer, I know it, I know I am. It's the most beautiful thing I've ever written or might ever write, please come read this.

And as she did I thought of what Janine, Carrie, and Clarice and now Larry might think about when they read it. I believed that Janine in her heart was going to forgive me; I think she already did yesterday and I now looked forward to seeing her for the first time as her big brother in our adult lives. I hoped that I could help her with whatever pain she had from the trauma from her childhood, I wondered if I was right about if it was Tom's kids that had done that to her. If she would be willing to possibly explore some professional help for that. Answers I would soon find out, maybe she'll see me Sunday.

I don't things will ever be ok with Carrie but hopefully livable after what I did to her; but she had her part in all of this too and did things and acted in ways that leaves her with her own fate. I can not change the course we are on with the lawyers, I have too much respect for myself to allow her entitlement to what's mine any longer. I will continue to support the children in every way I can, ways that my father did not support me. I know that I have been true with my children as their loving father and I hope they can find the peace one day that I have now : if and when they possibly go through all of their own emotional struggles.

I thought of Clarice and how I had totally blown it with her. It was odd, but I was ok with that. If what I had done had brought me inner peace as well as maybe one day peace for my sister Carrie and hopefully even Larry. Well then, it was all worth it.

After mom finished reading the email she turned to me and smiled at me. I then showed her how I had forwarded the email to Clarice telling her how sorry I was and hopefully she could understand things as now I did. And that I had forwarded the email to Larry asking if I could help him in whatever problems he had when he was ready if ever I guess, I can't force him and he might not be able to get past what was said between us when our friendship ended or his own personal problems.

Mom then returned to bed and you told me, Charles would go get some sleep now please. I replied I can't, I'll probably be writing again soon, I got 4 hours so I'll be ok. I then went downstairs to watch a little TV and flicked around the dial a bit. Ah Meanstreets, Scorsese, DeNiro, great movie, this will help me relax; can I relax? I wonder what Roberta meant by the email with "Dear Charlie" in it, is that an invitation in some way to return to our friendship, more? Should I wait and see if maybe she is at the softball game Monday and talk to her then? Does she have her own pain? Can I help her with that : pain just as she helped me with more than she'll ever know with the speaking of some kind words. The kind of words that sent me on this inspirational journey? Can I find love with her?

I think Janine is right, I don't think I'm going to find love with Clarice. She needs to heal herself like she said, and that could take years. What she does after that, well who knows? I know that for me I can't wait around, I love her so, but I need to live my life too.

I excitedly look forward to today; hopefully everyone reads their emails this morning. I hope I spend the day talking on the phone to Carlos, Connie, Don (who I need to let in more, I don't give him enough respect), Janine if she can get to a phone damn it, playing with my kids and trying to deal with mom, oh mom. I look forward to telling Vince all about this and allowing him to help me with guidance in the pursuit of my dream of becoming a writer and an artist, well a published writer anyways.

What's going to happen next I don't know, but I look forward to it. I look forward to playing some more basketball, well a lot more basketball, (I've missed it this last week). I look forward to the softball doubleheader on Monday and maybe seeing Roberta. The concerts I have lined up for the summer, getting my house in order and having my house warming party with all my old friends. I look forward to a new tomorrow my friend, I look forward to the future and I hope. I hope peace can be with you as well my friend as it is with me. Take care of yourself and your families. Find your god in what ever or where ever it may be and don't let your devil take hold of you as mine did me. Let go and be happy, be strong, it's ok, its ok, its ok.

Chapter 12

<u>Return</u>

Gaze out into the unknown,
float away tiny bit of spirit blown.
Continue dying a little inside,
tear away everything that you hide.
Analyze every detail so deep,
path of return will be jaded steep.
Purge away all the pain,
forvever more now truly sane.
Once a whisper in the distance,
happiness returns at this instance.
It is your choice,
find your voice.
Into the depths of total darkness,
a beacon of light for all the helpless.
Sing out oh once quiet soul.

That was where I was going to leave it; that was going to be the
ending, again. Very appropriate I thought, poetic, worded correctly.
I thought that the Larry stuff was going to be too huge to take care
of and to include in this book; I was going to leave the Clarice
question unanswered, leaving the reader wanting more and then
possibly write a follow up or a sequel in the future if I felt inspired
to do so. I relaxed after writing to Janine and Carrie and then forwarding that email to Clarice and Larry. I watched a little TV and
had a nice cup of tea. I then organized more of my writing files,
thought for a while about the new outline for the book and then
took a long restful nap.

I talked on the phone to Carlos and read him the whole story as he didn't have access to his email. He was pretty surprised; especially at the stories of physical abuse on the part of my step father. The one story where I was choked by Bill; then ran away and stayed away for a week or so, that one was particularly scary to him. And wouldn't you know it mom was in earshot of me the whole time I spoke with Carlos and not one cross word did she say about it. Something was happening inside of mom and she started doing different things around the house than I was used to seeing. This would only progress over the next little while.

I called Vince and expressed my excitement to him but he was at his cottage and said he would check it out when he returned the next evening. I called Connie and she said she hadn't read it yet and was on her way out but said we would chat later when she had the time; she had some family stuff to take care of.

I then went to the computer and totally updated my facebook profile; I changed my relationship status to single from it's complicated, changed some of my interests making my children my number one interest and writing number 2 as they weren't listed in that order before. I added some music that I liked, in particular I needed Coldplay to be listed there as that has been the soundtrack to all of this. Lastly I changed my name back to my full name instead of just Charlie Foster.

I happened to see that Brenda was online in the chat area so I decided to try and chat with her. Larry was now going to become a big priority for me, by helping him in whatever way I could; but wouldn't you know it I couldn't connect to the chat option. I had found in the past that messages would be received but I wouldn't get any back if I couldn't connect to the chat option. So I messaged her about the email to Larry to prepare her for what might come that day and asked her to get him to read his email when he was home. I proceeded to get a shower and to get ready to pick up Paige from a sleepover she was on.

After I returned from my shower I checked the computer again as I was just so interested in what anyone of the major players might have to say about all this and at this time I found a message from Brenda which read:

Hey I'm replying. He hasn't been doing well these past 3 weeks. I'll get him to look. The last 2 days have been better. He's not here right now, he should be home soon. Then we have hockey but I'll get him to look.

I thought about it and wondered what the email might do to Larry if he wasn't in the right frame of mind to read it. I thought it could really stir up his emotions by hearing me making peace with all that stuff as he had lived through all the abuse and my father's death with me and at times had been my rock through it. I thought and thought and I became very worried, extremely worried. What if he had read it already and it had upset him in someway? I became more worried, very very worried; I told mom about the situation and decided that I needed to go and find Larry while retrieving Paige from her sleepover. Her sleepover was located minutes away from where Larry lived so it would be easy to see him, or so I thought.

I called Larry and Brenda's landline to speak to Brenda but only got their voicemail; so I left a detailed message telling Brenda what might happen if Larry read the email. I got in the car and drove to retrieve Paige and then headed to Larry's home. I arrived at his home, knocked on his door but there was no answer. Their dog came to the sliding glass door and barked but no one was there. I thought ok hockey; they must be at the Streetsville arena so I headed there next. As I arrived at the arena it was completely deserted and I knew there was no Hockey game going on there. Now what do I do I thought? I realized that Larry's parents house was just up around the corner and if anyone knew where their granddaughter's hockey game would be it was Larry's parents.

I arrived and rang the doorbell and Larry's mom came to the door; the surprise on her face to see me was evident and she immediately invited me in. We hugged as we had already chatted a little on facebook and I had always liked her. She was so nice to me when I was a child, paying me for chores around her house or inviting me on her family excursions. I quickly told her about the direness of the situation I might be in and asked where Larry's daughter's hockey game might be. She gave me the directions and I knew the location and headed out. I was almost at the location when my phone rang; at first I thought it was Connie calling me back, but I soon realized that no, it was Brenda. She said that she was at home and she said Larry was out at a friends house. I asked if I could come over and talk to her to which she agreed; I arrived with Paige in tow and she invited me in and it was just like old times; like almost no time had passed at all.

We chatted and chatted and I told her of almost every detail I could think of. It was just so easy to talk to her about it all; she already knew all the major players of the story except for Connie the newbie. I admitted everything to her, every last thing and then listened as she described everything that had gone on with Larry over the last few years. How the passing of her mother had triggered his mental illness and about his suicide attempt. She went on to describe how alone and isolated she felt in the situation and I listened intently to every word spoke. She described how she only had 2 girlfriends and her father in her support network. She spoke of how she only had the topic of all things relating to Larry to talk about with her friends and that she didn't like talking about it. She felt she was burdening or bothering them with her problems because her life had stagnated and there was never anything new to talk about.

I asked her to help me with Mary, as she was once one of Brenda's best friends. Mary had not responded to me since I had sent my soliloquy to her and I wondered if I had scared her with the talk of masturbation. I wouldn't blame Mary if she was scared or

upset with me and I asked Brenda to approach Mary about it for
me, that way she would have something different to talk about with
a friend for once.

I continued on with how things might not be so easy with Larry
due to the choices of his lifestyle and that I could in no way support
those choices; since it was involving a lot anger, hatred and racism
and I could not support that at all. Brenda expressed her concerns
about what negative effects Larry's beliefs were having on their
children and I concurred that would probably be true. We continued
on with discussing the possibilities that their daughters might also
inherit Larry's condition one day. And as Brenda continued to
describe how isolated she felt in her life I could see the tears begin
in her eyes. I smiled at her and opened my arms to her and she just
fell into them. We embraced as she cried and I told her I was going
to be there for her from now on as she sobbed.

I proceeded to tell her about her importance to me and in a way
that she and I went back just as far as Larry and I did. Brenda had
first become my friend when I was 13 years old and had become
friends ever since, while Larry and I had only truly became best
friends and started our path to brotherhood when I was 17 after four
years apart. I told her of how I remembered the times when she and
I ran in the same crowd of friends and how her 1st love was in the
tight knit group of guy friends I had at the time. We spoke of old
stories during the partying days and we laughed and laughed.

I told her of how saddened I was at the passing of her mother
and that I had hoped she had got the email of condolence I had sent
to her at the time as I had not found out about the passing until 1
month after it happened. I then told her about speaking to Carlos
earlier that day about how that I now remembered that it was
Brenda's house that I stayed at when Bill had abused me by choking
me all those years ago. I continued that I hadn't forgotten her and I
was sorry for not being there for her during her tough times with
Larry. I would be now no matter what happened with Larry in the
future.

She told me it was ok that I wasn't there as she would have probably done the same thing if she was dealing with the issues that I was. I knew that it would now be awkward if things didn't work out with Larry in the way that I hoped they would, but Larry would have to understand that Brenda was an important player in all of this now too and I was just now really and truly realizing how much so.

I was so worried about myself and my happiness in all this that I had somewhat lost sight of others. Not totally obviously; but I had an agenda and Brenda had not been on that agenda. Well she was now and very much so! I never gave the respect to Brenda that she truly deserves as she was there for me just as much as Larry ever was during the rough times and she never complained about it; even if I gave her grief or was mean to her at times which I was on a few occasions. There was this one time years ago that I threw Brenda out of my house for seriously criticizing me for the way I was dealing with Janine in a boyfriend respect issue; I still need to say sorry to Brenda for that. Brenda truly is my sister and I never realized that before; until right now. So now I have to call her and tell her so.

And wouldn't you know it when I called their home I got Larry and he was quite ready to start talking as he and Brenda were reading over the emails that I had sent at that exact moment. I explained to him that I wanted to talk to him in person as I didn't want to go through all the same troubles of communication that I went through with my sister in this same scenario. We decided that I would visit later that night once I got myself ready.

I thanked him ever so much but asked for the phone to be passed to Brenda. I explained to Brenda how I had now come to the realization that I thought of her as my sister and how much she meant to me. She then replied, Charlie I always thought that was just known between us. Looking back I'm so very happy that I took the time to speak to her, message her about Larry and ask her permission to do all of this. I just so love the idea having another sister and increasing the size of my family; especially by adding a loving sister who just might be stronger inside than any of the previously mentioned people in this story. And so I finished a little writing adding Brenda to the end of the book, had some dinner and it was off to Larry's house I went. When I arrived he came out outside to have a smoke with me and we started to talk.

He said he held no grudges and that I didn't have to worry about apologizing to him but I did anyways. I also told him I forgave him for what he had said and now I wanted him to forgive himself. He quickly replied there was no worries, and with that he began with his rant about life. And he went on and on and on, and then just for good measure he went on some more; oh my goodness I thought what the hell has happened to him? He spoke of anti Semitism, and he spoke about black people, and he spoke about conspiracies, and he spoke about religion and corporations ruling the world; it was just unbelievable the crap he was spewing out. And while this was going on Brenda came to the window and gave me a look saying see I told you. I couldn't believe my ears; it was like he was totally brainwashed. So I started in on him subtly at first but then slowly I built it to where I was going. To say every little detail would be impossible, it would be almost like another book, but in a very blunt nutshell the conversation went something like this:

I am back whether you like it or not because now Brenda is my sister and am I going to look after my sister and my sister needs me. And that makes Sherrie and Louise my nieces and I am going to look after them as well. No, I'm not threatening you I would never do that I'm just telling you this is the case. I would never ever hit you in anger; but that being said all that stuff that you are spewing out, all that hatred and anger, that's wrong man. I'm telling you that's wrong man and I don't believe in any of that. I have bigotry in me too; don't we all, but that stuff you're living with, that's wrong. What happened to you? How is it that that is what you believe in now? We were like brothers man, we shared ideas, we had all these theories, we were like, in a way, like hippies man, how

212

in the hell is that what you believe in now after all our time together? After all our thoughts and beliefs and where we took them? All that hatred stuff doesn't make one difference in life and if you are acting upon it, that doesn't make one difference either. We are in no position to change anything in the world; we have to take care of ourselves. You have to take care of Brenda and those 2 girls of yours, who in the hell cares about all of that? I don't care if it's in your neighborhood, if it is then move! You've been here too long anyways and Brenda wants to move. Oh yes she does, she wants out of here! You guys have been here 16 years and that's ridiculous, that has been way too long and she feels trapped and it's a prison to her. Yes she will, she told me so; she will pack you guys up in an instant and go wherever you want as long as it's out of this neighborhood. No you can't take your parents home, then your childhood trauma will hold you and you will have a different type of anguish, it has to be somewhere new. She needs to be happy, you need to be happy, and don't you see that you guys are intertwined. Whatever one feels, so does the other. As long as you are like this, with all these ideas and thoughts, she will be unhappy, and as long as she still lives here, you will be unhappy. So what's more important; all this anger and hatred garbage or her because I can't believe she's still here, I can't believe it and I told her so. She says that's what everyone says to her, leave him; but you know what, she loves you more than anything in the world, she always has always will and she can't leave, she doesn't want to. She takes disrespect from your family, she has no friends, and she feels like a single mom at times. Why she is here is beyond me, but she is and she always will be. So what do you think, can you commit to moving? Ok and if you aren't feeling right then you've got to go to the doctor and try to get those meds dosages changed and if the doctor isn't helping you then you need to find a new doctor and another new doctor; until you feel as normal as possible. You have to do that so that Brenda can be happy no matter what.

And he agreed to it all; he was just as intelligent and as strong willed as I, but I cut through all his anger, hatred and fear. Larry truly is my brother, I know him inside and out. I knew that he didn't fully believe in all that crap he spewed. He had allowed his devil of bigotry to expand and to take complete hold of him. It had a hold of Brenda too and she couldn't get out from under it all because of her devotion to Larry. She was combating him using Christianity but it was to no avail because of his strong will. We continued on like that for a while but be sure to understand that the conversation that I wrote was not as blunt or as aggressive as it sounds.

I invited Larry to speak to me about his religion conspiracies because I can speak about religion to no end. Once after I said that organized religion is a curse upon mankind Larry said he would rather not speak about religion as it only upsets him. I will expand on my thoughts about religion though; as it disgusts me to think of what has been and is continuing to be done in the name of religion in the world and throughout the history of mankind. The stories in these doctrines, (I studied religion a great deal in high school); especially in the bible which I am obviously most familiar with, are great stories, but they are stories plain and simple. They are stories that inspire and set a good example to live your life by, but with all the corruption and evil in history and the world; anyone taking these stories to their most literal meaning and acting in an aggressive or violent fashion in their name is someone I do not wish to know. There is so much shame on almost every single religion in the world, especially Christianity, that I do not, or can not support any organized religion that was created by mankind. Although I can say that I respect the people who have the purest of faith in their religion.

I reiterated my forgiving of what he had said to me that had ended our relationship; that he had disrespected my family, myself and had used my childhood trauma as a weapon to hurt me. Once I had realized I could no longer deal with his drug and alcohol abuse, severe mood swings and the constant subtle verbal abuse I received from him in the form of jokes I became incensed. I believed that he did this to make himself feel better about himself, by putting me down. I explained him so and he said he understood.

Once the initial part was over and I started to see the person who is my brother again, I started asking him how he felt about his family members, those being his parents, his sister and brother. I don't think he fully understood the gravity of how those relationships affect his everyday life. He said that everything was ok with his dad and that his mom and him were at the same place that they always were. He added, that he and his brother had no relationship whatsoever and that his brother would attempt to pick fist fights with him periodically and that there was nothing in him but resentment towards his sister.

I started to express the significance of the bond between he and I and that I thought of him like family, that he was my brother. I told him that I would have done anything for him before and as an example of this I reminded him of a story from many years ago involving his actual brother. The scene happened at Patricia's one night when the bar was open for business and Larry's brother was absolutely wasted out of his mind on liquor and LSD. For some reason that night and I don't remember why, I think it was play fighting and wrestling that just got out of control, but Larry and his brother had a fist fight. After that had happened, and emotions were still running very high, Larry's brother told us that he was going to return home to get his father's gun and was going to kill himself. It was at that point that I stepped in as Larry and Patricia were both very drunk and very upset, so much so that they couldn't deal with their brother. I prevented Larry's brother from leaving Patricia's home and kept him trapped in the basement right up until he vomited and passed out. I took enormous amounts of physical and verbal abuse from his brother and just laughed and shook anything off that he threw at me and did not let him leave no matter how hard he tried. I asked Larry why would I do that and he replied because that was what a man of honour would do and I said no, that it was because Larry was my brother.

I knew that there was a lot of healing to be done inside Larry's whole family and I knew that it was far beyond the scope of anything I could handle even if I was invited to be involved in it. So I left his family issues be and started to ask Larry about Brenda, and about his one on one relationship with her. Their Intimacy and communication was my primary focus, and I found that he felt there was little to none of either aspect in their relationship. Thankfully I was able to show Larry that Brenda had hope for the future because he recognized that she had kissed him twice since I had been there, to which he said that the frequency of shows of affection from Brenda these days were seldom. I asked him about ways he thought he could improve their one on one relationship and he started talking of some unrealistic ideas; specifically with the renting of land in Costa Rica for a honeymoon after 16 years of marriage. I thought a honeymoon was a good idea but I told him to just keep it simple and to do an all-inclusive somewhere nice and just be with Brenda. It woudl just be Larry and Brenda the tourists in love and not to worry about being world travelers. I said you don't have to make it so complicated the first time out; just walk before you run.

I further talked with Larry about the barriers to communication and especially about anger and defense trigger mechanisms. I asked Larry if he knew Brenda's trigger mechanisms because it seemed to me that everything Brenda felt communication was not present in their relationship but Larry thought the exact opposite. He said he was trying to express things to Brenda all the time and I figured that either she was shutting him out or his message was getting cluttered by his mental issues. He said he would put a lot of thought to barriers to communication and trigger mechanisms in the future when having conversations with Brenda and would ask about and try to understand Brenda's mechanisms.

And so we sat and chatted, had a couple of beers and smokes, and reminisced about the old days. There were so many stories such as making super killer sandwiches at my house (as many different types of meat and cheese possible with liverwurst mmm). The time at our friends Cliff and Erin's wedding where Larry ended up vomiting on all fours right outside a cab and spent the night hugging a toilet. There was the time I was all high and choked on a lollipop and projectile vomited it across the room. Later that same evening Larry walked me home after I passed out by putting his finger in my back to keep me balanced. There was the Jethro Tull concert where we used Brenda being pregnant with Sherrie to our advantage. Brenda pretended she was my wife because I knew where the good general admission spots were and we were let into the venue before anyone else. There were so many great and funny memories and I stayed so very late that night to the point where neither of us could really focus any longer. When the time came to leave Larry extended his hand to me and I pushed it away and hugged him. I reinforced what his future plans were and how he was going to approach and achieve them, I told him I would call him the next day and with that I left.

The next day I sent the following message to Larry's mom on facebook following up on my quick visit with her and the online chatting I had also done with her about my helping Larry:

Hi Deborah, so everything yesterday went exceptionally well, even beyond that. I spent 3 hours with Brenda in the afternoon and then later on 5 hours with Larry in the evening. But this is only the beginning, just only the beginning. I cut through everything negative that is holding Larry (and Brenda for that matter) and really got to the heart of everything, having the knowledge of him that I do. They were both completely honest with me as I was them and I can see many ways that I can help them to at least find some sense of normality and then some happiness in their lives. It won't change Larry's condition and I can't do that; but this all involves Ken and you a great deal as well. If at all possible I would like to sit down with Ken and you to try and explain things more and possibly get you guys to really help them in every way that you can as well. It shouldn't be that hard honestly, it's just to recognize things and let them happen. It can only be Ken, you and I that talk and it can be anytime; it should be soon though. Brenda needs hope, and Brenda's happiness is intertwined with Larry's fate. She needs it now before it's too late; I have given her that glimpse of hope as well as have given hope to Larry. But I can't do it alone, I need your help. This Wednesday all day, Thursday all day, the following Monday all day and the following Tuesday all day I am available to talk at your convenience. Please realize that this is not me being nozy or any other negative ideas that you might have about my intentions. This is; like I said to you in person, that I am now truly ready to try and help Larry and Brenda. I never realized before how much Brenda needed my help too, and all I want to do is just that. Please oh please can you and Ken help me to help Larry and Brenda; you really only just have to allow things to happen at the end of the day. Charlie XOXOXO

On the exact same day Janine sent me a hugely significant email that really put everything I was doing into persepctive as she truly is a genius and it really made me step back and further evaluate my thinking:

Charles, I just want to mention something to you; I think you may have to choose a more cautious path in bringing everything on when discussing what you're feeling and going through right now. It's a bit overwhelming to be expected to go along with what you're thinking. I understand that you feel the need to help the people that you've mentioned but everyone has their own pace. Like I said, last week was VERY hard for me and I am not one who is comfortable with my emotions or talking about things. I have one person in my life that has made himself responsible for taking care of that and it's Phil and it did not begin by my choice but it just happens that he is ten times stronger than I am and can handle whatever I throw at him. I do want to heal our relationship, of course I do; but it is VERY hard for me to address anything from my past and I am not at a point in my life where I am ready and willing to open that door and deal with all of it at once; (or even little by little) I need to be normal with you. It's what I'm comfortable with and I know your focus is on helping everyone right now but I am really okay with everything. I felt like I couldn't BREATHE last week and it was too much all at once. Your happiness is important to me and I hope my comfort is to you; please be cautious with everyone. I can't imagine what Brenda is going through but she's been going through it for YEARS and Larry too and I wouldn't want anyone to get hurt. You've already had some negative feedback from Clarice, Carrie, and Mary (?) and especially me. It would suck to see rejection on any side in the Larry scenario and it could be just as simple as being an ear for Brenda or being a friend to Larry again, I don't know; but I just wanted you to know how it was for me, ok?

And Janine was exactly right and furthermore Brenda and Larry were upset with me after I had returned home and wrote about Brenda. The next day I tried and tried to call Larry and Brenda with no answer; for one stretch I was calling almost every hour and still I got no answer. Then finally at one point Brenda answered the phone and told me that yes they knew that I was calling but that they were initially very upset with me when they read what I had written. After time I guess all of my phone calls and even another call to Larry's mom made them kind of realize that they were somewhat wrong about their thinking on what my intentions were, that being that I was exploiting them for my book and that once I had my material for my story that I was out of there.

Brenda felt betrayed that I had written about what she felt she had told me in confidence and after Janine's email I totally understood her point of view. I told her I was so sorry and by this time she was not as upset. Still, however misguided I might have been at times, she was my sister and she knew me and knew that I didn't want to hurt her or Larry. She also told me that Ken was starting to get upset as he was still of the old school mindset about not talking about Larry's condition as was Brenda and Larry in a way. That really made me think a lot more about my upcoming meeting with Deborah and Ken that was to take place in a couple of days as Deborah and Ken had agreed to meet with me:

Hi Deborah, I've been thinking for 2 days about what I might say to you and Ken when we meet, it's been dominating my thoughts truly. I thought about how I would tell how you about how upset Brenda is and how I was able to breakthrough so much that was holding Larry, to truly be able to find the person I once and do know inside and out and call my brother. When I got into that panic I was in yesterday because I thought that maybe Larry had put his and I, (mostly I's) plan for him into action Sunday and that there was a crisis going on and that I had caused it, I then found out different. Brenda said no it was that they felt I had violated them in a way by writing about their true feelings shared in confidence. I had a hard time coming to grips with this because I never had the intention of exploiting anyone and I was so excited about seeing them again and so happy about everything that had taken place with them. Then Brenda told me how Ken was becoming upset too and it makes me think do I really have to meet with Deborah and Ken; is it such a monumental thing that I am going to tell them? No, like I said before this shouldn't be too hard honestly for anyone, it just has to be allowed to happen if they so choose. The thing is your generation and somewhat still Larry, Brenda's and my generation still believe that Larry's condition is something to be embarrassed about and to be hidden, getting past that thinking is the first thing. Larry's condition is not something to be embarrassed about and you shouldn't be embarrassed by it at all; just like I'm not embarrassed any longer about the physical abuse I suffered at the hands of my step father or by the abandonment of my real father. I was embarrassed for the longest time and just got past that embarrassment myself. So at the end of the day what do I have to say to you and Ken about Larry and Brenda? Well at it's most basic idea; the idea that I think will help Larry and Brenda the most right now is "pick the low hanging fruit". They need to move out of Streetsville and as soon as possible, they must. They need to go on a honeymoon, an all-inclusive trip somewhere ASAP. And Larry needs to learn to admit when he does not feel right; admit it and get those doses of his meds changed when he does not feel right and everyone has to accept and understand this. That's it, it's not my place to tell you how Larry and Brenda feel. Just know that the person that I knew, the one that is my brother, well he's still there under it all and I will not accept him using his illness as a crutch to spew out racism, anger and hatred towards mankind. I don't care what he says, I'm somewhat versed on this stuff, and I know my brother is still there inside him whether he thinks so or not. I will share with you what happened to me. Love, Charles Christopher Foster

I called Deborah to confirm her receipt of the message and she hadn't read it yet so I further explained things to her over the phone and she was taken aback by the talk of embarrasment to which I was not surprised, but it was a nice conversation. I further talked about Patricia and the grief she inflicted upon Larry and Brenda and further explained how I was sympathetic to them in that aspect having my own personal issues from when I had lived with Patricia for nine months previously in my life. Deborah knew about the issues with Patricia and of course it was hard to talk about her children in this manner as she was their mother and I expressed understanding of that but I asked her to keep Patricia out of the loop when it came to Larry and Brenda.

The next day I went by Larry and Brenda's home again to talk and to try and explain myself further and Brenda and Larry were still a little upset with me and got a little self righteous which was understandable. I deserved to be on the receiving end of some grief from them so I took it but tried to get them to understand me too. When I returned home I was still thinking about things with Larry and Brenda and I still felt I hadn't fully explained myself or had given them the respect they deserved since they were going to go along with my book. So I sent Larry everything I had written up until that point with the following email attached:

Larry, I owe you a lot more to truly tell you about how this whole thing came about; all you've seen really up until this point is two snippets and I never really explained it all to you guys. Sorry about that and I don't want you to think I'm exploiting you as this was quite the journey. I think you need more info and we need to talk a lot more about the book itself; so here's everything I have up until this point now. Again only the most important people in the world to me belong in this book. I wonder that if you don't realize that I personally believe that any kind of mental illness is nothing to be ashamed of or to be hidden, it's just like the abuse I went through. I guess that's why it didn't cross my mind about Brenda and your thoughts of exploitation and I'm so sorry about that. It bothered me all night at my softball game and I'm really sorry man. Read away please; you are my brother, I need to tell you more about everything. The book motivated me to come see you but not for content; it's that I believed in the effect the book's existence was having on myself and those around me. Please know that at the end of the day I'm not going anywhere and am with you forever more. There are very sensitive materials here to really really show you my commitment to the book, so be careful there is some really bad stuff in it. I guess I never brought you up to speed really as to how I got to that point where it was like ok I need to talk to Larry now. Sorry again I don't want to hurt anybody.

Larry's response almost made me cry and filled up my heart with joy and we are growing closer and closer again with each passing day. I don't see that initial person I saw at that first meeting any-more; I only see my brother whom I love so very much.

It's ok Charlie, this is an important journey for you and every-one you touch on the way; don't let me or anyone, including you, slow or stop you on this journey. It's funny that you keep saying that we are brothers because we are. As I sit here typ-ing this I can feel your energy and all these years I've felt your energy. Very few humans are, or have been fortunate enough to comprehend the extent of this connection between us. Please don't let anything bother you; if I have an issue, you know me; I will eventually communicate it to you. You can send me your softball schedule and we will probably come watch one night.

It was during my initial conversation with Brenda that I came to discover what has to be the biggest coincidence of the entire book, a coincidence that has made me come to believe that there is some-thing more to all of this than I will probably ever know in my life-time. While reminiscing with Brenda about the old days, the topic of Larry and her wedding came up while discussing Clarice and funny stories. Brenda reminded me that the previous day had actu-ally been her 16th wedding anniversary. My brain immediately clicked on to it and told her oh my god you have to be kidding. On the same day that I had stayed awake for 36 hours, on the same day that I found and took the first steps on my path to redemption, on the same day that everything blew up with Clarice; that very same day was Larry and Brenda's 16th anniversary and the 16th anniver-sary of the exact day I first fell in love with Clarice. I was and still am totally blown away by that and honestly and truly believe that fate or the will of god has set all of this in motion for some reason. To emphasize this numerical coincidence, there are also 16 poems I have written at this point in time, I kid you not. What is going on? Why a higher power would set me on this course I am still not sure, but from that point with Brenda going forward I was going to finish this book and take it all the way no matter what happened to see where it would take me in life, I had to, how could I not, I ask you?

I think people can find their devil in a lot of things in their life. I believe it again has a lot to do with the 7 deadly sins of Saint Francis of Assisi: Sloth, Gluttony, Wrath, Pride, Envy, Lust and Greed. My own personal sin which became my devil initially was obviously being consumed by my lust but there was a little bit of each one of the other sins in the mix too; especially pride being the second sin that I fully recognize. My pride prevented me from repairing so many relationships for so many years and I have lost so much time with Larry, Brenda, Janine, and my mom because of it. I can see devils in each one of them too and am trying to help them to break free of theirs as well but it's a long complicated process and sometimes things don't go all too well, well who am I kidding. I love them all so much and will never ever let anything in my control come between us again.

Chapter 13
<u>Embrace Despair</u>

Throughout this grey dark day,
I'm penetrated by the distance.
Oh why,
to my terrible dismay;
must I require a daily light,
for my existence?

Grant freedom from this destructive inkling,
that's locked inside and forever mine.
Oh tell me,
precisely whom is stealing;
the sensation that everything,
is just truly fine?

It's so uneasy to explain,
why this lit soul could be slowly fading.
Oh can I,
find a way to contain;
my implanted memory's,
consistent persuading?

Awakened totally alone,
without any real semblance of compassion.
Oh it's only,
that emptiness forever known;
so remember,

the forgotten passion.

Haunted again by my heart,
that's somehow gone inexplicably quiet.
Oh please
won't you depart;
this teetering insanity's endless mind riot.

And so I continued on for a couple of days, happy even though I thought Clarice was gone. I thought I had totally blown it with her by messaging her and phoning her and emailing her and getting upset with her that she couldn't see my point of view so I started to make peace with it all. I accepted it and I started thinking of other women, I thought of how I was possibly going to pursue Roberta again. One thing was for sure though, I thought Clarice was gone and then just when you think it's done, 4 days later Clarice replies to a book snippet I sent to her:

Hey Charlie; sounds awesome! You have everything falling into place it seems and the puzzle pieces are now all fitting in together. I have to say though; I love the way you write it's very deep and expressive. I know that this is your calling for sure. Take care and talk soon Clarice

And I'm like oh no she's back again, well maybe not oh no, but the relief I guess I had that I was going to be able to get on with things was gone; but nope here she is again and she's not going anywhere, this is just going to keep on happening over and over again with her. And so I accepted it and the first email I sent to her was aloof but I knew I was going to accept her back into my life and that things would get all revved up again; how could I ever say no to Clarice.

The next day I was at work and one of my friends Rob commented to me just how happy he had noticed I had been lately. He knew of my personal situation so I briefly ran down that I had found god and that there was this woman in my life named Clarice. And I started to tell him all about her, about how beautiful she was, and how connected we were and how in love with her I was. But after the conversation was over and I walked away I thought about it and I said to myself, why the hell are you talking about Clarice to someone? She's not your woman, she's not your girlfriend; she's someone you have a crush on, that's it! And I then found something else inside at this time. It was something that I had only had once before and for a little while and had lost it long ago. Self confidence, self respect and self esteem!

It was at this time that I decided to blow everything up with Clarice and tell her that she has to go. It was for so many reasons; because I needed to get on with my life, because I have children and I can't be like this for them and because I have too much respect for myself to let something like this kill me a little bit everyday with stress. So I told my sister and Connie what I was going to do in an email and before they could even respond, I put my plan into place to break free of Clarice once and for all and so I started the text messages:

I've been thinking about your email a lot and how nice it was; I can't do this with you anymore. You know how I feel and that will never change but I need to get on with my life. What I said in the book was true all true. Please go away because I can't take it any longer. One day we can chit chat again, but I can't see or talk to you anymore. I can't control myself when it comes to you and I can't change nor do I want to. Good luck in Alberta with your dad. Peace.

Well Clarice didn't hear what I said, all she heard was that I was leaving her for good and she got mad, very very mad. And so started the cursing and to tell me how much that I was hurting her. The exact words are unimportant and I don't want to disrespect her by saying how she conveyed her anger, but the whole time I was messaging her, whoa, mad is definitely the word. But I continued anyways:

That's the way it has got to be. You can not have your cake and eat it too. After all I went through inspired by loving you; great ending, goodbye sweet Clarice.

If you want to change things I don't have to tell you what it is that you have to do, you know what you have to do. Either way leave me alone or stop lying to yourself about that I could go on like this. What do you want to do kill me? What makes you think that I could go on like this? You know how I feel and I know how you feel and we are done unless you have got something new to say.

And I want to make sure that we are clear; I would do anything for you: marriage, kids and a family. I'm in love with you that much. But don't play innocent with me; you know what you did in this. This game that we've been playing for so long, I just can't keep doing it. It hurts too much Clarice.

Well forget about me then, if that's the easy way to deal with pain. I will always love you, but this is your decision. I will do just as we planned.

And she continued with her angry rant, she just didn't hear me or what I was trying to express to her as the instant messaging was barring our communication. All she heard was I was leaving her life again, just like two times before and that I was hurting her all over again. And then she said something that really stuck to me, she said that she is not deep she is just a regular girl; you are all wrong about me. To which I replied that I wouldn't be in love with just a regular girl. I wanted to make sure she heard it and my phone kept screwing up so I think I sent her that message three times. Afterwards I thought well; it will give that message a strong effect, because, there is no way that Clarice, the pillar of strength and beauty, is just a regular girl. So I left things at that for the rest of the day until I got home where there was an email from Clarice waiting for me. A really nasty one and she blasted me all over the place, she just ripped into me:

Dear Charles; Ok I thought we were on the same page but obviously your emotions have gotten too far for me to handle. I really believe that I have been clear enough on just being friends but you have gotten too far ahead of me so that I cannot help with how you are feeling about me. I have no idea what your intentions are either when it comes to us, but there never was an us and there never will be! All I ever offered you was friendship and I thought that I was quite clear on that but it seems to me you cannot handle us just being friends. This is the 3rd time that you have walked away from our friendship due to the feelings that you have for me and I will no longer accept such behaviour and head games coming from you. I thought that back in the day it was an immaturity thing but I see quite clearly now that it is a hurt thing. That you cannot have me in the way you want me so to hurt me you leave me, and that's unfair, consider someone else's feelings for a change! I believe that if you cannot be with someone the way you want to, that I personally would want to remain friends with that person so I could remain in their life. Not everyone feels the same way I do or can handle situations such as that but only the strong survive! So if you cannot remain friends with me that's your loss and at this point I really don't care because your emotional distress scares me. This is not DEEP to me its emotional abuse! So now that I have said my peace; I will leave you alone as long as you leave me ALONE! Please leave me out of the book as you do not have my permission to say one thing about me or about my past. I HAVE BEEN HURT BY YOU FOR THE LAST TIME! It hurts me that you have rejected me as a friend because of your feelings for me, which I believe that you are just rebounding from your divorce and that your emotional instability is getting the best of you. You are going through a lot and taking it out on everyone and I didn't give you permission to shit on me! I'm sorry it has come to this, but this was your decision; so be it! I hope you find what you're looking for.

But I could hear truly what she was saying even though again she had hit upon another one of my anger trigger mechanisms by calling me Charles, only my mom and sister call me Charles and whenever anyone else does, especially in a critical manner it just enrages me for some reason. It probably has to do with my child-hood trauma as I first started getting people to refer to me as Charlie in grade three. So I started writing an email to Clarice; and then just for good measure I started drinking! I wrote so much to the depths of how much I loved Clarice that I even impressed myself with how much I could write about how much I loved her:

From your text and I quote "If things go the way they I think they are, then we should focus on becoming best friends which is the basis of a great relationship, then in the future we can complicate things." That was after lunch when I told you I had horrible feelings. I can't be around you because I can't function normally because I am head over heels in love with you. Holding your hand makes me cum. Do you really understand how totally infatuated and obsessed with you I am? You are my whole world and everything I did with Carrie and Janine and Larry and Brenda was because I was inspired by the love I feel for you. I am at even keel now, back to normal and I can't go on like this with you. I have to get on with my life, and I never will be able to as long as you are around. A couple of phone calls, I see you 3 times, some chatting, messaging and I'm through the moon. This isn't a new feeling for me when it comes to you, it's just that I can express my feelings better now. This is how I felt before but you don't get it because I've never told you like this; I've matured. I have to let you go because obviously you're not going to tell me to leave you alone. You just keep coming back for more. Why? I don't understand why? If you don't want to be with me then why do you keep coming back when you know how madly in love with you I am? Does it make you feel good? To toy with my heart! I never want to hurt you, but this is killing me, I have to move on. I love you so much I can't be with you any longer or ever again, unless you have something different to say other than I have a good heart, or we'll see, or I'm not sure. I will wait just like I said, I will wait. But give me something to wait for, no guessing games, and no hidden meanings; no you might have my heart. You have mine and my soul; I need them back so I can live. I'm not angry at you at all, I just can't do this with you anymore; the book did change one thing about me, and it gave me some self respect. You need to choose me or let me go; you can't have me as an integral friend; I can never be that to you. As soon as I see you, I'm dumfounded, retarded or whatever you want to call it; in love with you is the end result every time. How can you ask me to control that, how do I control that? Tell me, how do I control my love for you? I have no idea how, so what else do I do? I thought you were gone as of Friday, I thought that was it, I put it in the book and then you come back for more? Why? Why Clarice? Why do you keep coming back when you know I'm in love with you? It had faded over 10 years and now it's worse than ever, it's killing me, it's ripping me apart. Why Clarice?

And then I wrote her a second email after drinking five beers:

You can say everything you want to hurt me, say it all because I know deep down inside you that you don't want to hurt me. I don't want to hurt you at all ever; I don't want to hurt you Clarice. I'm ever so sorry that this is the way you are taking this; that I want to hurt you in any way. It is not my intention at all to hurt you. Please believe me I do not want to hurt you.   You destroy me, each time you are in my life it gets worse and worse. This time I am older, I am bolder than I was before; my ability to express myself has matured. My heart has not changed in 16 years and I can still describe to this day flawlessly the moment I fell in love with you; I can describe moment for moment what it would be like to make love to you. I know you say you are not deep, but I am. Your strength, your inner strength is what draws me to you, what's inside you. Physical beauty is just that, superficial; what is inside of you is what I am drawn to; it's where my connection lies. I don't know how to control this, and I don't know how to exist like this. Remember smack hello, someone might get suspicious. Why do I do that, why do I do that to you? Why do I lose control when it comes to you? Why do you make me so pathetic, a blubbering fool? Tell me why you Clarice? Why does this happen every time? Like I said now I'm bolder, by shocking you by grabbing your hand, I can express myself now. And I want it all with you, with you and only you. Just being your friend is not enough, I'm sorry I wish that it was. I truly wish it was enough that I could love you from afar. But it's not enough, I can not do it. I've drank 6 beers for the 1st time in six months, I never drank anything for losing Carrie; Carrie is nothing compared to you. You are sweet, kind, sensuous, funny, feminine, cool, and everything that I want, EVERYTHING THAT I WANT AND DESIRE. Lightening struck me at Larry and Brenda's wedding and stayed with me always, it won't go away unless you go away and I have to live; I can't live pining and hoping that one day we'll be together. I DO NOT WANT TO HURT YOU FOR THE WORLD, I LOVE YOU AND I AM IN LOVE WITH YOU, but I don't want to kill myself, it hurts so bad not to have you. It's brutal to see you and know you and not have you. You don't understand since you are Clarice, how could you understand truly how desirable you are. That's all, what can I do, what can I do except stay away from you once and for all? 4 other times have I felt this pain in my life, the abandonment of my father, the death of my grandparents and the second rejection of my father, the death of my father, the rejection of Laura and now this with you. Emotions are high, sure they are? You need to comprehend the effect you have on me and until you understand that you totally, TOTALLY blow my mind, then you just won't understand why I'm like this. Do you think I pulled those poems out of the air, that I built those feelings from a day or two? I can describe hanging out with you on Stan's balcony on Mapleview and you smoked a joint, and making you dinner at your apartment, and the cd's I took from Burt's collection; Queensryche & Deep Purple, and you bringing Christina to my apartment in Milton, and yelling at you because Janine was on speed at your home, and obviously dancing at the wedding, and seeing you outside of Wal-Mart for the 1st time again, and seeing you at the Bread and Honey festival and not knowing if to talk to you or not. More ok; how about you on the top bunk at Brenda's parent's trailer in Shelburne and telling me of cramps and wanting to go home, or in the pit at Tool and on the bus ride home. I remember everything Clarice; every moment, every single one, this is not a rebound; this is 16 years since one moment. What do you really think I would have said no to you in Milton had you not said no to me first with Sean? I knew then I loved you and yes when you approached me in the bedroom I wanted to hurt you, you had killed me. Can you even fathom how much you hurt me when you went to Scarborough to think about Sean and me and then came back and chose him? I knew all about Christina and Children's Aid, and I knew about the crack, and I knew and know about everything else. I hear every word you say, every word, I see every move, I see it all. I had to let you go again and again; and I have to let you go now because no matter how much I try and I want, you will never be with me. How can I go on like this? This time has been the worst ever because this time you are say-ing stuff, truly whether you admit it or not but still it does not happen for us, not even inkling. This is my life, I have to look at myself and say are you going to live for nothing, are you going to watch her, love her, want her, listen to her, let your heart fly at every moment and then crash another? Is this what you are going to do Charlie or are you going to live life? I don't want to kill myself! I want you so to understand, that in my brain, and in my heart, and in my soul; every ounce of me loves you. When I'm with you I feel whole and when you leave "I get this horrible felling, like someone just stuck a knife in me. Like someone just took away everything in the world to me. I need to be free of you if I am to live. I NEVER EVER WANT TO HURT YOU EVER. I JUST WANT TO HOLD AND KISS YOU ONLY! I HAVE TO LIVE, I HAVE CHILDREN and they need me." So now can you start to understand truly how much I love you? And of course now I sound like a psycho, but maybe now you will not hate me when I walk away, ok. PLEASE I DON'T WANT TO HURT YOU, again and again and again I will say it, it's not like that ever It's not like that EVER when I walk away. PLEASE TRY TO UNDERSTAND, it's hard when we're on different levels. You make me cum with a touch, a touch damn it! You inspire me to write beautiful poetry, you inspired me to repair everything that is wrong in my life, you inspired me to write a book, and you inspired me to be a man! Gorgeous you are, Beautiful you are and a Goddess you are! How can I live without you? I have to go, let me go. Please Clarice.

When I awoke the next day I read over the emails I had sent to her and thought they were a bit clouded and might not get my message through to her (they've been edited since). Then it hit me about how much my Grandpa loved my Grandma and that was where I was getting all this passion from; from, my Grandpa or so I believe. It all became clear to me and I knew I had time before she would check her emails for the day so I wrote an email entitled "Please read this one first, please":

Every morning I seem to come to some sort of realization Clarice and that's no different today. By reading those other 2 emails maybe you can understand the depth of the love I feel for you and just how in love with you I truly am.   A love I have not felt since Laura. When I said I knew about bad stuff going on with you, it wasn't to hurt you, it was that I knew about it all and didn't come running to save you, I had to stay away. I thought of what I knew of love, or maybe tried to compare it to someone else. Do you remember me saying that my Grandpa smoked himself to death after my grandma passed; he lost his will to live.   He loved her so much that he gave up and I can see myself in that, maybe that's where I got all this from. Clarice, do you hear me saying I'm smoking so much? Do you get that as I'm inadvertently harassing you it's not that I'm saying "come see me come see me"; it's me wanting to share every moment I experience with you, every thought. I want to share these things with you because I love you. And with smoking, I have tripled or more how much I smoke in the last week and at the same time I have all this love and I can't touch you, or kiss you or make love to you.   It hurts like nothing I can describe.   When you left after our lunch it honestly felt like someone stuck a knife in my heart. And later when you sent those messages, it calmed me almost instantly. I can't do it with you anymore because I have children to think of, they need their dad. I'm still willing to do what was outlined over the phone when I read you my soliloquy and told you that I am in love with you.   Meaning that I will wait wait wait for a while and take it slow after you leave Steve, but you have to leave him and choose me. Otherwise we have to return to a quick hello; how are you and I can never see you again. I love you so much and never want to hurt you. I miss you every moment you are gone.

And so I started writing Clarice's chapter in the book and what I came to realize later on that day while talking to Mary was that Clarice's chapter was actually the start of the book. It just flowed out of me, it was just like how writing the poems about Clarice had easily flowed out of me. And it was while I was writing the chapter, that Clarice responded:

Dear Charlie, Ok I get it, yes I finally understand. It just hurts so very much that you would walk away from me; but yes if you're in love with me that much then I finally get it. I really do and I'm sorry that I have done this to your heart, believe me this was not my intention. I just wanted you to be in my life because I truly care about you and am your friend and you always will be a friend to me. I'm sorry if I seemed harsh in my notes yesterday but I guess the reality of it all didn't hit me until I read your notes this morning. I guess I was angry at the thought of never seeing you again my friend. Do what you have got to do Charlie to get on with your life. I wish you nothing but happiness and I hope that you can find what you're looking for; I understand now. Maybe one day we can meet again. Take care and best wishes. Your friend always, Clarice

And so I sent her what I was writing up until that point after describing to a T what it was like when I first fell in love with her. I now felt that passion for her grow again and it was bigger than ever. So I stopped writing the chapter and wrote this email to her:

You know Clarice I've always believed there was something more between us; really now Clarice be honest. And I know I've hurt you badly over the years, really badly by walking away from you with Christina and the children's aid thing and the crack and I SHOULD HAVE BEEN THERE FOR YOU and then later by rejecting you for Laura. I really want you to think about what this book has been all about; about forgiving people and telling the truth once and for all and, to try and get past everything between them and I (Larry, Janine,

Carrie, Mom) and to get back to where they should be with their relationship. It hasn't always worked out well. Fuck obviously not! Ahem; Janine, Larry and Brenda, and even Carrie, but they are all on the right track. But the only one that really matters at the end of the day; the one who inspired me to do it all is YOU. While you are gone; I don't know if you can find it inside yourself and your heart to forgive and get past those things with me, but I am truly sorry. I was messed up, really really fucking messed up and I SHOULD HAVE BEEN THERE FOR YOU. If you decide to choose me, then yes marriage, and kids if you want a family. A goddess you will be to me till the day I die. Just like my grandma was for my grandpa. I will wait for you until you return from Alberta and I hope you have a wonderful time. And if you do choose me we can do it exactly the way I outlined it to you after I read you my soliloquy, whatever way you want I don't care, as long as at the end of the day you end up my partner, my wife, my lover and my friend. That's all in the texts I sent you yesterday. I love you and I'm so sorry for what I did and am doing to you. Charles Christopher Foster

And I left it, I wasn't neurotic about it, I just went about my day. I went to meet Mary for coffee as she wasn't upset with me after all and I finally got in contact with her. Her husband had gotten pneumonia and was horribly ill and she did not have the time to speak with me. I read Mary the whole string of emails between Clarice and I and she was blown away by it all, her eyes welled up and she was very inspired by the story. She further said that she also found the part of the book when I was at my grandparent's grave and the observations about the clouds to be very thought provoking.

We went for a walk and talked about everything and it was like we had known each other intimately for our whole lives. And then we discovered another huge coincidence; Mary and her husband CHARLIE and Carrie and I both became involved intimately for the first time on August 14 1998. It was at separate locations mind you, but we both had hooked up with our spouses at bars on that same day. We discovered this when I told Mary the story of how Carrie

235

had given me a hard time about kissing me on that day last year during the last days of our relationship and how I considered it to be a second anniversary for Carrie and I and how Carrie did not. It was mind blowing, another huge coincidence. COME ON!!! Why Mary, why was I talking to her after all these years, we were never that close before. As Mary and I parted ways that day I knew in my heart that we should have been close friends all along, and would be just that.

And so I went on about more business for the day; I had to pay a bill at the bank and this woman who served me, well wow! She was absolutely totally gorgeous; an eastern Indian woman who looked like she could be a model. Somehow I got up the nerve to call her breath-taking, after asking her name, for which she thanked me and smiled. The euphoria continued; I knew I was going to be alright no matter what happened with Clarice and that I had found self respect, self confidence and self esteem. So I returned home to find Clarice's awaiting reply:

Dear Charlie, I got your message and yes I have read every-thing. I have only one thing on my mind right now it's my dad and my trip and it is soooo hard to think about everything else. I'm sooooo nervous, anxious, and excited and my stress levels are making me feel icky. I will check in on everything when I have a moment in Alberta as I have so much to do right now today for my flight tomorrow. So give some time ok and I will respond. Thanks for your well wishes for me in Alberta and wish me a safe flight. Clarice

And I thought to myself, I knew she loved me, I knew it in my heart, I always knew it, I had hurt her so bad in the past and that's what was holding her back from passion. I knew she loved me. She never said you're crazy, or I don't think about you like that, or I'm not attracted to you or I can't see this with you, she just said let her think. Well I hope she does love me because until I get that first kiss I'll never know. So I responded:

You take your time sweetheart and have a safe trip, I'll miss

you and I love you. I hope you find everything you are looking for in your dad. I'll be here when you get back with open
arms. Remember the book had a place for all of us, but in
the end it all came down to you and me. I still hope slowly
but surely that my sister will get professional help before her
and Phil get married. I hope that Larry and Brenda can
speak the truth to Deborah and Ken, and move to a new
home and go on a honeymoon. I hope Carrie can get on
with her life and maybe get herself some help too as she's got
shit to deal with too. I hope I can find the time to write this
fucking book, I hope I find you and I miss you already.

The next little while of course I was still being neurotic. I wish
there was an off switch for my mind at times and I was running
down so many theories as to what I thought Clarice might decide. It
was during that time I wrote the following email to Janine and
copied Connie:

So the best way I could possibly forecast Clarice's decision is
by doing a pros vs. cons scenario as to how I see it:

Pros:
Our compatibility: Interests- music, food, movies; Intimacy- SEX
SEX SEX, friendship, romance; My sobriety and that she will be
easy to integrate into my life and my friends as she already
knows so many of them specifically you Janine and the
prospect of having you as a sister-in-law must make Clarice
happy Our history that speaks for itself and that I gave my
sincerest apologies to Clarice for walking away from her 2
times previously Steve and his attitude towards her; his drug
abuse, and that she is not in love with him and has not been
for a long time. They have little to no sex life and right now
have not been together since early May and that there is a
very big prospect that he has been and is cheating on her.
She was already talking this up before I apologized for what I
had done previously, as in thinking she wanted to leave
Steve. At the end of the day the #1 pro is love, she knows that
100% for sure I am head over heals in love with her.

Cons:
Steve and the 12 years with him and her loyalty towards him

for everything he has done for her.

My neurotic crazy behaviour.

Her fear of abandonment and what I have done, by walking away from her twice to foster those fears in her further.

Her sweet setup at home.

Her inability to deal with pain and then smoking a joint every night to be able to sleep; so this might not bother her so much if she says no to me.

Morgan and taking her away from her dad which is probably tied for the #1 con.

At the end of the day tied for the #1 con is love, does she truly love me?

So I have to have faith, honestly Janine faith in god, well you know love. This all happened for a reason, and it's like once I sacrificed all of my own wants for the betterment of others, ie: us being close, mom being happy, Larry and Brenda being happy and Carrie being, well whatever she feels; once I said that all those things are more important than me being with Clarice, well that's when someone, be it god, said alright Charlie now you get what you want too.   And if at the end of the day if it doesn't happen, well I hope and wish it does sister; but if not, I am now brimming with self confidence and self respect and have flirted with women on 3 consecutive days before this.   That is something; I've always been so shy around women and couldn't do anything except for a little while there after Laura.   So again, I'm really ok; but I hope things work out with Clarice. I'm thinking of when an engagement ring will come into play, if she gives me any strong indication before she gets back that it will be me she chooses, I might have a ring ready for her when the time comes that she returns.   I know I know, but that would be fitting and soooooooooooo romantic, which is me sister.   Come on I am not going to change and I won't expect her to wear it; but if things work out and she says yes I hope that Clarice and I will be married in 2 years or so but I have to get my divorce done first, that's for sure.

Janine's response:

Charles, Clarice has been in a relationship for 12 years with no ideas about marriage. I can't imagine that she is marriage minded at this point. Has she indicated to you that she loves you in a forever sense? I wouldn't run out and get a ring just yet. You two left things on not so good terms and I sincerely think you may not even be talking for awhile after she gets back. I'm worrying now that you're not seeing things really clearly, be open to other women the ones that are available for you. You seem pretty obsessive about the situation and I know that you consider yourself a romantic and neurotic; but it's time to chill on it for awhile. You're going to over think this thing to death (and make Clarice run forever in the process) so trust me, chill. You don't know anything right now and she is in Alberta and only thinking about her Dad and her family, just wait and see if she's even willing to talk to you when she gets back.

My response:

Why does everyone look for the hidden meaning or seem to only be reading every other line, Janine really really read what I wrote. I'm holding myself back now until I know what the end with Clarice will be. I think I could have easily asked this woman on a date the other day and she would have accepted. This is it for me and Clarice; she has to get over her pain, her fears and put herself through some bad times too if she wants to be with me. I think, no Janine I know she does want to be with me, but I'm not going to make this easy on her any longer. We can wait, wait, wait, for as long as is necessary, but the first and most important step is she has to put a plan in place to leave Steve and this will probably involve getting a lawyer. Really hear me sister, I am going to be OK and happy; I have self confidence, self respect, self esteem and I feel worthy of receiving love. The book has changed me; I'm still neurotic, loud, boisterous, opinionated; but I've accepted who I am, I love myself and all those around me, meaning my family and friends. This has been and is the greatest year of my life and it's only onwards and upwards from here! I want her, I desire her, I love her, I am in love with her, I want her to feel exactly the same way I do; but funny I don't need her. I do need a partner, a lover, and I sooo want that to be her but if not her, then someone else.

Winning this Seinfeld contest is killing me! And if she doesn't choose me well then it will be all systems go at the end of it all; but these six weeks are going to kill me, lol. It's beard growing time, I'm all bushy.

I thought about things some more and Connie also responded to the email and was far more blunt with her opinions as she thought I was absolutely crazy for my thinking as she still believed I was on the rebound from Carrie. But she was wrong and I further explained my mind set to her and she said afterwards that she wished she could feel so confident about someone else's feelings for her as I was in believing in Clarice's feelings for me. And I set my facebook update that day as such:

How could you know, you're crazy, how could you possibly know that? Well, it all became clear once I put everyone else in front of me, that they were more important than what I wanted. When I reached my lowest darkest hour; that's when I got tapped on the shoulder and was told, ok you've done it, now you get what you need too. Go out and get it and have faith.

I have never been as confident in my life as I have been with something such as knowing that Clarice loves me. The only thing though is with as much sound advice as all those around me were giving me, I still can't control myself at times. I just had to send that 1st pro/con email to Clarice, although I edited out the engagement ring part. On a whim from speaking with Carlos I also picked up the new album from Shinedown and I was totally blown away by tracks 2 & 3 on the disc as the choruses to those two songs read:

I created the Sound of Madness. Wrote the book on pain. Somehow I'm still here, to explain, that the darkest hour never comes in the night. You can sleep with a gun. When you gonna wake up and fight... for yourself?

Tell my mother, tell my father, I've done the best I can, to make them realize, this is my life, I hope they understand, I'm not angry, I'm just saying, sometimes goodbye is a second chance.

It was like those 2 songs were speaking directly to both Clarice and I. Why I bought that cd on a whim having not even heard a single track; when at the exact same time everything was peaking with Clarice was absolutely beyond me.

So many were advising me otherwise in regards to Clarice, telling me I was crazy even; but everything I saw was pointing me in the path I took, I guess I just can't do things any other way. I now invite you my friend to give my favourite song of all time a listen to, it's my own personal anthem that was played at the end of my wedding and that holds more meaning to me than any other song possibly could:

Freebird: by Lynard Skynard

If I leave here tomorrow,
Would you still remember me?
For I must be traveling on, now,
'Cause there's too many places I've got to see.
But, if I stayed here with you, girl,
Things just couldn't be the same.
'Cause I'm as free as a bird now,
And this bird you can not change.
Lord knows, I can't change.

Bye, bye, its been a sweet love.
Though this feeling I can't change.
But please don't take it badly,
'Cause Lord knows I'm to blame.
But, if I stayed here with you girl,
Things just couldn't be the same.
Cause I'm as free as a bird now,
And this bird you'll never change.
And this bird you can not change.

Lord knows, I can't change.
Lord help me, I can't change.
I know I'm not going to change either, nor do I want to.
Hopefully I can learn to moderate myself a little, but in the end, do
I really want to? What's so wrong with being passionate about life
and a romantic? Yes it does lead to a lot of heartbreak and lows,
but the highs are well worth it. I forgot that it was exactly that, love,
for which I live for; for far too many years I had forgotten.

It also helps that the song Freebird totally rocks beyond belief. I
only wish the band was not involved in that plane crash in 1977 as I
would have loved to have seen the original band perform in concert.
This is who I am, take me or leave me; I'm not going to change
other than just becoming happy and being more assertive, (God
help those who know me). I think it's also now appropriate that I
include this prayer, SERENITY NOW, SERENITY NOW!:

Serenity Prayer
God grant me the serenity
to accept the things I cannot change
courage to change the things I can;
and wisdom to know the difference
Living one day at a time;
enjoying one moment at a time
accepting hardships as the pathway to peace
taking, as he did, this sinful world
as it is, not as I would have it
Trusting that he will make all things right
if I surrender to his will;
That I may be reasonably happy in this life

and supremely happy with him
forever in the next
Amen.
Reinhold Niebuhr

Chapter 14

Golden Mispronunciation

The true appreciation of the passion,
that produces exquisite art.
It generates the stare,
that penetrates straight to the heart.
Oblivious everyone is,
all except one.
The never ending pursuit,
now has begun.
Cruise along so curious,
to the powers from above.
Chase that gold oh man of renaissance,
to find the pure love.
Please teacher share with me,
everything that is inside.
To a man of honour,
her feelings she can no longer hide.
Rolling around in the turmoil,
it is ever so great.
She is now willing to risk it all,
even the return of so much hate.
Never a purchase made,
that she could call mine.
Comfort achieved now and forever,
their story etched in the winds of time.

And then 6 days later there was Clarice in the chatroom on face-book; so I clicked on her to start a conversation and said hi. I had already attempted to chat with her once before but she said she only had a moment and said she would talk to me later in the week and I said ok and she left. She replied to the initial contact saying that I thought you didn't want to be friends anymore and I said no that's not true, not true at all. I thought to myself here we go again with her changing her tune as she damn well knew the last thing I said to her was a round-about proposal of marriage and she had said give me time to think please. I asked her if she had read the newest emails that I had sent to her and she said no that she hadn't checked her email since she had left on her trip. So I told her that there would be a bunch of emails waiting for her and some book updates whenever she checked. I then asked how she was and she said she was fine and that it was beautiful out there in Alberta.

I asked how things were going with her dad and she said ok but that she felt uncomfortable at times even though her dad was trying his best to make her feel at home. She continued that she missed her home and that she was experiencing strange emotions around her dad; that sometimes she thought he was great and that they were so close and then other times he would say things that she didn't like and she would feel a lot of anger towards him. She wondered if this was normal. I explained that what she was feeling was perfectly normal and that she would probably feel a lot of resentment to him and that they would still have a long way to go in forming their relationship.

I told her about a new crisis I was going through with Carrie. Carrie decided she had wanted to move her degenerate ex-boyfriend that just got out of prison after serving a term for a variety of violent reasons into her home because of financial reasons. Clarice was just as shocked when I told her, as I had been previously. Yeah you read it right, I couldn't dream up a better scenario, honestly. We chatted about it for a while but then I changed the subject to her and me. Just then the messenger messed up and I could only send messages to her and not receive any back. That was just perfect as it would give me a chance to say what I wanted to her just like when I read her the soliloquy.

I told her that everything I had said to her recently was absolutely true; that I loved her, that I was in love with her, that I desired her, that I wanted her to feel the exact same way I feel, that I would marry her. I then continued with what I recently had said in an email that I didn't need her. I now thought that had changed because when things went into crisis mode with Carrie and I was in trouble; I started rhyming off who my support group was and who I wanted to talk to and who I needed at that time. Well the number one person at the top of that list that I wanted to be there with me when all hell was breaking loose was; Clarice. And with that I realized that yes I do need someone and that I needed her. I could then again receive her messages and she interjected that was ok as long as I realized that all she could offer was friendship.

So here it was; the moment of truth and I asked, is that it, friendship? Is that all it will ever be between us? And she paused for quite a while and I could see that she was typing, and then she stopped and then continued and this went on for a couple of minutes but then the message came. I've only been gone for six days and I miss him so much; I can't walk away from a man after 12 years. So I said that I understood and I hoped that she would in turn understand that I now had to go away out of respect for myself, for the sake of my children and out of respect for the next woman that will come into my life. Any woman that I was to be involved with in the future would probably have a huge problem with Clarice being involved in my life in any capacity after reading this book and I wouldn't blame anyone for feeling that way one bit.

And I know dear friend, I heard it too; is it Steve that Clarice misses? Or is it the comfort of her home and the routines that she's developed over the years that gave her the stability in her life that she had never known? That had now grown accustomed to and now she had lost that coveted stability while visiting with her father. Was she confusing the two things? I also heard that number six again too!

And further to the point for that matter what does it say about me and the depths of my love for Clarice if I'm not willing to wait to find out. Well I ask you my friend what should I do? Should I continue to bang my head up against the wall and rip away at my heart until sooner or later I shut down inside again? If Clarice does love me back and she doesn't realize it or she can't face it because of her own fears, would she truly want me to do that for her? There are a lot of theories to be discussed with regards to Clarice's thinking but what am I to do because I flat out directly asked the questions that needed to be asked and out of respect for myself and for Clarice I have to respect the answers I was given.

She said that she hoped that we could talk in the future and have some sort of friendship and I said that I thought that maybe one day we could talk. She said I'm sorry if I've hurt you and that she didn't mean for all this to have happened and she never meant to play with my heart. I found myself to be ok with all that she said. I did understandably get a little misty and I told her that I would send her a copy of my book through email once I completed it. She said that she looked forward to receiving it and with that I said goodbye to Sweet Clarice and closed off the site. Later that night I deleted her from my friends list on facebook for closure.

After I left the computer I went downstairs and outside for a cigarette and called Janine to tell her what had happened. She asked are you ok? And I guess that's the big question right? How did I feel? It was over; Clarice said she was staying with Steve and I had said goodbye and it was now done. So how did I feel? Well after all my speeches and after being so pathetic in love for so many years and after all my promises to myself; well...I did it! I was absolutely positively fine. Honest. I joked around with Janine on the phone and just continued on with my day as if it was like any other. I called mom to tell her I was going out that evening and that things were over with Clarice and then I called Vince to confirm that I was coming over to his home. All the while I was feeling totally fine and ok with everything that had just happened with Clarice.

Did I ever feel welcomed at Vince and his wife Kathy's home when I arrived; what a nice and friendly couple they are. Vince and Kathy put out this huge spread of food and we ate, drank and chatted till all hours of the night. I told them almost every story that I have put in the book that night and I now wonder if my book is to be published what will I have to talk to people about once all my stories are known? For the first time that night I saw Vince's paintings in full size rather than in his portfolio or on the internet and was his artwork was ever gorgeous. His religious motifs really appeal to me as does his choices of colour and subjects. He is a spectacular artist and I am so lucky to have met him, become friends with him and then to have him agree to be my mentor. Vince and Kathy listened intently to all I had to say and we laughed and joked all night. They also shared their own stories with me; in particular the story of how they met and became a couple, and that story inspired me to write Golden Mispronunciation in almost one hour.

The exact details of Vince and Kathy's story are beautiful but not entirely that relevant to my story. But it does need to be touched upon as it was just one more coincidence that is very fitting to the flow of the story. After I had told many of my stories, during the course of the night I asked Vince and Kathy to share one of their stories and they said ok what should we tell you and I replied tell me how you guys got together and became a couple so that I know more about your history together and so they did. Kathy told most of the story and Vince would interject or offer details whenever Kathy would lose track, but the story itself was intriguing.

What happened was that Kathy went to one of Vince's exhibitions and when she walked up to the gallery Vince was outside having a smoke with the gallery owner. When he saw Kathy there was an instant attraction and he told the gallery owner that he was going to marry her. As Kathy walked up she saw Vince staring at her and was very aware of it and scared by him as she felt the electricity between them. Her aunt recognized it too and said to Kathy look at the way that guy is staring at you; but Kathy had already felt cupids arrow hit her and that was it for them. There was one big problem though as Kathy was married to a very good man whom she cared for a great deal and they had two children together. She wrestled and wrestled with the thoughts of Vince even though they had just barely met. She would drive by his studio and asked the gallery owner, whom she also knew, about him. The gallery owner decided to set up art lessons for Kathy with Vince. Well that lead to further deeper feelings between Vince and Kathy and they could not fight it, nor did they want to and they slowly became lovers.

Kathy went through so much turmoil because of the thoughts of her husband and her children but she could not ignore how she felt about Vince. She eventually threw everything away and left it all for Vince. Her husband was furious at her and so was her entire family but her love for Vince was all encompassing. She had to be with him even if it meant losing her fabulous home and her children; as her husband was rich and he destroyed her in the courts.

Isn't it fitting that on the same day that things end with Clarice and she chooses to stay with her husband of 12 years; that the first story I hear that motivates me to write my first poem in over two weeks, that I write in one hour no less, is that of a man and a woman in similar circumstances to me, with the woman making the exact opposite decision that Clarice did.

Chapter 15

<u>Patience</u>

Every word she speaks completes my existence;
every note,
each lyric,
now make perfect sense.
It's been one long dance between her and I;
now my heart,
and my soul,
are starting to fly.
A squeeze of my hand becomes pure ecstasy;
a beautiful smile,
the only one,
now stands next to me.
So many trials now lay ahead;
but the most important things,
no longer,
need be said.
Before her I stand with nothing to hide;
whole I feel,
with her,
at my side.
Each memory of her is still so captivating;
one day so soon,
two hearts and two souls,
intertwined and soaring.
Now and forever;
the one,
and only,
true thing.

I guess at the end of it all when looking back there was one bond that I never really gave enough consideration to in my path to redemption; and that was a bond that lies within myself. It's the bond between my mind, my heart and my soul and that is the bond that has been the hardest one of them all to repair. I learned so very long ago how to hate myself so easily and how to cleverly hide all that hatred and then to continually convince myself that I loved myself but all the while I was ignoring my hearts true desire. I let my soul become black and cold, and right up until Roberta came along it was; and there was almost nothing there. Once I emailed everything that was going on in my life to Connie; that's when I started to realize what had really happened to me and to how many depths that my self hatred really went.

I know now that I deserve better than being the one who is always driving the bus; I deserve to be the one who is being pursued for once. I deserve a woman who will do something crazy like send me flowers or write me poetry or think of special ways to impress me. I deserve to be the one that inspires someone else to challenge themselves to be a better person. I deserve so much more than I have received over the years. From now on I intend on accepting no less than that and why shouldn't I deserve that? Why shouldn't I get what I want out of life too?

So that's why I was ok when Clarice told me no because I have learned to love myself and accept who I am; and then to forgive myself for every rotten thing that I think that I have ever done. I've tried to make amends and repair the damage that I've done to those close to me as best I possibly can. If in the end Clarice is not going to choose me; well then I am not going to stay around pitching woo at her anymore, it's time for me to move on. She's a wonderful person but I deserve better than what she is willing to offer. I no longer need anyone to tell me that I'm special or attractive, although I sure do like hearing that as much as possible. I've found that I'm just happy all the time now, even when things do go wrong, and geez sometimes they just do go so terribly wrong. I hope I never lose this feeling of happiness again, it's been dulled a bit over the last two weeks since the initial feeling of euphoria but it's still there nonetheless and I love it. I will continue to keep searching for that one woman out there who's the right one for me; so that hopefully one day I will stand in the presence of my god again and truly feel like the complete person that I want to be.

Yeah, yeah and I know I have to quit smoking too; and get it to stick once and for all. It's going to be very hard this time though as I really do enjoy it so much, but I've done it before; many times and I mean like at least 50, but I always get pulled back when I'm drinking or when I would go away on vacation. For the last ten years every winter I have quit and every summer I would start back up again, except this year I plan on giving it up for good, once and for all, so cut me some slack ok. Just like I said to my buddy Greg recently, I'm a big boy and if I wanted another wife I would get one ok, so give me some time.

I guess an important question would have to be what would happen if Clarice ever changed her mind or if Steve ever decided to leave her. I've spoken about this with all the important players in my life and I just don't know what I would do? Can I be second choice for Clarice after all I've said? Could I really close the door on Clarice if she ever was to come to me? I don't think I could ever walk away from someone I'm in love with and I think I proved that by rejecting Clarice once before for Laura; So I guess the window of opportunity is very small for Clarice and I as I intend on pursuing every woman I'm interested in that comes my way. I think if she ever did come back, that it would have to be a monstrous gesture that would make me accept her if I was single. After all her rejection of me and accepting advances from me, how could I ever feel secure in a relationship with her. The insecurity would eat me up inside far worse than anything I ever experienced with Laura, could a relationship with Clarice ever work? I guess that it's all in god's hands now and I just have to go on with my life wherever it may take me.

Janine and I are well on the way to being friends and I hope we continue down the path we are on as it will be a long one. Mom is really coming to grips with her own issues and I do believe that she has changed so much and will continue to improve the quality of her life as time goes on.

Larry and I are brothers again and it's just so amazing to have him in my life again without all that baggage from the past; but I still have to learn to deal with his illness as best I can and that will be a long journey.

Janine just said to me today that she felt most of the best books she has ever read always seemed to have somewhat similar endings. What she said those endings were, really rang true to me after I put some thought into to it. Looking back over my life, somehow I survived every grueling detail and sometimes I really don't know how I even did it, but I did and strangely enough "it didn't kill me". Peace.

<u>Selfish Reward</u>

There it finally rests,
his hand,
upon my tired shoulder.
I can see now,
the footprints,
since I have grown older.

Out of the depths,
of my despair,
do my sisters,
I retrieve.
The mask of anger,

on my brother's face,
I choose not,
to believe.

Gone away,
is the one,
who I thought,
I would live to please.
Only silence,
from the beautiful muse,
whose words,
surely could put me at ease.

The sacrifice,
of my wants,
has selflessly,
been made.
The confession,
has been heard,
and now the debts,
are being paid.

As I approach the end,
have I found,
the lightening rod?
So that one day,
I will again, stand in,
the presence of god?

Eat Away at Anything for Redemption

David James Watt

Eat Away at Anything for Redemption

David James Watt

CPSIA information can be obtained at www.ICGtesting.com
Printed in the USA
LVOW071942291211

261529LV00001B/153/P